Journeys Within

Journeys Within

The Contemporary
Spiritual Autobiography

Kerstin W. Shands

Södertörn University
Library
SE-141 89 Huddinge

www.sh.se/publications

Cover artwork: *Self Love* by Mimo Listerfelt 2015
Graphic form: Jonathan Robson & Per Lindblom
Layout: Jonathan Robson

Stockholm 2016

English Studies 6
ISSN 1651–4165

ISBN 978–91–87843–52–5 (print)

Contents

Acknowledgments

I would like to thank my colleagues at the Södertörn University English Department for the support they have offered during the writing process, with special thanks to our Department Head, Dr. Martin Dvorak.

Heartfelt thanks to Dr. Philippe Gasparini for reading and commenting on my manuscript.

I thank Karen Ferreira-Meyers, Senior Lecturer and Coordinator of the Institute of Distance Education at the University of Swaziland, and Dipti Ranjan Pattanaik, Professor of English at the Banaras Hindu University, India, for their support and feedback.

Special thanks to Dr. Giulia Grillo Mikrut for her valuable feedback on the manuscript, and also for our great and rewarding collaboration as conference organizers at Södertörn University.

I have appreciated the kind encouragement given by David Westerlund, Professor in the Study of Religions at Södertörn University, Wesley Kort, Professor Emeritus of Religious Studies at Duke University, Bruce Hindmarsh, James M. Houston Professor of Spiritual Theology at Regent College, Vancouver, and Sister Mary Rachel Capets, Dominican Sisters of St. Cecilia in Australia.

Many thanks to Professor Anders Ekenberg and Associate Professor Tord Fornberg at the Newman Institute in Uppsala, and to Mikael Larsson, Senior Lecturer in the Department of Theology at Uppsala University, for their inspiring courses in Theology.

I would also like to thank the international colleagues I have met at conferences organized by the University of Silesia, Poland, the University of Bucharest, Romania, Dublin University and Galway University in Ireland, the Sacred Journeys conferences in Lisbon and Prague, and the Christian Literary Studies Group at Oxford University, for highly stimulating discussions. Earlier versions of parts of some chapters have been published as conference proceedings: "Shedding Stones, Reaching Peace: William Schmidt's Pilgrimage in Walking with Stones" (*The Glass*, Oxford: 2014); "Journeys

Toward Grace: The Contemporary Spiritual Autobiography (*The Glass*, Oxford: 2013); "From Paradise Lost to Paradise Regained: Homecoming in Anne Rice's *Called Out of Darkness*" (Interdisciplinary Net, Oxford, 2013); "Journeys Toward Grace: The Contemporary Spiritual Autobiography in English" (Interdisciplinary Net, Oxford, 2012).

Many thanks to the Birgit och Gad Rausing Foundation for Humanistic Research and to the Harald och Louise Ekman Foundation for scholarships that allowed me to take some time off from a full-time teaching schedule. The Sigtuna Foundation has offered a wonderfully peaceful and stimulating oasis in which to work on this project, for which I am deeply grateful.

Preface

In recent decades, critics and theorists have embarked on studies of the myriad forms autobiographical writing may take: traditional autobiographies, diaries, journals, letters in print or in manuscript, autofiction and autobiographical dimensions in fiction, at the same time as new types of autobiography have been emerging. Encompassing a huge, interdisciplinary area, autobiography studies have expanded tremendously, and ground-breaking studies have been published.

And yet, there is one subgenre that has not received sufficient critical attention: the contemporary spiritual autobiography. This is the territory that will be in focus in the present study. A selection of spiritual autobiographies from the most recent decades will be explored thematically and conceptually from comparative and contextualizing perspectives. An attentive reading and interpretation of key images, themes, and metaphors that imaginatively mark the narration of inner and outer spiritual journeys, this study will propose, may add to our understanding of the contemporary spiritual autobiography and of spirituality in postmodern times.

Although there are important works on the classical spiritual autobiography and on the evangelical conversion narrative, there are surprisingly few book-length studies of the spiritual autobiography after 1995, even though an exploration of this area would seem important if, as is often stated, religion is 'returning.' "Sociologists of religion now generally speak of the 'desecularization' or the 'reenchantment' of the world," as Ola Sigurdson puts it in "Beyond Secularism? Toward A Post-Secular Political Theology" (177). It has been predicted that the twenty-first century is going to be a century of religion. Of course, as Jeremy Carrette and Richard King point out in *Selling Spirituality: The Silent Takeover of Religion*, "[m]ost of the people on this planet" "have not experienced the 'death of God' that so many secular theorists and political activists in the West have proclaimed" (177). Similarly, as Karen Armstrong underlines in *A History of God: The 4,000-Year Quest of*

Judaism, Christianity and Islam, "our current secularism is an entirely new experience, unprecedented in human history" (3).

But if religion is indeed 'returning,' the question is how. Theologians such as Hans-Joachim Höhn have pointed to the aesthetic and therapeutic aspects of a subjective and experience-oriented post-secular spirituality and wondered if the return of religion is merely a new form of secularization. If western society expects anything at all from religion these days, it is comfort and therapy, according to another theologian, Werner Jeanrond, who perceives a paradoxical coexistence between scientific and political globalization on the one hand and a privatization of religion on the other. In literature, too, religious themes are returning. For example, there is a fascination with the miraculous, and in *Contemporary Fiction and Christianity*, Andrew Tate asks: "Is this eclectic spirituality indicative of a postmodern 'Great Awakening' or simply the death-throes of sentimental, decadent late capitalism? If modernity banished mystery from the world, should we regard its return with hostility or with cautious optimism?"(9). At any rate, Tate concludes, "Lukács' emphasis on the absence of God from fiction now seems charmingly obsolete" (7).

In *American Grace: How Religion Divides and Unites Us*, David E. Campbell and Robert D. Putnam regard religion's role in America as a puzzle. They observe that "America peacefully combines a high degree of religious devotion with tremendous religious diversity including ranks of the nonreligious" (4). In "Protean Identity: Religion and Contemporary American Autobiography," Melissa Knox notes that autobiography devoted to religious identity flourishes in America. Even though "U.S. Americans write more autobiographies than the citizens of any other nation," as Knox goes on to say, "surprisingly little has been said specifically about autobiographies concerning American religious conversion." According to Campbell and Putnam, religion in the United States is malleable and fluid. Knox traces this flexible approach back to Thomas Jefferson, who "constantly changed his religious preferences, as his letters amply demonstrate" and whose "remarks on the *Virginia Statute for Religious Freedom* reveal that he wanted to protect persons whose religious volatility approximated his own." Proposing that "[r]eligious malleability, indeed the personal stamp of both Jefferson and the Founding Fathers, has become a central characteristic of U.S. American culture, and holds considerable sway in the U.S. today," Knox concludes that "[f]luidity of religious identity in a country whose population overwhelmingly claims to be religious means … fluidity of all forms of identity, or a stereotypically American optimism about the ability to change one's identity, religious or otherwise," and she finds it unsurprising "that autobiography, and especially autobiography devoted to religious identity, flourishes in this atmosphere. The less U.S. Americans know who they are, the more they write autobiographies in order to discover and establish these shifting identities." Along similar lines, Wesley A. Kort affirms in *Textual Intimacy: Autobiography and Religious Identities* that "the rise of self-accounts continues, and they have become major texts in contemporary American culture" (43).

While research on autobiography has produced studies on marginalized groups from feminist, postcolonialist, and poststructuralist perspectives focused on issues of power, authority, and representation, and while the searchlight in the most recent decades has been directed toward autobiographical writings concerning social justice, testimony, trauma, and ethics, so far, religion and spirituality have not been areas of primary interest. If the assessments made by Campbell, Putnam, Knox, and others are correct that autobiography devoted to religious identity is in fact flourishing in America, and if Kort is right that these autobiographies have "become major texts in contemporary American culture," the contemporary spiritual autobiography ought to merit more scholarly attention than it has hitherto received.

Looking back in time in *Protestant Autobiography in the Seventeenth-Century Anglophone World,* Kathleen Lynch suggests that the "inward aspects" of early modern spiritual autobiography are "well recognized" (4). Lynch's conclusion is that the narratives from this period indicate a "change from conventional forms of worship to an experiential worship," and that "a semiotics of salvation" was "established by the beginning of the seventeenth century" (5, 7). When it comes to the present, to the contrary, it cannot be claimed that the 'inward aspects' of spiritual autobiographical writing are 'well recognized.' Such aspects will be the focus of the present study.

Introduction

The contemporary spiritual autobiography is an as yet understudied aspect of autobiography. In this study, a selection of contemporary spiritual autobiographies written in English and published after 1995 will be in focus. After a consideration of the genre of autobiography more generally and an exploration of different theories, perspectives, and definitions, we will turn to the sub-genre of the spiritual autobiography. Via a discussion of what constitutes spirituality, an attempt will be made to determine how the spiritual autobiography differs from the secular autobiography. Before embarking on individual analyses of a selection of contemporary spiritual autobiographies, an overview of theories of spiritual development of relevance for the texts selected for this study will be given.

While it has sometimes been suggested that autobiographical writing is a modern, 'Western' thing that is absent in older or 'primitive' cultures, recent scholarship on autobiography indicates that this is not the case. Rather, we need to rethink our definitions of what constitutes autobiographical writing. Dating back to the eighteenth and nineteenth centuries, the term 'autobiography' appears to have been used first by William Taylor in a review published at the end of the eighteenth century. It was used by Robert Southey in 1809, and from the 1830s, it has become the most frequently used term. Regarded as a literary genre since the end of the eighteenth century, autobiography has been "an important testing ground for critical controversies about a range of ideas including authorship, selfhood, representation and the division between fact and fiction," as Linda Anderson asserts in *Autobiography: New Critical Idiom* (1–2). Autobiography is at the same time "the simplest of literary enterprises" and "a very daring, even foolhardy, undertaking," as James Olney puts it in "Autobiography and the Cultural Moment: A Thematic, Historical, and Bibliographical Introduction" (4). But due to what Anderson calls the "pervasiveness and slipperyness of autobiography" (1–2) and what Geoffrey Galt Hartman in "Conversion and the Language of Autobiography" calls the "luminous indeterminacy" of autobiography (49), the genre of autobiography has been difficult to distinguish from biography, on the one hand, and from auto/fiction, on the other. James Olney paints a vivid picture: "In talking about autobiography, one always feels that there is a great and present danger that the subject will slip away altogether, that it will vanish into thinnest air, leaving behind the perception that there is no such creature as autobiography and that there has never been" (4).

Traditionally, the authors of autobiographies have been cast as cultural role models for readers to emulate. This is the straightforward, utilitarian, and didactic function of the *Autobiography of Benjamin Franklin* (1771), to take one example of an autobiography in which the author explicitly assumes the position of a role model capable of imparting knowledge about self-improvement. Franklin states:

> From the poverty and obscurity in which I was born and in which I passed my earliest years, I have raised myself to a state of affluence and some degree of celebrity in the world. As constant good fortune has accompanied me even to an advanced period of life, my posterity will perhaps be desirous of learning the means, which I employed, and which, thanks to Providence, so well succeeded with me. They may also deem them fit to be imitated, should any of them find themselves in similar circumstances. (16)[1]

Another pertinent example of a role-modelling autobiography is that of Jorian Simons, an Anabaptist weaver "who was burned at the stake as a heretic at Haarlem in Holland on 26 April in 1557" and who wrote a last will and testament in which he "offered a spare and unembellished conversion narrative as part of an admonition that he hoped his son would read when old enough to understand such matters," as Bruce Hindmarsh explains in *The Evangelical Conversion Narrative: Spiritual Autobiography in Early Modern England* (29).[2]

---

[1] As Edwin S. Gaustad points out in his Introduction to *Memoirs of the Spirit: American Religious Autobiography from Jonathan Edwards to Maya Angelou*, many critics have seen Franklin's *Autobiography* as a "transition from a salvation story to a secular one" (xvi). However, in Gaustad's view, it should "be regarded as but an adaptation of the more explicitly spiritual 'pilgrim's progress.' Franklin tells of another kind of salvation: from obscurity and poverty to fame and an agreeable station in life, from ignorance to illumination, and from intense activity to calm reflection" (xvi).

[2] Drawing upon archival sources, *The Evangelical Conversion Narrative* discusses conversion narratives and issues of identity among Wesleyan Methodists, Moravians, Anglicans, Calvinists in the Church of England, and Particular Baptists as well as evangelical Presbyterians.

While all genres including autobiography involve culturally conditioned transactions between writers and their readers, autobiography, then, has been marked by expectations of exemplarity. In 1829, a reviewer in *Blackwood Magazine* made a distinction between what he called a "legitimate autobiographical class" and the "vulgar" who tried to "excite prurient curiosity that may command a sale": "[v]ocation would seem to be the key to authorship and it is also the way in which 'serious' autobiography, that written by the few who are capable of sustained self-reflection, is to be distinguished from its popular counterpart" (Anderson 7). Already in the late eighteenth century, a time when modern autobiographical writing took off along with Romantic notions of the heroic artist, there was criticism of autobiographical stories that seemed not worth reading and of stories written by people who could be dismissed as narcissistic exhibitionists. Historically, then, a prevalent opinion was that autobiographies should be written only by people who had achieved something important in life and whose reputation was untarnished. In the period examined in *La tentation autobiographique de l'Antiquité à la Renaissance*, Philippe Gasparini shows how early autobiography in China would hold up exemplary lives and how noblemen in Europe aimed to increase their prestige by writing memoirs. The lives of saints were of course the most exemplary of all. While the modern autobiography arising in Europe has been regarded as separate in form and content from hagiographic narratives in relating the lives of secular and fallible people as opposed to saints, roots in sacred stories and biblical narratives may nonetheless be detected in the teleological drive of modern autobiographies narrating stories of 'nobodies' who become 'somebodies' or even celebrities. Perhaps one could even claim that some modern autobiographies are remakes of older hagiographies. "Au sens large," Gasparini suggests, "on peut soutenir que toute autobiographie est travaillé par une tentation hagiographique" (120).[3]

Besides expectations of exemplarity, autobiographies also seem to hold out the promise of something real, genuine, and intimate. Indeed, intimacy has been seen as a crucial component in both autobiographic and spiritual

---

[3] Gasparini goes on to say that "le terme *hagiographie* fut d'abord réservé aux vies de saints qui se multiplièrent à mesure que le christianisme se propageait et jouèrent un rôle majeur dans sa stratégie prosélyte. Les Évangiles et les Actes des apôtres en fournissaient les paradigmes. 'Biographie excessivement élogieuse', l'hagiographie érige la vie d'un 'saint' en modèle afin de susciter l'émulation des destinataires. Se réclamant d'une vérité supérieure, elle n'est pas tenue à l'exactitude historique et fait volontiers intervenir le surnaturel sous forme d'ingérences divines ou démoniaques, de prémonitions, de miracles" (121).

expression. For William James in *Varieties of Religious Experience*, religion means "*the feelings, acts, and experiences of individual men in their solitude, so far as they apprehend themselves to stand in relation to whatever they consider the divine*" (29–30, italics in original). The feelings, acts, and experiences of human beings in their solitude have a great deal to do with intimacy. Taking place in a space of intimacy, confessions involve sharing one's innermost thoughts about the most important moments and experiences of one's life. Intimacy, then, is another significant aspect of autobiography. Attempting to understand autobiography and its 'textual intimacy' through metaphors of space, Wesley Kort suggests that autobiography as a genre is located in a space between conventional and complete disclosure, a space he calls textual intimacy. But we cannot expect complete exposure in autobiographies. Rather, Kort suggests that "intimacy in autobiography is similar in social standing to flirting, a personal interaction that takes place at a level below the ordinary but without the consequences of full involvement" (2). Nonetheless, autobiographies do "give us knowledge not usually accessible," and "[t]he craft of autobiography lies, among other things, in knowing what and how much of the personal and informational to divulge in order to move from ordinary toward complete while remaining in … a space between the two" (2). Kort is probably right that "we generally think of personal self-disclosure as more related to relational and especially sexual matters than to religious identity" (3). Inspired by John Sturrock, for whom autobiographical writing is "an invitation to intimacy" and by Wayne Booth, who, interestingly, uses the term intimacy in his description of the mutuality between (implied) writers and readers, Kort suggests that intimacy is a key ingredient in autobiographical writing (46).[4] Intimacy, then, is a central aspect of autobiography on levels of reading and writing, and many readers would claim that they read autobiographies precisely because they feel that this brings them closer into contact with the author than any other form of writing. Proposing in 1975 that autobiographical reading and writing rest on a pact, Philippe Lejeune launched the term *le pacte autobiographique*. In such a pact the encounter between author and reader is uppermost.[5]

---

[4] It is an ingredient that John Henry Newman, in *Apologia Pro Vita Sua*, saw as a mixed blessing: "It is not pleasant to be giving to every shallow or flippant disputant the advantage over me of knowing my most private thoughts, I might even say the intercourse between myself and my Maker" (Newman, Preface I).

[5] Not all critics see intimacy as primary. In "Self-Evidence," Michael Ryan calls for politically significant methods that are antagonistic to capitalist thought and that demystify 'idealist' claims to transcendence. Since Ryan's Marxist perspective questions the right to private

The genre of autobiography has been linked to the rise of individualism and to western notions of a rational and conscious self, with author-protagonists who enter into unwritten contracts with their readers, contracts that are marked by mutual assumptions and expectations about seeking, expressing, and listening to a truthful representation of a life and the events that have marked it, a contract that for a majority of readers (if not for a majority of critics) still seems to be in place. Early autobiography criticism, as Olney puts it, might "reflect no more than the critic's view of the content narrated" or discuss the truthfulness of the account, assuming that the "recollected life" was "transmitted through the unclouded, neutral glass of the *autos*" (21). In his Introduction to *Memoirs of the Spirit*, Edwin S. Gaustad wonders if autobiography "[offers] us the worst of all possible worlds so far as the potential virtues of memory and history are concerned" and he asks: "Is every autobiography of necessity a hopelessly egocentric *Song of Myself*, to cite Walt Whitman, or unseemly *Advertisements for Myself*, to name Norman Mailer?" (xiv). But perhaps the self-centeredness is illusory: "Is Whitman perhaps speaking for a young nation, and Mailer for a sorely tried generation?" Collective autobiography may, Gaustad suggests, "transmute itself into the necessary myths by which peoples and nations live" (xiv).[6]

Georges Gusdorf was among the first critics who problematized the apparent simplicity of the *autos*, turning to questions of how the *autos* in the course of writing both discovers and creates itself and "[t]he *bios* of an autobiography" becoming "what the 'I' makes of it" while "neither the *autos*

property, notions of a self linked to private property must be criticized, and his critique of Lejeune's vision of the autobiographical self is scathing. According to Ryan, Lejeune's "antediluvian" norms promote "the values of ownership and property" (15, 6). In Ryan's stridently dogmatic view, "Lejeune's theory advances the interests (theoretical or ideological as well as practical) of a patriarchal, white, western ruling class under the guise of such concepts as validity, authenticity, universality, property, legality, etc." (10). Ryan, for whom "deconstructive and Marxist critiques of idealism overlap," finds that "Lejeune's text is ideological … in the sense of being one active, effective part of the machinery of class dominance. The text (en)acts—by performing and effectuating—the idealist philosophy which is a necessary component of capitalist class rule" (11). As Ryan concludes: "It is not surprising that a critical philosophy such as Marxism, which questions the right to private possession, should also question the bourgeois model of private self-possession" (14–15). A Marxist analysis of autobiography, then, wants to disturb "our conception of the ostensibly private nature of its discourse," as Paul Jay comments in "What's The Use?: Critical Theory and the Study of Autobiography," and property becomes a "key word upon which [Ryan's] argument about the relationship between capitalism and conceptions of the 'self' pivots" (49).
[6] Following Arthur R. Gold, Gaustad points to the Hebrew scriptures as an example of national autobiography of importance for a people's investigation of its own identity (xiv).

nor the *bios* is there in the beginning" (Olney 22). Olney continues: "Here is where the act of writing—the third element of autobiography—assumes its true importance," and it is here that, for poststructuralist critics "the text takes on a life of its own" to the point where "the self that was not really in existence in the beginning is in the end merely a matter of text and has nothing whatever to do with an authorizing author" (22). Gusdorf argues that autobiography is "limited in time and space: it has not always existed nor does it exist everywhere" (28–29). It is "a late phenomenon in Western culture," he goes on to say, coming "at that moment when the Christian contribution was grafted onto classical traditions" (29). Autobiography thus "expresses a concern peculiar to Western man," according to Gusdorf, "[t]he conscious awareness of the singularity of each individual life is the late product of a specific civilization" (29). Autobiography "becomes possible only under certain metaphysical preconditions" (30), and a distinction (that in Gusdorf's view is important for a comprehension of what autobiography is) should be made between the interdependent, communal and repetitive role-performativity of earlier historical times and the increasing individualism of the period from the Renaissance to modernity.

Building on Robert Folkenflik's understanding of the eighteenth century as a time when autobiographical writing was given "separate attention and cultural importance" (something that happened because of Romanticism's emphases on origins and because of an "erosion in authority of more estab-lished genres" [42]), Wesley Kort adds another important factor: urbaniza-tion also influenced the development of the genre of autobiographical writ-ing, and since then, self-disclosure, telling other people who we are, Kort suggests, has played a part in "resisting the obliteration of personal parti-cularity and significance by pressures and controls that encompassing and powerful social, political, and economic structures and processes exert on us" (16).

Apart from dealing with memory, as the term memoir indicates, autobio-graphy may have many other purposes, as its extensive terminology reveals. Rousseau called his work *confessions*, while Newman chose the term *apologia*.[7] Terms such as memoir or life were used by writers during the

---

[7] Rousseau wrote: "Je veux montrer à mes semblables un homme dans toute la vérité de la nature; et cet homme, ce sera moi." Similarly, Augustine wrote about his *Confessions*: "Here see me as I am and do not praise me for more than I am" (Letter to Darius). Similarly, in Preface I (1865) to *Apolgia Pro Vita Sua* Newman addressed an 'accuser' according to whom Newman seems not to prioritize the truth. Newman's reputation is at

nineteenth century even when critics and scholars started using the term autobiography. A later term, life-writing, has been regarded as more inclusive (it might also include oral histories). With so many theoretical views on autobiography[8] there is, not surprisingly, a plethora of terms, such as memoir, life-writing, self-narrative, ego documents,[9] self-accounts, autrebiographies, nouvelle autobiographie (Robbe-Grillet), autofiction, faction (literary genres that mix fact and fiction), égolittérature, and circonfession. More recently, Philippe Gasparini has introduced the term autonarration. In his view, the term autofiction can be misleading precisely because of the word fiction. Autonarration, by contrast, he suggests, is a wider and more neutral term that may include both autobiographical stories and autofiction. As Rosamund Dalziell suggests in "Speaking Volumes: About Auto/biography Studies in Canada," further, terms such as self-portraiture or self-performance may be useful, in particular when discussing the autobiographical mode of reality TV where "individuals without a script act the part of themselves" (225).

One of the pioneering theorists in autobiographical studies, Philippe Lejeune, has offered the following definition of autobiography: "*Retrospective prose narrative produced by a real person concerning his own existence, where the focus is his individual life, in particular the story of his personality*" (4, italics in original). Further, there has to be "identity between the *author*, the *narrator*, and the *protagonist*" (Lejeune 5). Lejeune's concept of an autobiographical pact rests on the idea of a contract and "an intention to honour the signature" (Anderson 3). Concepts of intention and sincerity could in turn be seen as problematically linked to issues of authority and gender as well as to notions

---

stake and he wants to defend himself specifically against the charge of untruthfulness. In Preface II he underlines that he is primarily explaining himself: "I am not expounding Catholic doctrine, I am doing no more than explaining myself, and my opinions and actions. I wish, as far as I am able, simply to state facts, whether they are ultimately determined to be for me or against me." John Barbour comments: "Newman's *Apologia Pro Vita Sua* is one of the clearest examples of an autobiography motivated and shaped by the writer's desire to vindicate his moral character" (11). While Rousseau presents a "new ethic of authenticity," his "ideal of authenticity of feeling leaves much to be desired as a standard of moral truthfulness" (Barbour 33).

[8] In *Derrida and Autobiography*, Robert Smith comments: "The theory of autobiography has become very well trodden terrain. So much so, in fact, that there are now not only many theories of autobiography, but there is also a growing number of theories of those theories" (51).

[9] Historical analysis may be based on egodocuments including oral memorabilia, letters, diaries, and other archival material such as English nineteenth-century autobiographies written by laborers or those of artisans in early modern Europe.

of property and possession. Troubled as they are, truth claims continue to be central to autobiography. First of all, as Elizabeth Bruss argues in *Autobiographical Acts: The Changing Situation of a Literary Genre*, "the autobiographer purports to believe what he asserts" (10–11). For Gusdorf, notions of truth are as crucial in autobiographies as they are complicated. A biographer can never know the full truth about his subject, a biography is "always related to the detective story," and "it is precisely in order to do away with misunderstandings, to restore an incomplete or deformed truth, that the autobiographer himself takes up the telling of his story" (36). However, although "[m]any critics have attacked the very idea of truthfulness as a useful concept for understanding autobiography, for they see it as imposing a narrow and unattainable standard of resemblance to an irrecoverable past," as John D. Barbour points out in *The Conscience of the Autobiographer: Ethical and Religious Dimensions of Autobiography*, truthfulness is nonetheless "a crucial goal of most autobiographers," and "assessments of truthfulness or its lack are a crucial element in the distinctive mode of reading that autobiography engenders" (26).

Furthermore, "autobiography is a second reading of experience," in Gusdorf's view, "it is truer than the first because it adds to experience itself consciousness of it. In the immediate moment, the agitation of things ordinarily surrounds me too much for me to be able to see it in its entirety. Memory gives me a certain remove and allows me to take into consideration all the ins and outs of the matter, its context in time and space," whereby "the reconstruction in spirit of my destiny bares the major lines that I have failed to notice, the demands of the deepest values I hold that, without my being clearly aware of it, have determined my most decisive choices" (38). The importance of memory for subjectivity and mental health has been underscored. Exploring how research on first-person epistemology has "been directed toward understanding the part played by memory in the experience of self" (461) and on autobiographical memory and neuropsychological disorders resulting from their loss, Stanley B. Klein, Tim P. German, Leda Cosmides, and Rami Gabriel, considering "the weighty problem of the ontology of autobiographical first-person experience" (482), argue in "A Theory of Autobiographical Memory: Necessary Components and Disorders Resulting from Their Loss" that the self is constructed from our memories of personal experiences. They propose that "one's sense of self depends, in a fundamental way, on memories of one's past experiences and the capacity to call those experiences to mind" (461).

Memory and narration, then, are intimately connected and crucial aspects in autobiographical expression. Comparing writing and painting, Gusdorf suggests that a painting captures a moment in a person's life and not a life in its totality. Autobiography, on the other hand, "requires a man to take a distance with regard to himself in order to reconstitute himself in the focus of his special unity and identity across time" (Gusdorf 35). For Paul Eakin in *Fictions in Autobiography: Studies in the Art of Self-Invention*, narrative is central in identity formation. Eakin argues that "self-narration is the defining act of the human subject, an act that is not only descriptive of the self but *fundamental to the emergence and reality of the subject*" (quoted by Kort, 39, emphasis in original). Galen Strawson, on the other hand, does not accord the same importance to narrative. Wesley Kort disagrees with both Eakin and Strawson because he finds that both narrative and non-narrative are important in autobiographical writing. Contending that there *is* compatibility and correspondence between life and narrative, Kort, in contrast to many postmodern scholars, proposes that what he sees as the four aspects of narrative (character, action or plot, place or location, and tone or teller) can be found in our lives, too, and that both depend on the beliefs we hold, since these beliefs shape our understandings and evaluations of people, places, events, and possibilities as well as our decisions and selections regarding if and how we include and present certain things in autobiographical writing.

Another aspect concerns what Karl Weintraub in *The Value of The Individual: Self and Circumstance in Autobiography* sees as the main tasks of autobiography, that is, self-representation and self-realization. In James Olney's view, "autobiography is a self-reflexive, a self-critical act, and consequently the criticism of autobiography exists *within* the literature instead of alongside it. The autobiographer can discuss and analyze the autobiographical act as he performs it" (25).[10] In Linda Anderson's estimation "there is little apparent difference for these critics between realizing the self and representing the self, and autobiography gets drawn seamlessly into supporting beliefs and values of an essentialist or Romantic notion of selfhood" (4). For Anderson, who views "the unified subject of modern liberal ideology" with suspicion, a

---

[10] Moreover, "the student and reader of autobiographies … is a vicarious or a closet autobiographer," and as to the authors of autobiography criticism, "their autobiographies have already half emerged in the act of living and writing about the autobiographies of others," thus reading a work by a critic in the field of autobiography criticism "will reveal a half-obscured, half-emergent autobiography that has been profoundly implicated in determining the particular critical or theoretical attitude being expressed" (Olney 26).

fascination with the mysteries and possible transcendence of the self is part and parcel of a "Romantic view of art" (4–5) that must be discarded. Pointing to the "revealing paradox" in autobiographical criticism and theory of the 1960s and 1970s of the idea of an ineffable and irreducible self, on the one hand, and the prescriptive demand for clear genre limits (in order to distinguish autobiography from fiction), on the other, Anderson finds that the seeming neutrality and objectivity of the approach of critics in this period "both disguised and supported their critical authority" (6). Fortunately, in Anderson's view, with the advent of critics influenced by feminism, psychoanalysis, and poststructuralism, "the theoretical temperature hots up" (6). "[B]y positing language or discourse as both preceding and exceeding the subject," poststructuralism, as Linda Anderson sees it, "deposed the author from his or her central place as the source of meaning and undermined the unified subject of autobiography" (6). Genre, as Anderson emphasizes with a reference to Jacques Derrida's "The Law of Genre," "is necessarily too general, but it also never general enough" (9). Autobiography, then, as Linda Anderson concludes, following Derrida, "turns itself into a genre in order to 'place' the subject, the 'I', only to be undone by the instability and difference already instated within the law" (11). On one level, moreover, knowledge "depends on figurative languages and tropes" and autobiographies "produce fictions or figures in place of the self-knowledge they seek," as Anderson comments on Paul de Man's "Autobiography as De-Facement." What de Man's essay ("a supremely deconstructive moment for Romantic selfhood") does is to invert the idea of a unique and unified self and emphasize instead a self that is "fatally divided" and "threatened by representation" (Anderson 13). Similarly, the "pre-existing subject of autobiographical theory" was "presented as an illusion, unmasked" in Roland Barthes' death of the author as the origin of meaning (Anderson 13).

As to spiritual processes from religious and theological perspectives, there are important studies of classical texts and narratives of conversion. In *The Evangelical Conversion Narrative: Spiritual Autobiography in Early Modern England*, Bruce D. Hindmarsh looks at the large number of conversion narratives written in England from the mid-1730s to the mid-1780s and observes that great numbers of people who underwent evangelical conversions sought to express their experiences in spiritual autobiographies in order to try to understand their experience. Another major study is David J. Leigh's *Circuitous Journeys: Modern Spiritual Autobiography* that examines ten religious autobiographers of the twentieth century.

In one of the few recent book-length publications on modern spiritual autobiographies, *Textual Intimacy: Autobiography and Religious Identities*, Wesley A. Kort analyzes nine modern autobiographies, choosing works where religion plays an important part and dividing these accounts into separate but overlapping groups according to the ways in which religion is important for each writer. Kort's first category, Religious Debtors, includes writers for whom religion has played a major role in the past or when they were growing up. Writers for whom religion is central in the present are placed in a second group, Religious Dwellers. Dwelling is strongly associated with place and location, and in the case of Religious Dwellers this is reflected in terms of their religious affiliation. Religious Diviners, finally, are writers who tend to be more oriented toward the future. The nine texts analyzed in *Textual Intimacy* are all are from a Judeo-Christian tradition. Two are by Jewish writers, and five by Christian writers from different denominations (Catholic, Presbyterian, and Unitarian). In Kort's view, "the discourses in and by which negotiations and constructions that relate religious and American identities to one another have been largely shaped by Protestant, Catholic, and Jewish writers." The autobiographies analyzed are presented as examples of the three categories established by Kort.[11]

Focusing on how religious traditions are appropriated by individuals and how religious voices enter into narrative constructions of the self, *Religious Voices in Self-Narratives: Making Sense of Life in Times of Transition*, finally, an anthology edited by Marjo Buitelaar and Hetty Zock, was published in 2013. This volume of essays deals with religion and biography, in particular, as the title indicates, 'religious voices in self-narratives in times of transition.' While *Religious Voices* foregrounds the views of psychologists, anthropologists, and historians, it does not delve into the literary and theological perspectives that will be at the centre of the present study. The authors come from disciplines such as psychology, anthropology, history and religious studies, but, surprisingly, since character, tone, imagery, and plotline are said to be of interest, there are no literary scholars. Generally speaking, there is an avoidance of a discussion and evaluation of aesthetic and formal aspects of autobiographical writing such as language, tone, narrative perspective, and

---

[11] A question that could be raised is if Kort's tripartite analytical framework could be applied to *any* spiritual autobiography and whether it is equally useful for all religious orientations. In *Textual Intimacy* works by African and Asian immigrants have been excluded since "there is a paucity of self-accounts by these Americans" and "discernible patterns have not been established" (6).

instead, a focus on content and themes from social and rational perspectives. The irrational and passionate aspects of the human psyche, that are also essential in religious voices, tend to be lost.

In David Leigh's definition in *Circuitous Journeys*, autobiography is "a narrative that embodies the life story of an author as self-conscious subject present to itself but also reflectively exploring and affirming the interrelationships of his or her interior, interpersonal, and social world" (26). A spiritual autobiography is a narrative where the interior and spiritual aspects are uppermost. If we build on Philippe Lejeune's definition, we might say that a spiritual autobiography is a retrospective and introspective prose narrative produced by a real person concerning his own existence vis-à-vis an ultimate or transcendent reality and placed within an actual or imagined, religious or spiritual community, focusing on the development of his spirituality in particular and relating inner and outer events and milestones in his individual life to a religious, theological, or spiritual dimension approached through particular concepts, symbols, and rituals.

Certainly, spiritual paths and experiences can be hard to capture and convey. In *Understanding Religious Conversion*, Lewis Rambo asks: "How can we understand, predict, and control that which is generally invisible to the outsider, mysterious and sacred to the insider, and more often than not subject to debate within the tradition itself?" (11).

One window open to a deeper understanding, the present study will suggest, is that of the spiritual autobiography. Indeed, as Wesley Kort emphasizes in *Textual Intimacy*, we read autobiographies "*because they give us knowledge not usually accessible*" (2, my italics). As Gaustad points out, "many American autobiographers blend their own story with that of their society and their nation. An inner, private history becomes a window through which to see more clearly the complexities and ironies of the modern world" (xiv). In *Religious Voices in Self-Narratives: Making Sense of Life in Times of Transition*, moreover, Marjo Buitelaar and Hetty Zock argue rightfully that "self-narratives are the medium *par excellence* through which to study the rich variety of manifestations and functions of religion" (3). "In pluralistic and individualized cultural contexts," Buitelaar and Zock go on to say, "the question of how religious voices are appropriated by individuals has become particularly relevant" (2).[12] From the perspective of psychology

---

[12] In Wilhelm Dilthey's view, as James Olney puts it, "autobiography occupied a central place as *the* key to understanding the curve of history, every sort of cultural manifestation, and the very shape and essence of human culture itself" (8). Similarly, in *The Value of the*

of religion, similarly, Ulrike Popp-Baier suggests in "Life Stories and Philosophies of Life: A Perspective for Research in Psychology of Religion," that if one is "interested in how people relate to whatever they or other people call religion or give meaning to their lives or find meaningful in their lives," "the life-story approach provides the best methodology to this end" (59). Whereas one can rely on theological or philosophical works when exploring stories of spiritual development, as John Barbour asserts in *Versions of Deconversion: Autobiography and the Loss of Faith*, finally, "autobiographical narratives express the interplay of cognitive, volitional, and emotional factors within the individual and the writer's commitments within a particular society and broader cultural context" (7).

Whereas the spiritual autobiography is often in one sense a success story, the texts chosen in this study will focus on introspective works by writers who embark on genuine quests and who do not know beforehand where they will end up. Spiritual autobiographies that are sermons whose main purpose is to enlighten readers and set them on the right path, that are providence tales, wonder tales, or conversion narratives designed to convert others, are not a primary concern here, even though such aspects will surface in some of the texts, in particular in the near-death narratives analyzed in the final chapter. Further, the intention here is to explore individual spiritual development as expressed in autobiographical narratives, not to enter into contemporary religious debate. The focus will be less on what William James in *Varieties of Religious Experience* sees as the 'ordinary' religious believer, the person whose "religion has been made for him by others, communicated to him by tradition, determined to fixed forms by imitation, and retained by habit" (11), and more on seekers on a spiritual quest. Complex and conflicting as they might be, self-accounts are, in Wesley Kort's view, "oriented to if not determined by three areas": the personal, the social, and the ontological, and "any account that [one gives] can be primarily located within one of the three" (20, 21). In the present study, it is primarily the first and the third arenas, the personal and the ontological, that will be explored, in relation to social arenas.

This study will neither evaluate the experiences or descriptions of union, communion, and communication with a higher power or divinity described

---

Individual: Self and Circumstance in Autobiography (1978) Karl Weintraub has treated autobiography "as an epiphenomenon and mirror of cultural history" (Olney 13).

in the texts selected nor attempt to establish any objective truths about the reality of such experiences. Instead, through a focus on narrative, metaphor, style and tone, the aim is, rather, to study autobiographical descriptions of spiritual journeys and transcendental experiences. It will be proposed that a deeper understanding of the inner and outer journeys narrated in the contemporary spiritual autobiography may open up through a close reading of directional images and key metaphors.

While researchers such as Karl F. Morrison (in *Conversion and Text: The Cases of Augustine of Hippo, Herman-Judah, and Constantine Tsatsos*), see the gap between spiritual experiences and their representation in language as surmountable only in silence, since rational thought is unable to communicate such experiences, in Harold Bloom's view, metaphors can function as bridges between different registers and different kinds of experience, even those of transcendence. Ever since I. A. Richards published *The Philosophy of Rhetoric* (1936), metaphors have been regarded as fundamental structuring principles in language, and not just added decoration or ornament. Since metaphors speak to readers' emotions, moreover, their aesthetic and rhetorical effects become powerful.

In matters of faith and spirituality, metaphors may be crucial, since they offer a way to express that which is otherwise difficult to convey. In *The Interior Castle*, Teresa of Àvila likens God to a "burning furnace" or a "vast blazing fire," to take one example, and she describes the "delightful fervor" that can overcome the soul as a "fragrance so powerful that it diffuses itself through all the senses" (75, 76). Apart from images of movement, waters, boats, and pilots, Teresa also draws upon erotic unions of rapture, ravishment, inebriating union, and ecstasy to convey the encounter with God. Augustine begins his *Confessions* with a reflexion on the oxymoronic difficulties of conveying something about the nature of God. It is as impossible as it is necessary: "What can any man say when he speaks of you? But woe to them that keep silence—since even those who say most are dumb" (Book One, Chapter IV). Similarly, Teresa finds it almost impossible to convey how souls are aroused by God, that is, how "the Bridegroom treats the soul before uniting her entirely to Himself": she does not think she can explain these ways "except to people who have personally experienced them. These desires are such delicate and subtle impulses springing from the inmost depths of the soul that [she knows] of nothing to which they can be compared" (74).

It has been suggested that metaphors can help us understand our images and models of God. If that is the case, metaphors could bridge what David Leigh calls "the inevitable gap between the human signifier and the divine signified" (22). In *Metaphorical Theology: Models of God in Religious Language*, Sallie McFague makes a case for a metaphorical theology. Even though metaphors infuse and underpin all our thinking (with dominant root-metaphors becoming models and "abstraction[s] of the similar from a sea of dissimilars" becoming concepts [16]), metaphors—"seeing one thing *as* something else, pretending 'this' is 'that' because we do not know how to think or talk about 'this'"— are even more relevant and unavoidable when "speaking about the great unknowns" (McFague 15). Indeed, in McFague's view, metaphorical thinking is prophetic, while symbolic thinking is priestly, and she writes: "good metaphors shock, they bring unlikes together, they upset conventions, they involve tension, and they are implicitly revolutionary" (17). Proposing that religious language in the Bible is fundamentally relational (between God and Israel in the Old Testament and between persons in the community in the New Testament), McFague argues that the Judeo-Christian tradition is primarily personalistic and relational and, less frequently, naturalistic and impersonal: ("God as rock, fortress, running stream, power, sun, thunder" [20]). Calling for a multitude of metaphors, McFague sees the task of a metaphorical theology as an attempt to "chart the relationships among metaphors, models, and concepts," to "investigate possibilities for transformative, revolutionary models," and "to question the *didactic* tradition of orthodoxy over the more flexible, open, *kerygmatic* point of view epitomized in the parables and Jesus as parable" (28, italics in original). Since the central, absolutized models in the Christian tradition have been hierarchical, further, it is the task of a metaphorical theology to reform and transform.

So how does a non-fictional genre work that purports to express that which, in verbal communication, is expressed only with difficulty or perhaps not at all? Before turning to an exploration of a selection of contemporary spiritual autobiographies, the next chapter will explore definitions of spirituality and theories of spiritual development that might be useful for a deeper understanding of the spiritual autobiography, past and present.

Spiritual Autobiography and
Stages of Development

Since autobiography theory generally has focused on the secular autobiography, the question arises if and how the spiritual autobiography is different. In order to explore this question, it may be useful first to consider what spirituality is. Although it has gained wide currency in recent decades, 'spirituality' is a slippery term whose meanings range from the banal to the transcendent. In what follows, terms and definitions offered by Lewis Rambo, John Hull, Patrick Love, Paul Wink and Michele Dillon, Kelly B. Cartwright, and Robert C. Atchley will be discussed.

Spirituality and religion are terms that are difficult to define in part because there is no consensus and in part because these terms tend to be regarded as synonymous. In "Differentiating Spirituality from Religion," Patrick G. Love cites the *Random House Dictionary of the English Language* (1979), which states that religion "is a concern over what exists beyond the visible world (operating through faith and intuition, as opposed to reason)"; it "generally includes the idea of the existence of a single being, a group of beings, an eternal principle, or transcendental spiritual entity that has created the world, that governs it, that controls its destinies" and "the idea that ritual, prayer, spiritual exercises, or certain principles and conduct arise naturally as a human response to the belief in such a being or eternal principle" (qtd. by Love 2015). Spirituality has, according to the *Random House Dictionary*, more to do with "seeking personal authenticity, genuineness, and wholeness as an aspect of identity development," with "continually transcending one's current locus of centricity (e.g., egocentricity)," with "the process of deriving meaning, purpose, and direction in one's life," and with "an increasing openness to exploring a relationship with an intangible and pervasive power or essence or center of value that exists beyond human existence and rational human knowing."

Concerned with participation in communal activities such as church service, religion is often seen as an institutionalized system of thought, ritual, theological doctrine, and structure aimed to bring its adherents toward what they consider the ultimate. In *Introducing Feminist Theology*, Anne M. Clifford defines spirituality as a "[s]triving to integrate one's life in terms of self-transcendence toward what one perceives to be the ultimate value" (272). John Hull suggests in "Spiritual Development: Interpretations and Applications" that "whatever you take as ultimate will become your religion" (176). On this view, religion is an instrument that is useful in the development toward true humanness. Although, as Hull points out, spirituality and religion are not attitudes, people engaged in religion and spirituality will evince certain attitudes among which faith is central. Faith could thus be seen as an "attitude of acceptance directed toward the transcendence of the human, and faith in the narrow sense of religious faith would be directed toward the symbols of ultimacy," and Hull concludes that "[r]eligion is the instrument; spirituality is the goal; faith is confidence that the instrument will lead to the goal" (176). Ritual, authority, and hierarchy have marked many religions negatively, and this brings the risk of what John Hull calls 'religionism,' which may emerge when religion "seeks to build up collective identity by constructing negative images of the religions and faith of other people" (Hull 176).

The meaning of the term spirituality has shifted over the centuries and the term itself began to be used only in the seventeenth century. Before that, distinctions were made between (morally charged) conceptions of spiritual and material matters and between spiritual and temporal aspects in a legal sense (concerning, for example, church or worldly property). While the older associations of the word have been carried over into modern usage, the word *spiritualité* was coined in France in the seventeenth century due in part to the influence of Madame Guyon. As Carrette and King explain in *Selling Spirituality: The Silent Takeover of Religion*, "a new sensibility began to emerge which specifically associated *spiritualité* with the interior life of the individual soul" (37). Guyon's method of *orison*, "a silencing of self in order to experience the divine within" (37), sounds like a precursor of modern methods of meditation. Following Principe, Carrette and King find that the term spirituality has been used more widely from the 1950s, a time when, thanks to the development of American humanistic psychology, there was increasingly an "interiorized and psychologically inflected language of 'spirituality'" (43). However, as Carrette and King argue, "[t]he dichotomy between the secular and the religious, so central to the Western project of modernity and liberalism, may well be in the process of unraveling" (180–81). Today, the term spirituality may just as often have secular as religious connotations.

In *The Meaning of Lives: Biography, Autobiography, and the Spiritual Quest*, Richard A. Hutch makes a distinction between 'implicit' and 'explicit' religion. While implicit religion is similar to the concept of spirituality, explicit religion is "the corroboration of implicit religion by means of interpersonal interaction and collective life" in a community "giving (usually) institutionalized vent to their shared implicit religion" (2). In Robert C. Atchley's definition in "Everyday Mysticism: Spiritual Development in Later Adulthood," spirituality "is usually defined as a holistic inner domain within which people deal with existential issues such as the meaning of life, the nature and existence of God or the Absolute, the causes and cures of human suffering, the meaning of death, and identifying right courses of action" (125). Building on Atchley's theories, Paul Wink and Michele Dillon propose in "Spiritual Development Across the Adult Life Course: Findings From a Longitudinal Study," that spirituality "connotes the self's existential search for ultimate meaning through an individualized understanding of the sacred" (79). Contrasting the spiritual and the biological, John Hull suggests in "Spiritual Development: Interpretations and Applications" that human potentials transcending the biological are spiritual, whereby spirituality becomes a rather vast category that also includes language, conscience, and creativity. Hull suggests further that we visualize the concepts of spirituality, religion and faith

> as a series of three concentric circles with the outside, largest circle being spirituality, the middle ring being religion and the inner circle being faith. Spirituality includes religion but is more comprehensive. Religion as a whole is concerned with spirituality but not all spirituality is concerned with religion. (171)

Hull defines religion thus: "In religion we transcend our humanity itself, postulating a transcendence beyond which there is no further transcendence. When we encounter or conceive of a transcendence beyond which no higher transcendence can be conceived, we call this the ultimate, and we name it the divine, the absolute or God," and he goes on to say that:

> Religion relativises all our human achievements by placing them under the domain of the transcendent itself. Religion sets human life against its ultimate limit. Thus, through religion, the finite discovers itself as finite in the presence of the

infinite. The temporal discovers itself through religion to be faced with the eternal. (173)

At the same time, when it comes to "religion as a distinct and universal category," as Ulrike Popp-Baier points out, this "is more or less the intervention of scholars in the 19th century," whereas more recently, the "concept of religion as a universal category has been seriously challenged" (57). Focusing primarily on individual spirituality, the present study will rely on the definition offered by John D. Barbour in *The Value of Solitude: The Ethics and Spirituality of Aloneness in Autobiograhy*:

> Spirituality involves encounter or intimate relationship with something outside the self, whether a part of the natural world, God, or the cosmos as a whole, it also entails self-discovery, self-acceptance, and new understanding of who one really is. These two components—knowing oneself more fully and being better related to an ultimate reality beyond the self—are often fused in spiritual experience, so that, in the paradoxical language of mystics, a person may speak of a new awareness of the divine both within the self and beyond it. (4)

Following Rambo & Haar Farris, Bruce Greyson and Surbhi Khanna suggest that "Americans seem to be more comfortable with the freedom associated with spirituality, and implied in this distinction is the emphasis on personal choice and independence from the constraints of religion" (302). Building on research by Koenig, King & Carlsson, further, Greyson and Khanna argue that

> [t]he United States in particular has witnessed a polarization of religiousness and spirituality, with the former representing an institutional, formal, outward, doctrinal, authoritarian, inhibiting expression and the latter representing an individual, subjective, emotional, inward, unsystematic, and freeing expression. (302)

In Margaret Placentra Johnston's view in *Faith Beyond Belief: Stories of Good People Who Left Their Church Behind*, finally, traditional religion is often "exclusionist, ethnocentric, judgmental, and triumphalist" (278), whereas Johnston would like to see a development towards heterodox, mystery-centred, and "post-critical" spirituality.

Spiritual development towards self-transcendence has been seen as a crucial part of human development. While both religion and spirituality are concerned with matters beyond the physical and visible universe, spirituality may or may not include an idea of or belief in a supreme being. There may be a sense that there is something beyond the physical world even though we cannot determine exactly what this is. The spiritual journey, then, could be seen as a movement towards a dimension beyond the corporeal where communication with God, a supreme being, or a Higher Power is uppermost, a movement marked by a desire for wholeness and authenticity stemming from a sense of dissatisfaction and an attempt to find meaning and purpose in one's life. A spiritual search may be prompted in midlife by a sense of dissatisfaction with what may have been a hyperactive life focused on work and family to the detriment of introspection. At midlife, the horizon shrinks, and mortality adds a sense of urgency to one's existence. In this often difficult passage spirituality may become a more important aspect in the maturational process due to a need for growth and development. There may also be losses and traumas that trigger spiritual journeys.

The spiritual journey is often visualized as a journey consisting of stages, with a beginning and an end, a goal reached. This is how spiritual development is described both in classic texts such as Teresa of Àvila's *The Interior Castle* and in modern developmental theories such as James Fowler's *Stages of Faith: The Psychology of Human Development and The Quest for Meaning.* One departs from a certain point, traverses different stages, and arrives at a desired point of insight, maturity, illumination, and transformation, whereby major changes have taken place. Not that stasis or stagnation beckon at the end of the journey (although they might), but some things are definitely left behind, be it immaturity, depression, doubt, or irresolution. Conceptualized, too, through metaphors of health and illness, or maturity and immaturity, the stages of spiritual development may range from unawareness or nondifferentiation to unity consciousness, from egocentricity to cosmocentricity, from selfishness to selflessness, from the subjective to the objective, from conformism to inner-directedness. The stages may be spatially conceived as in Teresa of Àvila's inner rooms or 'mansions,' they may be hierarchically organized as in Fowler's scheme, understood as geological layers, or viewed almost behavioristically as 'styles.'

Stages of spiritual development have also been discussed in relation to cognitive developmental theory. The fundamental view is that all humans evolve and develop on different levels over a lifetime in both predictable and individual ways. Thus, it has been posited that cognition and spirituality may develop along similar paths. Returning to the stages of development posited by Piaget, Kelly B. Cartwright notes in "Cognitive Developmental Theory and Spiritual Development" that Piaget's scheme does not include adult stages, something that has been addressed in postformal theories of cognitive development. Further, while Piaget stresses development towards cognitive mastery and objectivity, subjectivity has not been taken sufficiently into account. Other theorists have outlined stages of moral and cognitive development that have been applied to spiritual development, such as Lawrence Kohlberg's six stages of moral development from conformity, outer-directedness, and self-interest to greater principles of truth, or from a first to a second naïveté via a stage of critical distance as in Ricœur's *The Symbolism of Evil*. In *The Individual and His Religion*, Gordon Allport attempted to define mature religion, which, in his view, leaves behind literalism, magical thinking, and received religious ideas and reaches a non-egocentric, moral, and heuristic level. In *Religious Judgement: A Developmental Perspective*, Fritz Oser and Paul Gmünder outline five stages of religious judgment that in many ways recall the stages posited by James Fowler. Their first two stages could also be applied not only to individual development but to the Bible, whereby God in the first stage is seen as all-powerful and in the second stage as powerful but possible to influence through the right action. The next steps involve surrender, acceptance, enlightenment, transcendence, and union with God. The fifth and final stage brings compassion and a wish to serve humanity.

Teresa of Àvila's spatially conceived rooms or mansions in *The Interior Castle* include seven stages. The first mansion could be seen as a point of departure on the spiritual journey where unawareness and materialism ('reptiles') reign. It corresponds to stages visualized by modern developmental theorists where human beings occupied with careers and worldly affairs follow the rules laid down by society. In Teresa's second mansion people have been roused and are beginning to question conformist religion, and in the third mansion they are even more reflective. The fourth mansion brings increasing acceptance and less clinging to the material world. The fifth mansion leads to a more complete surrender to and trust in God whereby the ego and all its concerns take a step back. It is in the sixth mansion that the dark night of the soul may strike, which means that crisis comes relatively late in Teresa's scheme. Bringing balance and a commitment to serve God, the seventh mansion is where transcendence and deep spiritual insight is reached.

In *Stages of Faith*, James Fowler (drawing upon interviews with 359 adults), sees the development of faith as linked to cognitive and moral development. He formulates six key stages of spiritual development as reflective of meaning-making and relationships to other human beings and to a higher power, stages that are modelled on the theories of Piaget and

Kohlberg. Since Fowler's first four stages concern childhood and youth, they will not be relevant in the present study. Fowler begins with Stage 0, Primal or Undifferentiated (infants up to 2 years) which would correspond to Piaget's sensorimotor stage. Stage 1, Intuitive-Projective (from three to seven) would correspond to Piaget's preoperational phase, and Stage 2, Mythic-Literal (school children), to the concrete operational. The Mythic-Literal stage involves a literal attitude to faith and morality with God seen as a father figure. Stage 3 is Synthetic-Conventional faith (adolescence from age 12). It recalls Theresa's first stages of unquestioning adherence to authorities and is marked by a lack of analysis (which is why Fowler calls it 'synthetic'). Actually, in Fowler's view, many religions and church-going people remain in this stage and do not move beyond it, something that may even be encouraged by the churches.[1] Stages 3 to 6 correspond to Piaget's formal operational stage. As in Piaget's theory, postformal stages are not included in Fowler's *Stages of Faith*. Since stage 4, Individuative-Reflective faith (mid-twenties to late thirties), is the first stage of independent assessment, reflection, and a questioning of authorities, it may evoke anxiety, and it may take several years to move through. Stage 5, Conjunctive faith, normally occurring around midlife, can lead to a confrontation with the paradox of reality and the elusiveness of transcendence and allow for a greater acceptance of paradox and complexity as well as openness toward other faiths. Seldom occurring before the mid-forties, stage 6, Universalizing faith, the highest stage, leads to a broadening faith that embraces individual as well as universal and abstract principles and values, could be compared to enlightenment.

In *Integral Spirituality*, Ken Wilber visualizes twelve stages in terms of colour that recall traditional chakra systems. Marked by egocentricity and aggression, the first and most primitive level is red (infrared, magenta, and red). Amber, the next stage, recalls Teresa's first mansion in its conventionality and conformism. Egocentricity here becomes group-centricity. The third stage is orange, and involves individuating steps toward world-centricity. While these first three stages could be compared to Piaget's first stages—sensorimotor, preoperational, concrete operational, and formal operational—it may be misleading to see them as chronological and age-related, since many people remain stuck in 'early' stages most of their lives.

---

[1] Along similar lines, Margaret Placentra Johnston suggests in *Faith Beyond Belief: Stories of Good People Who Left Their Church Behind* that "much of traditional religion promotes a spiritually immature message" (5).

Recalling the heart chakra, Wilber's green stage brings compassion and a wish to serve others. Since an individual at this stage seeks connection rather than division, Ken Wilber suggests that the green stage resembles Fowler's fifth stage. The next colours, teal and turquoise, are associated with a 'cosmo-centric' view, a stage reached by very few. As in Ken Wilber's highest stage in *Integral Spirituality*, Fowler's final stage is reached only by exceptional individuals such as Gandhi or Martin Luther King Jr.

Whereas factors for spiritual development such as personality and intelligence have been underlined, the factor of age has been less examined even though it, too, plays an important role in spiritual development. In "Spiritual Development Across the Adult Life Course: Findings From a Longitudinal Study," Paul Wink and Michele Dillon examine the role of spirituality across the life span, looking at two cohorts that were interviewed on four occasions over four decades. Their research shows that "all the participants, irrespective of gender and cohort, showed a significant increase in spirituality from late middle (mid-50s/late 60s) to older adulthood (late 60s/mid-70s). There thus appears to be "a general tendency for individuals to become more concerned with issues of spirituality in older age" (91). Spiritual development "tends to occur in the second half of adult life," and it is "enhanced by the combination of being a psychologically minded and unconventional individual who has also experienced discontinuity and adversity" (Wink and Dillon 93). Studies by other researchers, such as D. M. Hamilton and M. H. Jackson's "Spiritual Development: Paths and Processes," see the role of adversity as a catalyst in spiritual development, a view with which Fowler concurs. Similarly, in "Everyday Mysticism: Spiritual Development in Later Adulthood," Robert C. Atchley underlines the connection between older adulthood and a deeper spirituality, something that other historical epochs and other cultures have recognized. Examples are the Hindu stages of life, with the fourth stage reserved for a lessening engagement in and even renunciation of worldly affairs. The notion of increased interest in spirituality in old age goes back at least to Confucius. Premodern Western societies, too, have endowed older people with spiritual wisdom, and in colonial New England elders held special positions in the church, something that was lost with the increasing meritocracy and specialization that followed in the wake of modernization. Building on previous studies as well as on his own research, Atchley concludes that "[s]tudies of aging individuals indicate that spiritual growth does indeed occur in the later stages of adulthood," and he proposes that "contemplative, mystical experience is at the heart of adult spiritual development" (124).

James Fowler, too, in *Stages of Faith*, found a greater sense of unity and transcendence in older people.

Looking at the stories of nonbelievers, post-organized religion, and 'spiritual but not religious' categories and examining theories of spiritual development by thinkers such as James Fowler and Saint Teresa of Avila, in *Faith Beyond Belief: Stories of Good People Who Left Their Church Behind*, Margaret Placentra Johnston (who herself left the Catholic church of her childhood) posits four stages of spiritual development that she calls the lawless stage, the faithful stage, the rational stage, and the mystic stage. Johnston's stages seem to be inspired mainly by F. Scott Peck and James Fowler, and it is difficult to determine exactly how her stages differ from those delineated by Peck. Whereas the four stages proposed may be reasonable and realistic, the terminology is confusing since terms such as 'lawless' and 'faithful' often imply strong value judgments (negative or positive), as does the term 'rational.' Even Johnston's fourth stage, 'mystic', is partly misleading. It is problematic, then, that the terminology is so charged, and the sense of progression that the division into stages implies is partly undermined by Johnston's conclusion that in the end all levels hold partial truths about God or an ultimate reality. There is certainly a sense of progression in Johnston's scheme, however, and the first two levels are clearly less developed. Organized religion tends to be found on what Johnston calls the faithful level, with "literal believers in traditional religion" and sometimes religious leaders who do not encourage spiritual growth to the Mystic level in their congregations" (96). Worse, these religious leaders

> preach the Faithful level of religion not because they have not been taught about—or cannot understand—the Mystic level, but rather because keeping people Faithful is better for the longevity of their institutions. If people didn't feel they needed a certain church and set of beliefs, they would be free to conduct a spiritual search on their own. (Johnston 96)

Even though Johnston emphasizes that groups are porous and that one can belong to more than one group, with characteristics such as mature and immature, external or internal, separate or unitive, or theological understandings of God as literal or metaphorical, the development categories she proposes are oriented toward the very binarism she wishes to avoid.

Whereas people at the faithful and rational stages crave certainty (as do the new atheists who are certain that God does not exist), people at the Mystic level have embraced doubt and ended up accepting the fundamental mystery of the universe. If they speak of certainty it tends to be more in the terms of *certitude* rather than certainty:

> They are certain "there is something out there," some sort of divine Presence, even though they can't prove it and have very little idea of what that presence might be like. *Certitude* means something more like trust. Whereas the "certainty" grasped at by the other levels arises out of a *fear* of the unknown, the Mystic is more likely to trust that whatever is out there, it is benevolent. (Johnston 198)

As individuals develop through the four stages, their worldview changes and becomes broader. Whereas the first stage is marked by egocentricity and selfishness, the second is characterized by exclusivity, ethnocentricity, a tendency to see one's own group or congregation as superior, and, not infrequently, a measure of triumphalism. At the third (rational) level the perspective becomes worldcentric, something that often leads to a greater sense of inclusivity and social engagement. At the mystic level, finally, there is a universal and unitive worldview "encompassing everyone and everything, including the spirit world" whereby the mystic "has transcended the walls of his own culture, his own faith tradition, even his political party; to the Mystic, everyone and everything in the cosmos deserves the same attention, respect, and concern. The overriding trait of the post-critical person is his all-inclusive, universal worldview" (Johnston 200).

Whereas the lower levels are competitive and profit-oriented, the mystic level is marked by a profound sense of interconnectedness. Furthermore, mystics have moved from literal to metaphorical interpretations of Scripture and to a greater acceptance of ambiguity and paradox. Having moved beyond a need for what Johnston calls 'oracle authority' and through the 'conscience authority' marking the rational stage, mystics are able to listen to 'spirit authority,' something that brings a more accepting, humble, and forgiving attitude with gratitude replacing greed. But "the Mystic of the spiritual-development ladder is not a secluded hermit on a mountaintop," according to Johnston: "Rather, she is one who can put up with the vicissitudes of interacting with unsolvable situations, inconsistent people, and the frustrations of a largely imperfect world" (206). Thus, in Johnston's view, the mystic "engages in spirituality or a faith community to serve others and to better approach the Mystery of Spirit, however he or she might understand that" (207).

Following Fowler, finally, Johnston argues that the levels of spiritual development can be applied to the development of society as well, whereby "society progresses through essentially the same development trajectory that each individual must traverse in the move toward maturity, with the faithful stage "comparable to that of the pre-Enlightenment society" and the rational stage "comparable to Enlightenment-level thought" (260). Today, Johnston concludes, "if there is a transformation occurring, it is hurling our society toward the universal worldview of the Mystic" (261).

If we turn from theories of spiritual development to autobiographical writings, we will find that the pattern of moving from darkness to light or from sin to redemption recurs in classical texts such as captivity narratives. In Mary Rowlandson's *The Sovereignty and Goodness of God* (1682), there is a movement from the 'sin' of captivity to redemption by God. While the 'outer' events describe Rowlandson's experiences of captivity, the 'inner' experience is the insight rising from those experiences of the necessity of having complete trust in God, whereby Rowlandson learns to look beyond smaller and more trivial problems. Half a century later, Jonathan Edwards wrote his "Personal Narrative" (1739) about the ups and downs of his own religious development, the downs being periods of sin due to his 'wicked' inclinations to the point when he makes seeking salvation the main aim of his life and moves towards an "inward, sweet delight in God and divine things" (21). Orestes Brownson's nineteenth-century 'sketch' "aimed to record facts, principles, and reasonings, trials and struggles," to take another example, tells the story of "the personal history of an earnest soul, working its way, under the grace of God, from darkness to light, from the lowest abyss of unbelief to a firm, unwavering, and not a blind faith in the old religion" (the Roman Catholic Church) (79) to the conclusion that "religion is of the highest necessity to man and society" (86). But the pattern of moving from sin to grace found in many spiritual autobiographies may apply not only to the author's own sense of sin but to that of the world. In Thomas Merton's *The Seven Storey Mountain*, for example, there is a desire to leave behind a greedy, foul, miserable, and cruel world marked by desires, appetites, competition and conflict and to immerse oneself instead in a world of monks, which is seen as clean, ageless, eternal, poor, unvarnished, straightforward, and freed from the tyranny of the flesh.

While the studies and theories of stages in spiritual development mentioned above can provide a useful starting point, it is also important to remember that stage theory has been criticized for its positing of "invariant and irreversible succession of stages of increasing complexity," as Barbara Keller points out in "Toward a Multidimensional Conception of Faith Development: Deconversion Narratives in Biographical Context" (78). From life span developmental perspectives, multidimensionality and multi-directionality have instead been stressed along with historicity and context-dependency (Keller 79).

For the purposes of the present study, the stages outlined by Lewis Rambo in *Understanding Religious Conversion* would seem to be the most useful. Rambo's first stage is 'context,' which refers to a person's whole historical and educational background, culture and life experience. If one remains in this stage, there is a risk of stagnation and conventional understandings of religion and spirituality. Rambo's context stage could be compared to Teresa's first three stages. 'Crisis,' Rambo's next stage, may be triggered by loss, trauma, or a general dissatisfaction with life. When life has thus been destabilized, 'quest,' the third stage, may follow, leading to a search for new information or alternative possibilities as well as to new contacts. 'Encounter,' the fourth stage, involves significant meetings that show new options, and 'interaction,' the fifth stage, brings immersion in a new spiritual or religious environment. Then, 'commitment' is the stage in which the seeker joins a faith community formally and ritually. The final stage is 'consequences,' in which a person immerses himself or herself in the new community and makes an assessment as to whether or not this community will lead to the desired outcome.

While some of the autobiographical narratives studied here do explore what Rambo sees as the first stage (context), more commonly the main focus is on the crisis traversed and the quest for spiritual transformation. Since all three of Rambo's 'middle' stages—quest, encounter, and interaction—include significant encounters, further, they are really subtle gradations on the path toward spiritual transformation. For the purposes of the present study, then, three of Rambo's stages will be the most important: crisis, quest, and consequences.[2]

A different perspective is offered by Jeremy Carrette and Richard King in *Selling Spirituality: The Silent Takeover of Religion.* Frustrated with what they see as a lack of clarity in discussions of spirituality, Carrette and King

---

[2] These terms are more appropriate here than, for example, Larry Culliford's terms outlined in *The Psychology of Spirituality: An Introduction,* Belonging, Searching, and Homecoming (or conformist, individual, and integrating). Three stages of conversion are also visualized by G. K. Chesterton In *The Catholic Church and Conversion* (patronizing the Church, discovering the Church, and running away from the Church), but these stages are really pre-conversion stages that omit the starting point and the consequences stage discussed by Rambo.

argue that spirituality has become "a new cultural addiction and a claimed panacea for the angst of modern living" (1). To the extent that spirituality is "seen as a force for wholeness, healing and inner transformation" this may be positive (1). Viewing contemporary notions of spirituality with suspicion and arguing that privatization and corporatization colour everything, even religion, Carrette and King argue that capitalist ideologies have taken over religion. Whereas enlightenment philosophers such as Locke cordoned off religion and placed it within the private realm, for Carrette and King, religion and spirituality are not so much cut off from the rest of society as an integral part of it. They see an emergence in recent decades of a 'capitalist spirituality,' which, even though it may look radical and transformative, is an 'accommodationist' spirituality that fails to challenge the status quo of selfish consumerist lifestyles. Instead, Carrette and King propose 'alternative' and more socially engaged understandings of the term spirituality. Due to the institutional control enforced by politics, education, and media, they propose, we are the victims of 'thought-control' forcing us to accept the dominant versions of reality proposed by corporate capitalism. Increasingly, there has been not only a privatization but an individualization of religion, and today, the "commodification of religion as spirituality" is ubiquitous (15). In Carrette and King's view, corporate capitalism wishes to draw upon the cultural capital of religion for its own, sinister purposes, namely to endow products with a spiritual aura of authenticity in order sell or to enhance productivity at work. This use of spirituality, Carrette and King argue, may seem to "endorse the values of the ancient traditions that it is alluding to" but is in reality a "silent takeover of religion," "in order to support the ideology of capitalism," something that will lead to an erosion of cultural diversity (17).

Carrette and King make an important point when they argue that a problem with a "private, psychologized spirituality" may be that "it reinforces the idea that the individual is solely responsible for his or her own suffering" when the self in fact is a product of economic, political, cultural and social interactions as well. However, a relentless emphasis on the social, political, and collective aspects of spirituality misses the fact that there may be times of losses and traumas in the lives of human beings when economic, political, cultural and social factors are less relevant and when an individual may experience an existential aloneness that makes him or her embark on a personal spiritual journey.

Since such journeys will be in focus in the present study, as narrated in contemporary spiritual autobiographies, let us return to definitions of the genre of the spiritual autobiography. The classic spiritual autobiography is defined by *The Literary Encyclopedia* as follows:

> a non-fictional form which rose to prominence in seventeenth-century England, although its roots can be traced as far back as such works of the early Christian tradition as St. Augustine's *Confessions*. The form's basic concern is to trace the progress of an individual believer from a state of sin to a state of grace, where the conviction takes hold that salvation has been guaranteed by God. Given the concentration on the individual, the form appealed most to Protestants, in particular the more militant sectarian movements (Baptists, Quakers, etc.) who broke away from the Church of England over the course of the seventeenth century—a period of marked religious division in English history. (Sim)

In a chapter on conversion in spiritual autobiographies in *La tentation auto-biographique de l'Antiquité à la Renaissance*, Philippe Gasparini, further, distinguishes some traits introduced in Christian accounts: "Ce que le christianisme introduit de radicalement nouveau dans l'écriture du moi, ce n'est pas seulement la 'faiblesse', l'humilité, c'est aussi l'avenir, une perspective eschatologique qui surplobme et configure le passé" (100–01).

Of course, the secular autobiography may not necessarily concern outer achievements only. It may treat psychological dimensions and psychic processes as well. However, an ontological and spiritual dimension is usually foregrounded and becomes the *raison d'être* of the spiritual autobiography. In David Leigh's definition in *Circuitous Journeys: Modern Spiritual Auto-biography* (2000), it is when a "lifelong search for an ultimate reality that gives meaning to one's life in the face of evil, suffering, and death become the theme of a book" that a work can be called a spiritual autobiography (xi). It is often the "creation in symbolic form of the self-affirmation of the person as transformed from lost to found, from seeker to discoverer, from alienated to reunited with a higher and deeper One" (27). While 'worldly' memoirs often serve to emblazon the high points and admirable exploits of the authors and aggrandize them, spiritual autobiographies tend to be less prone to gloss over the difficulties and pains suffered or to suppress personal failures or mistakes that could be construed as sin (depending on how sin is defined). In Georges Gusdorf's view, "[t]he theological mirror of the Christian soul is a deforming mirror that plays up without pity the slightest faults of the moral personality" (34). Pointing to the importance of religion, more specifically Christianity, not only for the spiritual autobiography but for the genre of autobiography itself, Gusdorf suggests that "Christianity brings a new anthropology to the fore" as "Christian destiny unfolds as a dialogue of the soul with God" (33):

> Each man is accountable for his own existence, and intentions weigh as heavily as acts—whence a new fascination with the secret springs of personal life. The rule requiring confession of sins gives to self-examination a character at once systematic and necessary. Augustine's great book is a consequence of this dogmatic requirement: a soul of genius presents his balance sheet before God in all humility—but also in full rhetorical splendor. (33)

A memoir (from the French word for memory) is often held to treat aspects of a life worth remembering rather than life in its totality. From the nineteenth century, "there was a definite hierarchy of values in relation to self-representation with memoirs occupying a lower order since they involved a lesser degree of 'seriousness' than autobiography," as Linda Anderson reminds us (8). But autobiography has "came to be equated with a developmental narrative which orders both time and the personality according to a purpose or goal" (Anderson 8). Such a narrative structure is crucial to most of the texts examined here, and although most of the texts in this study could be regarded as memoirs, since they do not present an all-encompassing lifetime perspective, the term autobiography will be used in the view that also 'incomplete' autobiographical narratives should be regarded as autobiographies. Even Augustine, who narrates his own life from childhood, left many things out of his *Confessions*: "for I pass over many things, hastening on to those things which more strongly impel me to confess to thee—and many things I have simply forgotten" (Book Three, Chapter XII). True, spiritual autobiographies could in some cases be said to be more like memoirs since they tend to focus specifically or even exclusively on spiritual events and experiences. As Linda Anderson writes about Bunyan: "Retrospectively, he picks out those [events of his life] which reveal a providential design" (27); "He makes only a passing reference to the Civil War and says little about the specific reasons for his imprisonment" (29). Similarly, to take an example from a modern spiritual autobiography such as Anne Rice's *Called Out Darkness: A Spiritual Confession*, the author mentions, but does not dwell on, the death of a child and the death of her husband.

One of the earliest examples of autobiography is found in the Bible in the texts written by Paul. Subjectivity is an important aspect, as when Paul holds himself up as an example to emulate in Galatians (4:12; 'I'm asking you to become like me'), or when he presents himself, his thoughts and feelings in Romans. An important contribution to the development of the spiritual autobiography was made by the fourth-century bishop Grégoire de Naziane (whose texts Augustine may have read before writing his *Confessions*), who addressed God and asked for comfort in his autobiographical poem *Sur ses épreuves*. Grégoire de Naziane also wrote *De vita sua*, ostensibly with an educational purpose but at the same time expressing his own suffering. Grégoire, importantly, did not idealize himself, according to Philippe Gasparini in *La tentation autobiographique*: "au lieu de construire un moi social idéalisé, unifié, significant, comme ses prédécesseurs, il affiche ses contradictions et ses blessures avec franchise, sinon avec délectation. Il faudra attendre le XXe siècle pour voir cette veine reapparaître puis proliférer" (106). Paulin de Pella's *Eucharisticos*, another important contribution and one of the imitations of Augustine's *Confessions*, is a work that is original in the author's view of himself as an ordinary individual, something that was not the case with Saint Patrick's *Confessions*, a work which must be regarded as both autobiography and hagiography (Gasparini 130, 120). Looking back to early spiritual autobiographies that have influenced the development of the genre, the autobiography of Guibert de Nogent, a twelfth-century monk, writer, and theologian, describes his struggle with sin, finding grace, and becoming a monk in *De vita sua, sive monodiarum*. In the fourteenth century, Dante's *Vita Nuova* and Petrarcha's *Secretum* are important milestones in spiritual autobiographical writing. Interestingly, Petrarcha wrote *Secretum* in "a dialogue with Augustine over whether or not to withdraw from the world" (Hindmarsh 24). Other important works from the fourteenth century were those of Julian of Norwich, Margery Kempe, and Margaret Ebner. In the sixteenth century, Teresa of Àvila and Ignatius de Loyola wrote their influential works (such as *A Pilgrim's Journey: The Autobiography of St. Ignatius Loyola* and Teresa of Avila's *Way of Perfection* and *The Interior Castle*).

With references to biblical narratives, both Augustine and Bunyan modelled their spiritual development on the lives of Paul and Jesus (just as Jesus himself emphasized his connection with Hebrew prophets). Augustine's life story in *Confessions* encompasses thirty-three years, to parallel that of Christ, and Bunyan writes about the first thirty-two years of his life in *Grace Abounding* even though, as Robert Bell points out in "Metamorphoses of Spiritual Autobiography," "he recast and revised *Grace Abounding* six times between 1666 and 1688" (109). While such models no longer predominate in the contemporary spiritual autobiography, biblical stories do infuse modern narratives and references to biblical parables and the words of Jesus abound. As in classical spiritual autobiographies, the focus is on stages of development. Bunyan's story, as Bell writes, "contains sections corresponding to the standard stages of regeneration: conviction of sin, vocation, justification, sanctification, and glorification," and "the paramount narrative purpose" of Augustine's *Confessions* is "to trace the hero's gradual development in grace" (Bell 108, 111). In depicting these stages of development, however, the contemporary spiritual autobiography deviates from earlier life stories in their more individualistic narratives that aim to express unique experiences, while older narratives did not aim for originality. To the contrary, as Robert Bell affirms, "Puritan doctrine fixed the structure and content of all such accounts. Even the striking title turns out to be a formulaic epithet; many Puritans, including Cromwell, envisioned themselves as the 'chief of sinners,'" and "Bunyan conforms generally to a stock pattern of conversion" (108). Bell sees Bunyan in *Grace Abounding* as "in the process of becoming a spiritual *exemplum*" and Augustine in *Confessions* as "a representation, or figure, of spiritual regeneration" who, however, "never *literally* realizes redemption" as he ends Book X with the view of his situation as a trial in which he wages a 'daily war' against temptation" (115).

Autobiographical writing focusing on the spiritual journey began to flourish after 1640, in part because the state at that time no longer exercised the same censorship as before, and in part because of the printing press. For religious dissenters, the spiritual autobiography became a matter not only of testimony of individual expression but of legitimation, in particular in cases where the writer lacked institutional connections or formal credentials, whereby "personal testimony" endowed authority and became "an important form of religious propaganda" (Anderson 26). Bunyan, a prime example, was imprisoned in 1660, and published *Grace Abounding to the Chief of Sinners* in 1666. While it is difficult to know if Bunyan had read Augustine, his autobiography resembles Augustine's *Confessions* in its "emphasis on a search for unity with God which could redeem the self's sinfulness and hence its incoherence" (Anderson 26–27). After the Reformation there is a greater sense that an individual stands alone and must turn to God for help, something that leads to an even greater emphasis on an individual's personal relation to God.

Although Puritan spiritual autobiographies illustrated patterns of conversion in the seventeenth century, the conversion narrative in its popular form arose in Britain and in New England in the mid-seventeenth century. Interestingly, Bruce D. Hindmarsh writes in *The Evangelical Conversion Narrative* that "there was a deeply rooted sense within Western European

Christianity that the fundamental human predicament was one of conscience, guilt, and divine judgement" (59), and he suggests that "[i]t was the unique convergence among Protestants of heightened individualism and heightened guilt, of self-consciousness and conscience, that led to the emergence of the new literary genre of conversion narrative" (60).[3] Looking at the development that contributed to the Evangelical Revival, Hindmarsh perceives "a native tradition of Puritan and Nonconformist spiritual autobiography and teaching about conversion, related traditions in British and American piety, and Continental Pietism," and he comments:

> The emergence of popular conversion narrative in these antecedent traditions of piety took place within the larger phenomenon of an autobiographical turn in the early modern period and the rise of heightened self-determination, introspection, and individuality. But it also drew on very specific religious and theological sources. In particular, conversion narrative was predicated on what Krister Stendahl called the 'introspective conscience' of the West. (59)

Hindmarsh raises the question as to "whether conversion narrative is a genre that has been constant since the New Testament, present whenever and wherever Christian communities have existed, and whether there are, therefore, pre-modern precedents for the evangelical narratives" (16). Protestant reformers seldom wrote spiritual autobiographies whereas they did write tracts and catechisms. Luther did not write a spiritual autobiography, but there is an autobiographical fragment from 1545 about his spiritual breakthrough when reading Romans 1 about the righteousness of God (according to Hindmarsh, recent scholarship indicates that Luther may have telescoped a much longer spiritual process when looking back at his life decades later). Similarly, no spiritual autobiography was left by John Calvin, except for some lines from his Preface to a *Psalms Commentary* (1557), a cryptic allusion to his conversion (from *subita conversion* till *docilitas*) called forth not by any desire for self-examination or autobiographical expression but rather to point to the comfort one may find in the Psalms when one (like David) faces difficult times. Hindmarsh concludes:

---

[3] "Although the narratives themselves were surprisingly similar, the role and consequences of conversion differed depending on the context. Thus conversion functioned within English Puritanism as part of the ideal development to transform the church and nation, and complete the Reformation. In early New England, in contrast, conversion was the bedrock on which the church and state rested" (Hindmarsh 53).

> There is a peculiar gap in the long tradition of the conversion narrative. The tens of thousands of Europeans who in the course of the sixteenth century turned to Protestantism left very few accounts of their experiences of conversion. Hence, we may speak of the evangelical conversion narrative in the eighteenth century, or the Puritan conversion narrative in the seventeenth century, but there is no genre of sixteenth-century Reformation conversion narrative. (26)

One important work in Puritan theology that was to provide a structure for autobiographies to come was William Perkins' *The Golden Chain* (or *Armilla Aurea*), a text that visualizes a chain of salvation all the way to divine glory. Perkins, first of all, encourages or rather exhorts readers to take full cognizance of their state of sin, to examine themselves and their lives, to realize that they cannot rectify their own lives without the help of God. In particular, Perkins' insistence upon close self-examination becomes a model for conversion narratives. In *Cases of Conscience* (1606), further, Perkins outlined the steps to take and the responses from God that would lead to salvation, through stages that Hindmarsh (pointing to Edmund Morgan's *Visible Saints*, 1963) refers to as a morphology of conversion. This is a "geography of the soul," a "definite teleology to divine grace" that involved God's "[stirring] up the mind to consider seriously the promises of the gospel" and "to kindle in the heart some sparks of faith" but also to "test with doubt, despair, and distrust" and "to quiet the conscience and give assurance of final salvation" (Hindmarsh 37).

Foregrounded in writers such as Augustine, Guibert de Nogent, Grégoire de Naziane, and Paulin de Pella, then, self-examination is an important characteristic of spiritual autobiographies across time. One example among conversion narratives is Richard Kilby's *The Burden of a Loaden Conscience* (1608). Although (as already the title indicates) this is a self-examination according to the Ten Commandments and an exposure of a sense of guilt and fear of God's just judgment, Kilby's first book "is something of a hybrid or transitional genre: part self-examination and confession, part biblical exposition, part sermonic exhortation, and part factual narrative" (Hindmarsh 40). Autobiographical narration is mainly found interspersed and mixed into Kilby's theological reflections and advice to his readers, but in this early work "there is little of the larger narrative syntax of what Aristotle called *mythos*—of beginning, middle, and end" (Hindmarsh 41). In Kilby's second book, *Hallelu-iah! Praise Yee the Lord, for the Unburthening of a Loaden Conscience* (1614), conversion is a fact, and this volume (which describes Kilby's illness and suffering from kidney stones), similarly, lacks a beginning-middle-end structure. Indeed, this book and later evangelical narratives have a "labyrinthine quality," "so that just when it seems to the reader that Kilby has arrived at peace of heart and his conscience has been finally relieved, again he describes another layer of sin and descends into another period of lamentation and doubting" (Hindmarsh 42).[4]

In *La tentation autobiographique: de l'Antiquité à la Renaissance*, Philippe Gasparini eloquently sums up the development of the spiritual autobiography thus:

> Dès le début de son expansion, le christianisme assigna à l'écriture du moi une teneur, une fonction, une signification tout à fait nouvelles qui devaient marquer profondément son histoire byzantine et européenne. Ce 'je' chrétien trouvait dans la Bible des modèles qui rompaient avec la conception gréco-romaine du sujet-citoyen: les prophètes énonçaient la parole de Dieu, non la leur, Job se soumettait à sa volonté, les psalmistes imploraient sa miséricorde. Le sujet ne se définissait plus par sa fonction sociale mais à travers une relation privilégiée avec une entité toute-puissante située hors du monde, dans un rapport filial d'obéissance, de crainte, d'humilité, aux antipodes de l'orgueil de l'homme libre en sa cité. De la même manière, le 'je' chrétien aura pour fonction principale, sinon exclusive, de proclamer et d'illustrer les bienfaits de sa foi. C'est ainsi qu'en langage ecclésiastique les mots *apologie* et *apologétique* en viendront à désigner exclusivement la défense de la religion chrétienne. (98–99)

Raising the question in *Circuitous Journeys: Modern Spiritual Autobiography* as to what "marks the modern context of spiritual autobiography" and reading a selection of modern spiritual autobiographies together with Augustine's *Confessions*, David Leigh suggests that "the modern autobiographer is an alienated seeker struggling with unmediated experience, an autonomous searcher struggling with an unauthorized identity, a self-appropriating thinker struggling with a lack of a stable sense of the self, and an authentic proponent of social change struggling with a paralyzing environment" (xiv). Leigh examines the patterns in ten spiritual autobiographies[5] in the light of Augustine's *Confession* and finds that the patterns have "a remarkable similarity in their narrative form and literacy patterns" (x, xi), and he concludes that "the circular journey pattern provided Augustine with

---

[4] But "Kilby's account was still a rare example of the Puritan autobiography that would appear in larger numbers later in the seventeenth century"—"it was not until the end of the Civil War that conversion narratives began to appear in greater number in print, singly and in collections of spiritual experience" (Hindmarsh 41, 43).
[5] Leigh examines works by Thomas Merton, Dorothy Day, G. K. Chesterton, C. S. Lewis, Gandhi, Malcolm X, Black Elk, Paul Cowan, Rigoberta Menchú, Dan Wakefield, and Nelson Mandela.

a structural metaphor for several doctrines important to his theological understanding of his conversion story" (4).[6]

Augustine's *Confessions* has been a paradigmatic example that has consolidated definitions of the genre of autobiography for many critics including Georges Gusdorf ("Conditions and Limits of Autobiography"), Roy Pascal (*Design and Truth in Autobiography*), and Karl Weintraub (*The Value of The Individual: Self and Circumstance in Autobiography*). At the same time, as Philippe Gasparini argues in *La tentation autobiographique*, the importance of Augustine's role in the history and development of autobiography should not be overestimated: "l'écriture du moi leur préexistait largement sous des formes variées. Certes, Augustin l'a enrichie et renouvelée, notamment en ce qui concerne l'exploration de l'intériorité, l'assomption de la mémoire, la stratification des identités, l'intensité du style" (117). In *Confessions*, it is God who is the addressee, something that is complicated since God is already omniscient as well as outside time. Such an autobiography becomes an impossible task. Still, in his strong desire to share his experiences with readers who might be inspired to follow in his footsteps, Augustine attempts to pull it off. Augustine's *Confessions* reminds us of the dialogicity of autobiographical texts. His autobiography has been regarded as foundational, inspiring later autobiographies ranging from Rousseau's *Confessions* to Jacques Derrida's *Circumfession*.[7]

Linda Anderson emphasizes that the "developmental version of the self," although "socially and historically specific," has come to "provide a way of interpreting the history of the genre: all autobiography, according to this view, is tending towards a goal, the fulfillment of this one achieved version of itself" (8). Perhaps this is even more the case with spiritual autobiographies, where the fulfillment of a particular 'achieved version of itself' might seem even more peremptory. In *Understanding Religious Conversion*, Lewis Rambo points to the importance of *testimony*, whereby "conversion is in part the adoption of a new rhetoric or language system" (137). "Personal

---

[6] While Leigh's study is an important source for my own study, its focus is different. Most of the texts analyzed in *Circuitous Journeys* examine major religious autobiographers, spiritual and political leaders of the twentieth century, and most of the texts chosen are from the period before 1995. Leigh's study, thus, does not treat the contemporary spiritual autobiography that will be analyzed in the present study.

[7] Similarly, in *Circumfession*, Derrida returns to "the question of God's position as transcendent interlocutor, a God who knows everything in advance," and "draws attention to the fact that Augustine writes his confessions after the death of his mother, and like Derrida himself, could be said to be writing for his mother" (Anderson 24).

testimony is a common method for publicly displaying commitment," Rambo continues, and "testimony is the adaptation of this modified rhetoric to explain one's conversion experience, to tell one's own story" (137). Rambo's comments concern testimony within particular religious groups, whereby a convert may "[undergo] an experience of biographical reconstruction" (138). Apart from a brief mention of testimony in a chapter on commitment and a brief discussion of stories of conversion in a chapter on consequences, Rambo studies actual experiences, conceptualizations, and understandings of conversion, and he states: "Although all of ordinary human life can be seen as a subtle process of reorganizing one's biography, in religious conversion there is often an implicit or explicit requirement to reinterpret one's life, to gain a new vision of its meaning, with new metaphors, new images, new stories" (138). As to the idea that conversion can be pinpointed in time, however, in "Conversion and the Language of Autobiography," Geoffrey Galt Hartman—for whom autobiography itself is conversion, so that if "we are to understand autobiography, we must understand conversion" (47)—writes that "[c]onversion is a constant, ceaseless process" and "the unchanging condition of our existence," for which reason "conversion cannot be localized in a single event. No moment is 'pre-conversion.' Nor, we must remember, does the subject ever achieve a 'post-conversional' condition" (48).

Looking at metaphors, images, and stories in modern spiritual autobiographies, David Leigh detects what he calls directional images. In the "spiral pilgrimages" (5) he studies, Leigh finds directional images often related to childhood experiences that "[embody] the dynamic of the story" (1), images that "[provide] the dynamic of movement and the hint of a goal to be reached" (2) even though the journey may include several side tracks and "prolonged wanderings" (3). For the purposes of the present study Leigh's term will be useful, since a directional image designates not only a particular image, metaphor, or symbol, however complex, but a tensive site of cross-currents marked by the movement of underlying forces and emotions that propel the narrative from beginning to end. One example of a directional image is from Augustine's *Confessions*, where Augustine introduces the theme of the *cor inquietum* from the very beginning, a motif that "emerges from his earliest experience of hunger in his quest for language as an infant and a schoolboy" (1). In Leigh's view, "[t]he rest of the *Confessions* flows from this motif of the 'unquiet' quest for an object or person who will satisfy his hungers and his desire for dialogue" (1). A directional image, then, in the autobiographies studied by Leigh, "embodies the dynamic in their story, often associated with the motif expressed in the title or subtitle of their story" (1). For Thomas Merton in *The Seven Storey Mountain*, the metaphor of life as "a journey, in search of a permanent 'home'" is a directional image (1). In Nelson Mandela's *Long Walk to Freedom*, it is "the vision of an harmonious society modeled on the tribal unity of his childhood villages" (2). Most often there is one central directional image, although in T. S. Eliot's *Four Quartets* there are four. Interestingly, as David Leigh suggests, a directional image suggests that "the storyteller is going somewhere": "What it does not immediately indicate is what happens in all these modern stories of the wandering self (as in Augustine's *Confessions*): that, for most of the story, the direction is the wrong one. In fact, what intrigues many readers of spiritual autobiographies is that the journey consists primarily in wrong turns and dead ends" (2-3).[8] Regarding the texts he examines in *Circuitous Journeys*, on the other hand, Leigh concludes: "This overall pattern of childhood directional images of a goal, followed by adolescent and adult wanderings through illusory realizations of the directional image, and eventual achievement of the goal (often in a surprising place) fits most of these autobiographies within the Augustinian tradition" (3).

If, as Bruce Hindmarsh proposes in *The Evangelical Conversion Narrative*, "[t]he early evangelicals in the 1730s inherited the genre of conversion narrative not just from the Puritans and their Nonconformist descendants, but also from Continental Pietists and their descendants" (57), we may ask to what extent contemporary writers of autobiographies have inherited the genre of the spiritual autobiography from their predecessors. If, further, spiritual autobiography in the sixteenth and seventeenth centuries "took the form of religious apologia, or narratives of suffering and martyrdom, reflecting the religious and political strife of the period" (Hindmarsh 27), we may ask what the central themes in today's spiritual autobiography are. Turning to contemporary narratives that try to make sense of and relate modern lives to spiritual perspectives, the present study will propose that there is a renaissance in spiritual autobiographical writing today recalling the avalanche of spiritual writing produced during the Early Modern period. If that

---

[8] Perceiving not only wrong turns and dead ends, in *Archetypes of Conversion: the Autobiographies of Augustine, Bunyan and Merton*, Anne Hunsaker Hawkins argues that at least in the case of a modern spiritual autobiography such as Thomas Merton's *The Seven Storey Mountain*, a final destination is not reached and no ultimate synthesis is achieved, only milestones on the path of spiritual development.

is the case, a study of a selection of spiritual autobiographies from this period would seem to hold a promise for a better understanding of religion and culture in our own ontologically unstable, postmodern times. The temporal framework corresponds to a late postmodern era in which religion has become increasingly deinstitutionalized, globalized, deconfessionalized, and individualized at the same time as religious practice has become diversified, fragmented, as well as increasingly divisive.

Not infrequently, the point of departure for many of the texts studied here can be located in a wasteland of crisis, meaninglessness, suffering, and loss. In similar ways, early conversion narratives took their departure in biblical descriptions of sin. In the Old Testament, the books of Jeremy, Isaiah, and Ezekiel express God's anger against entire nations that must be severely punished for 'detestable practices' such as eating at mountain shrines, defiling the wives of neighbours, committing robbery, looking to idols and lending at interest (Ezekiel 18:11–13). Here, God states that "[t]he one who sins is the one who will die," "[b]ut if a wicked person turns away from all the sins they have committed and keeps all my decrees and does what is just and right, that person will surely live; they will not die" (Ezekiel 18:20–21). Old sins will be completely forgotten, but by the same token, the righteous things a person has done will be forgotten when he or she turns to sin. Turning away from the sin, then, becomes a crucial aspect of the 'turning' involved in conversion. In the New Testament, in Peter 2:24, we read about Jesus' sacrifice for our sins: "'He himself bore our sins' in his body on the cross, so that we might die to sins and live for righteousness." Although sin may still be a useful concept, people today may be more prone to talk about emptiness or ambivalence. As Eckhart Tolle writes in *A New Earth: Awakening to Your Life's Purpose*:

> *Sin* is a word that has been greatly misunderstood and misinterpreted. Literally translated from the ancient Greek in which the New Testament was written, to sin means to miss the mark, as an archer who misses the target, so to sin means to *miss the point* of human existence. It means to live unskillfully, blindly, and thus to suffer and to cause suffering. Again, the term, stripped of its cultural baggage and misinterpretations, points to the dysfunction inherent in the human condition. (9)

"In autobiography," writes Bruce Hindmarsh, "it is not only the patterns of action portrayed in the story (*mythos*) that reveal the moral qualities (*ethos*) of the subject, but also the patterns of narration" (9). Certainly, in examining these questions, we need to ask, as James Olney does with a reference to Roy

Pascal's *Design and Truth in Autobiography*: "Is there such a thing as design in one's experience that is not an unjustifiable imposition after the fact? Or is it not perhaps more relevant to say that the autobiographer half discovers, half creates a deeper design and truth than adherence to historical and factual truth could ever make claim to?" (11). As Georges Gusdorf argues in "Conditions and Limits of Autobiography," further: "The author of an autobiography ... sets out to ... reassemble the scattered elements of his individual life and to regroup them in a comprehensive sketch. ... [He] strains toward a complete and coherent expression of his entire destiny" whereby "autobiography assumes the task of reconstructing the unity of a life across time" (35, 37). It is through this act of recomposition and interpretation that the autobiographer can arrive at a form of self-knowledge. But, as Olney underlines, "no autobiography as conceived in a traditional, common-sense way can possess wholeness because by definition the end of the story cannot be told, the *bios* must remain incomplete. In effect, the narrative is never finished, nor ever can it be, within the covers of a book" (25). The self, as Olney comments, "(like the autobiography that records and creates it) [is] open-ended and incomplete: it is always in process or, more precisely, is itself a process" (25). At the same time, when it comes to the spiritual autobiography it could be argued that there is a difference since conversion narratives "achieve a kind of completeness by recording the death of the old individual—as it were, the Old Adam—and laying that individual to rest within the confines of the conversion narrative" (Olney 25).

Autobiographical writing from the most recent decades is particularly interesting to study not only because there are few book-length studies of spiritual autobiographies from this period but also because it is a time period that comes on the heels of important shifts on individual and collective levels in the understanding of the role of religion and spirituality.

In the present study, the themes and questions to be explored in the works selected will be related to a larger contextual framework concerning religion and spirituality in our time with the aim of providing a broad overview as well as in-depth analyses of selected texts. Key elements in spiritual autobiographies, developmental trajectories, conversion, epiphanies, mystic experiences of different kinds, experiences of transformation, will be theorized and explored, and each chapter will focus on a particular imagery or theme, such as pilgrimage or metaphors of marriage. Situating the autobiographies to be examined in this study within a network of ideas and reflections will lead to a deeper understanding of texts and contexts and enable us to observe patterns and discover relationships among those patterns relating to the spiritual journeys described: What sort of stages and milestones are depicted? How are narrative points of departure and arrival visualized? William James suggested that one must "judge the religious life by its results exclusively" (22). If so, some questions arise: What is the result of the transformative journeys undertaken in these autobiographical narratives? In what, more precisely, do experiences of transformation consist? How are processes of spiritual exploration, descriptions of the presence or absence of a kataphatically or apophatically understood divinity, and experiences of epiphany conveyed through narrative structure, intertextual reference, symbols and metaphors? Are apostolic or contemplative paths visualized? In the final analysis, what sort of personal and spiritual truths are articulated in these works?

Positing three major stages of transformation in the works selected—crisis, quest, and consequences—this study will focus, first, on autobiographies about experiences of conversion or deconversion. The first chapter will explore Lauren F. Winner's *Girl Meets God: On The Path to a Spiritual Life* (2002), *Still: Notes on a Mid-Faith Crisis* (2012), and *Real Sex: The Naked Truth about Chastity* (2006). The second chapter will examine central metaphors linked to the body, food, and communion in Sara Miles' *Take This Bread: A Radical Conversion* (2007). Whereas spiritual journeys tend to focus on the mind, the soul, and the emotions, in *Take This Bread*, the emphasis is on the physical and material, more particularly on food and the body.

Despite the difficulty of capturing and verbalizing experiences in a spiritual dimension, spiritual autobiographies often attempt to narrate concrete points of departure and arrival as well as specific corners turned. In pilgrimage narratives, journey metaphors are particularly important. Pilgrims arrive at the end of one earth and find another one opening up—or wish to do so. What is the deferred but fervently desired gratification that makes people walk hundreds of miles in all kinds of weather, carrying heavy material and metaphorical rucksacks? What kind of peace is sought in such an enterprise? In such a typology of purpose one could also turn the question around and ask what deficiencies there might be that trigger the idea of pilgrimage in the first place and propel it to its conclusion. Questions such as these will be explored in a chapter on modern pilgrimage narratives such as Conrad Rudolph's *Pilgrimage to the End of the World: The Road to Santiago de Compostela* (2004), Arthur Paul Boers' *The Way Is Made by Walking: A Pilgrimage Along the Camino de Santiago* (2007), Tony Kevin's

Walking the Camino: A Modern Pilgrimage to Santiago (2007), Linda C. Magno's *Bliss: My Pilgrimage to Santiago de Compostela* (2011), and Lee Hoinacki's *El Camino: Walking to Santiago de Compostela* (1996). In a chapter on William Schmidt's pilgrimage in *Walking with Stones: A Spiritual Odyssey on the Pilgrimage to Santiago* (2012), an interpretation of some of the spiritually charged symbols studding the path of pilgrimage will be offered. It will be proposed that numbers are particularly important for a deeper understanding of the sensory and symbolic aspects of Schmidt's pilgrimage narrative and that we can read his story as marked out within and ordered by four different ways or dimensions related to the cardinal directions and to the four elements of fire, earth, water, and air.

In Karen Armstrong's *The Spiral Staircase: My Climb Out of Darkness* (2004) commonplace views of religious life in the cloister as the most life-denying choice one could make are dismantled. Even though a few nuns in Armstrong's cloister are cold, reprimanding, and seemingly far removed from Christian ideals of love and compassion, most of them possess an admirable serenity. A life focused on God, prayer, and simplicity is never criticized in Armstrong's autobiography, but romanticized views of convent life as easy and safe (held by Armstrong's psychiatrist) are debunked in the descriptions of the rigors and challenges life in the cloister entails.

The final chapter will deal with a hitherto understudied sub-genre of the spiritual autobiography, the near-death narrative, stories that are often marked by soteriological aspects. This chapter will examine a selection of accounts of the near-death journey as described in publications such as Eben Alexander's *Proof of Heaven: A Neurosurgeon's Journey into the Afterlife* (2012), Dale Black's *Flight to Heaven: A Plane Crash ... A Lone Survivor ... A Journey to Heaven – and Back. A Pilot's True Story* (2010), Ned Dougherty's *Fast Lane to Heaven: A Life-after Death Journey* (2001), Crystal McVea's *Waking Up in Heaven: A True Story of Brokenness, Heaven, and Life Again* (2013), Mary C. Neal's *To Heaven and Back: A Doctor's Extraordinary Account of Her Death, Heaven, Angels, and Life Again: A True Story* (2012), Richard Sigmund's *My Time in Heaven: A True Story of Dying ... and Coming Back* (2004), and Freddy Vest's *The Day I Died* (2014).

The texts to be examined in this study—nine by male writers and nine by female writers—will be chosen from contemporary autobiographies placed within and related to new spiritual landscapes marked both by religious diversity and by increasing interfaith engagement inside and outside religious communities. In some of the texts studied here, the point of departure is the frustration of not finding what one has so fervently hoped to find, such as

Karen Armstrong's search for God during her convent years, described in *The Spiral Staircase: My Climb Out of Darkness* or the wish for the permanence of marriage in Elizabeth Gilbert's *Eat, Pray, Love: One Woman's Search for Everything Across Italy, India, and Indonesia* (2006).

If one visualizes the spiritual journey in these quest narratives as consisting of three (often overlapping) stages, the second part involves a search for a way out of crisis. In this stage we find directional images that are saturated with movement, a movement that is sometimes so primary as to become personified and endowed with an agency, as is the case with the Camino in William Schmidt's *Walking with Stones: A Spiritual Odyssey on the Pilgrimage to Santiago*. In Anne Rice's *Called Out of Darkness: A Spiritual Confession* (2008), the second stage involves extensive traveling, as is also the case in Gilbert's *Eat Pray Love*. Conversion or deconversion may be part of the second stage.

Suffering may trigger a movement away from an untenable situation. Or, a step away from the past may be completely unplanned or unexpected, as with Sara Miles' conversion in *Take This Bread*, and the motivations may be partly unconscious. When deciding to walk the Camino, for example, the real reasons may be largely unconscious, as in some of the pilgrimage narratives discussed here.

The descriptions of the third stage are shaped and underpinned by conceptually charged directional images such as food, matrimony, statues, cardinal elements, numbers, light and darkness. In Winner's texts, matrimony and incarnation involve complex, biblically inspired key metaphors. In Sara Miles' *Take This Bread*, incarnation, ingestion, and flesh constitute central images. In pilgrimage narratives, the physical and spiritual journey is directed towards an endpoint that is the furthest away at the same time as it represents a homecoming. Anne Rice's *Called Out of Darkness*, too, narrates a homecoming, resembling the "general pattern of ending where it began, but on a higher level," the "sort of chiasmic pattern within a horseshoe form (∩)" that can be traced back to Homer and Virgil" that David Leigh sees in Augustine's *Confessions*. Proposing that "[t]he circular journey [embodies] the Neoplatonic scheme of emanation and return, but with a solid base in personal and social history," Leigh suggests that the journeys in the modern autobiographical narratives he analyzes also "[parallel] several biblical narratives with circular patterns" (4), something that pertains to the story in Anne Rice's autobiography. It should be noted, however, that the three stages of crisis, quest, and consequences often overlap in terms of narrative structure, and the final stage may not be experienced as final at all. In

Bunyan, to take a classic example, the spiritual resolution and clarity he craves are neither certain nor permanent since he repeatedly "[returns] to a state of searching and uncertainty," his "progress [depending] on repeated backsliding, and the hope, rather than the certainty, that conversion has already taken place" (Anderson 28). As John Barbour points out in *Versions of Deconversion*, conversion had to be reenacted over and over again: "[s]eventeenth-century doctrine and preaching stressed the need for believers to imaginatively reenact their initial conversion in order to revitalize their faith," that is, "[p]uritan piety requires not simply conversion, but repeated conversion" triggered by recurring points of repentance (22). In later spiritual narratives, too, stages are not always as clear cut as stage theory would seem to suggest.

Metaphorically speaking, the starting point in many texts studied here often resembles a primal bog of despair, cluelessness, and stagnation that only profound spiritual transformation or divine intervention can remedy. In this way, many of these quest narratives, lacking a clear chronological order, could be compared to ancient creation myths depicting a transformation of the world from a primal, undifferentiated mass or chaos, a transformation leading (via a threatening dragon that has to be slayed) to an ordered world where things are named and distinct. "In almost all cultures," as Karen Armstrong writes in *A History of God*, "the dragon symbolizes the latent, the unformed and the undifferentiated" (17).

The personal metaphorical meanings expressed by individual writers, as this study will propose, can and must be related to shared spiritual and theological meanings. Keeping in mind the interdependency of an author's understanding or experience of God (the experiential) and the actions or consequences (ideological, ethical, or material) to which it leads, the metaphorization of spiritual experiences that resonate with central religious or spiritual concepts will be in focus here. Fundamentally investigating how human beings have responded to the great existential questions posed by life itself, studies exploring the place of, and individual relationships to, religion and spirituality in our society are of great interest.

In the search for the spiritualities of the twenty-first century, one place to look, then, this study will argue, is to the contemporary spiritual autobiography. An introspective quest narrative that bridges theology and literature in tracing the stories of authors who move from states of confusion, dejection, or loss to profound insights or epiphanies of spiritual revelation, from conversion to deconversion or from deconversion to conversion, the contemporary spiritual autobiography belongs to an as yet understudied genre of autobiographical writing. Shining an analytic light on individual texts placed within a broad spiritual perspective, this study will offer an illumination of the genre of spiritual autobiography while relating it to understandings of the role of religion and spirituality in our time.

Matrimonial Metaphors and Spiritual Bliss: Conversion and Deconversion in the Autobiographies of Lauren Winner

In the "perfect Christian salvation story, about God's hand and foreordainedness and teleology," "the telos, the end to which everything has been pointing, is Jesus, is the church, is the Cross."

(Lauren Winner, *Girl Meets God* 89)

Remain in me, as I also remain in you.

(John 15:4)

Spirituality has sometimes been imaginatively metaphorized as a life-long journey through which we discover not only God, but also ourselves in relationship to God. This chapter will examine the governing metaphors in Lauren F. Winner's *Girl Meets God: On The Path to a Spiritual Life* (2002), *Still: Notes on a Mid-Faith Crisis* (2012), and *Real Sex: The Naked Truth about Chastity* (2006), predominant among which are images of physical, emotional, and spiritual matrimony that could be linked to theological concepts of oneness, union, and unity. In *Genesis* (2:24) it is stated that a man "shall cleave unto his wife: and they shall be one flesh." While there are references to God's oneness in the Bible (both in the Old and the New Testaments), oneness is a debated concept in theology. For many evangelical Christians, the oneness of God is related to the number 'one,' as is the case in Lauren Winner's work.

Mixing personal reflection and spiritual commentary, Lauren Winner's first autobiography, *Girl Meets God: On the Path to a Spiritual Life* (henceforth abbreviated to *Girl Meets God*), is organized in a circular fashion around both the Jewish and the Christian calendars, following religious dates and seasons and commenting on the liturgical order and the prayers and sermons of the day. *Girl Meets God* is a learned tract offering reflections on religious ritual, rabbinical and priestly pronunciations and perspectives, and analyses of biblical stories. In her second autobiography, *Still: Notes on a Mid-Faith Crisis* (references below abbreviated to *Still*), similarly, along with her own life story, Winner offers an explicatory commentary on subjects such as epiphany, intinction, hymns, exorcism, and dislocated exegesis.[1] Winner's middle book, *Real Sex: The Naked Truth of Chastity*, is not an autobiography as such. Still, since it is informed by Winner's own life, it could rightly be regarded as at least partially autobiographical, and it does shed interesting light on the key metaphors in her two autobiographies. Among Lauren Winner's other books is *The Voice of Matthew*, a retelling of the Gospel of Matthew in contemporary story form, and *A Cheerful and Comfortable Faith: Anglican Religious Practice in the Elite Households of Colonial Virginia*.

Lauren Winner's spiritual journey is remarkable in its inclusion of two conversions, first to Judaism and then to Christianity. Showing her awareness of the requirements of the traditional conversion narrative, Winner remarks upon how her Evangelical friends want her to "shove" her spiritual story "into a tidy, born-again conversion narrative" (*Girl Meets God* 7). While the "datable conversion story has a venerable history" beginning with St. Paul, "the most famous Jew to embrace Jesus" and the one who "established the prototype of the dramatic, datable rebirth" (7), Winner's 'conversion story' does not have an exact date and time. Since she has not had an "epiphanic on-the-road-to Damascus experience" herself, she finds that her own "story doesn't fit in very well with this conversion archetype."[2] In her later book, *Real Sex*, Winner comments on the process of conversion:

> Something very dramatic and transformative happens when a person becomes a Christian, when a person is born again or baptized and gives her life to Jesus and the church. But conversion makes one a *new* Christian, not a mature one, and though it effects a change in one's heart and one's very being, it does not usually effect an instantaneous change in all one's habits or assumptions (23).

[1] Dislocated exegesis is "the practice of reading scripture in unexpected places, in places that might unsettle the assumptions you were likely to bring to the text" (*Still* 136).
[2] Winner adds: "A literature scholar would say there are too many 'ruptures' in the 'narrative.' But she might also say that ruptures are the most interesting part of any text, that in the ruptures we learn something new" (*Girl Meets God* 8).

Winner's first conversion is to Judaism. With a Jewish father and a lapsed Southern Baptist mother, Winner was raised Jewish, but from the perspective of Conservative and Orthodox Judaism, Winner knows that she will never count as a 'real' Jew, and she will never be able to marry an Orthodox Jew or move to Israel, should she want to. She decides to convert to Judaism, and goes all out in her effort to become an Orthodox Jew, attending Orthodox services every day and taking up all the Jewish rituals. Despite her efforts, however, she experiences a growing dissatisfaction, one that seems to have less to do with a vertical dimension of faith than with a horizontal, social dimension of Jewish life in New York where Winner feels that she will never completely fit in. She experiences a supremely subtle ostracism, a lack of total acceptance by Orthodox Jews in New York. There are subtle but sharp snubs from Orthodox girlfriends that are wounding: "There were lots of Sarahs, lots of pretty Orthodox girls who snubbed me, the convert, never mind all the rules the rabbis piled up forbidding Jews to remind converts of their background. Those small snide remarks, which I should have been able to overlook, those, I think, are where this story begins" (*Girl Meets God* 91). One man she dates, further, informs Winner that he cannot go on seeing her because he can never marry a convert, no matter how profoundly, devotedly, and ambitiously Jewish she has become (*Girl Meets God* 91–91). One Jewish boyfriend's mother, similarly, is unable to wholeheartedly accept Winner as a daughter-in-law ("I was not a proper Orthodox Jewish girl from Long Island who had been to the right Jewish summer camps and the right Jewish schools" [*Girl Meets God* 92]). Another boy with whom she somehow falls in love is completely out of limits, since he comes from a cohanim family, "the priestly class"[3] that, as Winner puts it, "must be kept distinct, and pure, and separate" (*Girl Meets God* 174). Although Winner's best friends at Columbia are "the most intellectually capacious people on earth," she finds that "many of the other Orthodox Jews at Columbia were the worst breed of intellectually insular" (*Girl Meets God* 93).

It becomes obvious that Winner's alienation from Orthodox Judaism has a lot to do with her own realization that, being barred from marriage to an orthodox or cohanim Jew, she is actually barred from a complete union with Judaism. Gradually, there are experiences that push Winner in the direction of Christianity and that lead to her second conversion. She has a dream that she interprets as Jesus rescuing her. Reading a novel by Jan Karon, *At Home*

---

[3] Dating back to Aron's being chosen as a priest by God (Mos. 27: 28).

in Mitford, further, plays an important role since it "[leaves Winner] wanting something Christians seemed to have" (*Girl Meets God* 8): "*I want what they have*," she affirms (*Girl Meets God* 60, italics in original). So what is it that Christians have and that Winner realizes that she is longing for? One answer is incarnation: "In Christianity," Winner writes, "God got to be both a distant and transcendent Father God, and a present and immanent Son god who walked among us" (*Girl Meets God* 51).

Another answer, I'd like to propose, could be found in the imagery embedded in Winner's texts, especially a range of metaphors wedded to the teleological aspect of the narrative of arrival. In accounts of the spiritual journey, certain metaphors are recurring. Light and darkness, firstly, are among the prevalent metaphors, and they are part of the directional images in Winner's books as well.[4] In one instance, employing a metaphor of light, Winner pictures the spiritual journey as a walk through a castle of seven increasingly bright rooms of crystal that symbolize stages of spiritual development recalling those described by Teresa of Àvila in *The Interior Castle*. While people in the first room "are making a beginning of humbly devoting themselves to God—they are turning their attention to God, but they are still vulnerable," in the second room they "are increasingly able to hear God—through holy conversation and holy reading, through prayer," and in the fourth room, "you begin to hear God's voice directly" (*Still* 197). The seventh room is "all light; in the seventh room is God" (*Still* 198).

While the journey metaphor is prevalent in spiritual writing, and Winner points out that "The Christian tradition is thick with metaphor for the journey to God" (*Still* 197),[5] this metaphor has not been without its critics. In *Women and Spirituality*, Carol Ochs has criticized the journey metaphor so common in traditional spirituality since she sees it as limited in "[carrying] with it the view that part of our life has meaning and value only insofar as it contributes to the goal of the journey. Living in itself is not considered intrinsically valuable—the only value is in the goal we are supposed to achieve. The journey model is not even an accurate description of

---

[4] Winner writes that her most recent autobiography, *Still: Notes of Mid-Faith Crisis*, "is not primarily a picture of darkness" but rather "of the stumbling out of the darkness into something new" (Still 202).

[5] There is a stretch of Winner's development towards Christianity that she calls her glory road, a road [she thinks will] "carry [her] forever" (*Still* xiii). "Sometimes, in the days when I felt furthest from God, I thought that my goal was to recover the kind of spiritual life I had once had, to get back to that glory road. Increasingly, I understand that I don't get to go back (increasingly, I don't want to)."

our experiences—we don't experience our lives in a linear, developmental manner" (*Women and Spirituality* 24).[6]

Another metaphor paints the spiritual journey as "a ten-rung ladder of love" that similarly passes through prayer, commitment and performance until "on the tenth rung [one's] soul is intertwined perfectly with God" (*Still* 198). A metaphoric journey that appears to have a stronger appeal for Winner, however, is the mountain of God "swathed in darkness": "This is what it is like to ascend God," she says, "you are standing at the edge of an abyss, at the foot of a mountain that seems impassable" (*Still* 198).

But the metaphor that is most central in Winner's work, as this chapter will argue, is the extended metaphor of matrimony. The matrimonial metaphor is a complex and capacious category encompassing the whole range of stages that can be part of the journey of matrimony and out of it as well: attraction, courtship and dating, nuptials, marriage, stagnation, infidelity, fornication, separation, and divorce.

Matrimonial metaphors are appropriate in spiritual writing. In the Bible, matrimonial metaphors are often used to depict the relationship between human beings and God. A well-known example is the marriage metaphor in Hosea. In The Old Testament, marriage represents the covenant of the Lord and his people. "For your Maker is your husband," we read in Isaiah (54 5:8): "'the LORD Almighty is his name—the Holy One of Israel is your Redeemer; he is called the God of all the earth. The LORD will call you back as if you were a wife deserted and distressed in spirit—a wife who married young, only to be rejected,' says your God. 'For a brief moment I abandoned you, but with deep compassion I will bring you back. In a surge of anger I hid my face from you for a moment, but with everlasting kindness I will have compassion on you,' says the LORD your Redeemer." In Jeremiah, the Lord says, "Return, O backsliding children, for I am married to you" (3:14). In the New Testament, Jesus tells parables about a wedding feast that symbolizes the coming of the kingdom. In the Epistle to the Ephesians (5:23), further, Paul says: "For the husband is the head of the wife as Christ is the head of the church, his body, and is himself its Savior." Here, it is the union of love between Christ and His Church that is described, that is, between Jesus and his believers. In *The Interior Castle*, similarly, Teresa of Àvila draws upon marriage metaphors when she writes about how "God

---

[6] Ochs sees no indication that "we are here on earth for some goal we may reach— that is, salvation or union with God"; instead, our existence is primarily relational on a human level: "we are here to act and to interact with others—to perform, not to escape" (24).

spiritually espouses souls: may He be praised for His mercy in thus humbling Himself so utterly. Though but a homely comparison, yet I can find nothing better to express my meaning than the Sacrament of Matrimony although the two things are very different" (69). The soul, in Teresa's comparison, "aspires to become the bride of God Himself" (71).

Let us turn to some examples of how Lauren Winner uses the image of matrimony in her work. Advent, first of all, is described through metaphors of love and courtship. Advent is "the season of expectation," a season "during which you are supposed to cultivate longing for Him, the type of longing you feel when your beloved has been out of town for three weeks but you know he is coming home tonight" (*Girl Meets God* 34). Here, waiting for Jesus is filled with intense longing metaphorically described through an erotic image of the lover "coming home tonight." The relationship between the religions that Winner is drawn to, further, is illumined through metaphors of matrimony. As Winner recognizes, increasingly, Judaism informs and remains an inextricable part of her understanding of Christian faith. Whereas she realizes that she has wanted to "find the key to marrying Judaism off with the cross" (*Girl Meets God* 17), something that is not possible, Judaism and Christianity remain locked into a reciprocal matrimonial relationship where a complete divorce can never be possible. Inevitably, aspects of Judaism and Christianity are interwoven. Winner's account also makes clear that divorce seldom is final even when there is a new marriage. For Winner, Judaism and Christianity continue to dwell side by side, and they turn up intertwined in the final chapter of *Girl Meets God*. If we turn to Lauren Winner's first autobiography, *Girl Meets God*, we see that the title itself seems to hint at romantic attraction of a kind one might associate with 'chick lit.' 'Girl' evokes a sense of smallness, immaturity, and beginnings in life, whereas 'God' represents greatness, omnipotence, ultimate truths, and eternity. If 'girl' meets 'God,' this is a meeting that could lead to a significant union. A meeting or union between the two evokes the relationship between God and Jesus, with Jesus' humanity relating to the divinity of God. In *Girl Meets* God, the process of converting to Christianity is described through metaphors of marriage, divorce, and remarriage. "If it was a marriage, [Winner] to Orthodox Judaism," Winner thinks, "[she has] failed from the beginning" (*Girl Meets God* 96):

> I had married Judaism and then I had an affair with a foreign God, another religion, I took another lover. And I realized I was in love with that other lover, and I wrung my hands for a while. I struggled through my own inner turmoil and angst and then I handed my shocked husband divorce papers, threw my stuff into

some empty cardboard boxes, and moved out, setting up home with my new love before an even passably decent interval elapsed (*Girl Meets God* 98).

In this passage, Winner's conversion to Christianity is conveyed through matrimonial metaphors of erotic passion, infidelity, divorce, and a new relationship of even greater passion. Winner is, as she puts it, "courted by a very determined carpenter from Nazareth," whose "dogged pursuit of [her]" wins out in the end (*Girl Meets God* 12, 89), and her spiritual desire is visualized through sexual metaphors of passion: the new lover, Christianity, is embraced before decorum permits; such is the irresistible passion he evokes.[7]

In the first chapter of her second autobiography, *Still: Notes on a Mid-Faith Crisis*, Winner, whose last name so far has seemed so spectacularly appropriate, is facing failure: "it is a mark of [her] charmed life that it [is] the first time [she has] ever tried to do something and simply failed" (7). What she has failed at is her marriage, but she also seems to be failing at religion. Winner's spiritual impasse—that might be construed as a form of spiritual burnout resembling the condition Karen Armstrong describes in her autobiography, *Spiral Staircase: My Climb Out of Darkness*—is marked by anxiety, hypochondria, and compulsivity. Winner comes to a point where she decides to "[s]it with the loneliness and ask what loneliness has for [her]" (*Still* 56). This being in the moment is a form of surrender and submission to the suchness of reality, even though, when Winner does invite loneliness to sit down, a surprisingly aggressive (imaginary) dowager turns up, "[taking] a letter opener from her bag and [telling Winner that] she can kill [her] if she wants to" (*Still* 59). If we take a closer look at this startling image, we discover that here, too, there is a hint of the matrimonial metaphor, since a dowager is a dignified elderly widow whose identity is forever marked by the *marriage* she once had.

This image of the dowager stands in contrast to the image of God as conveyed in another part of the book. Once again, marital metaphors are employed. The nearness of God resembles the proximity of a husband who is invisible for the moment but who is nonetheless present in another part of the house: "With this elusive God, there is a kind of closeness, one I did not know before God became elusive, one I did not know when God was still

---

[7] Similarly, reading an article in the *New York Times* on Roman Catholic priesthood and the prayer of seminarians, Winner is struck by the observation that they "talk about their prayer lives the way most people talk about their love lives" (Jennifer Egan, quoted by Winner, 139).

nearby as friend. It is the closeness of invisibility, of abiding presence, of your husband in another room of the house, also reading. Close, you do not have to speak" (*Still* 162). Since God is imagined as a husband, one could understand the image of the aggressive dowager as an image of the frustrations and self-deprecations of the author at having lost her marital and spiritual relationships, that is, the loss of her husband and the alienation from God that Winner experiences during the 'middle' stage of her spiritual journey.

Somehow, Winner's disappointment in marriage is not allowed, and she takes most or all of the failure entirely upon herself, depicting her husband in rosy tones of deep spiritual commitment and great personal charm and herself in dark grey tones of negativity. The inadmissibility of acknowledging that their marriage is falling apart or that it might have been a mistake from the beginning is reinforced by the conversations she has with Christian friends and clergy, some of whom chastise her and attempt to steer her away from even thinking of separation and divorce. Examples include the friend who says, "*Lauren, if you leave your husband, you are leaving Jesus,*" the pastor who tells her that she "would be stepping out of God's favor" if she divorces, and the seminary that cancels a class that Winner is going to teach (*Still* 8). Valiantly, she struggles on, intellectually aware of the importance of prayer and other good habits and disciplines and consulting dozens of books about prayer, grateful to the Episcopalian church that has "this incomparable liturgy that keeps us tethered to prayer when our heart's awandering" (*Still* 67), and remembering her days of vibrant prayer while feeling spiritually and emotionally dead.

Remembering the words in Luke 5:16 that "Jesus often withdrew to lonely places and prayed, Winner muses in a marvelously original metaphor of complete bodily and spiritual union that is as matrimonial as it is maternal: "*Maybe I can make my loneliness into an invitation—to Jesus—that he might withdraw into me and pray*" (*Still* 141, italics in original). With its gestational and erotic overtones, this metaphor conveys the depth of Winner's longing, picturing herself both as a temple and as a womb and Jesus as a foetus gestating in the body of her loneliness.[8] This inside/outside metaphor recalls, firstly, Jesus' words in John: "I am the vine, you are the branches. The one who abides in me while I abide in him produces much fruit, because apart

---

[8] Most often, however, her in-body resident is not Jesus in prayer, but anxiety: "As far back as I can remember, anxiety has been my close companion, having long ago taken up residence in the small, second-floor bedroom of the house that is my body" (*Still* 82).

from me you can do nothing" (John 15:5), and, secondly, the words in 1 John 17: "God is love. Whoever lives in love lives in God, and God in them." It also recalls Augustine's thoughts in *Confessions*: "And how shall I call upon my God—my God and my Lord? For when I call on him I ask him to come into me. And what place is there in me into which my God can come? How could God, the God who made both heaven and earth, come into me? Is there anything in me, O Lord my God, that can contain thee?" (Book One, Chapter II). Furthermore, it could be seen as an inversion of the vision of Julian of Norwich, who said that "Our Savior is our true Mother in whom we are endlessly born and out of whom we shall never come" (qtd. by Winner, *Still* 160).

Encapsulating a sense of mutuality and interdependency between divinity and humanity, this charged bodily metaphor is an image of a state of being *and* becoming. In the desire for union, the gap between Winner and Jesus is closed and movement into the womb coincides with the stillness and interiority of this small space. In this passage, we might see an *inversion* of the image evoked by the title of Winner's first autobiography, where girlish minuteness encounters the immensity of God. Here, instead, Jesus is small enough to lodge inside her body and Winner is big enough to house God. (A similar conception is put forward by Kathleen Norris in *Amazing Grace: A Vocabulary of Faith*: "There's a lot of *room* in Mary" [123, italics in original]). Since Jesus is God's son, this pregnancy must have resulted from a conception, immaculate or not, that is all about transformation and new beginnings. Like a latter-day Virgin Mary, Winner is literally creating space for Jesus, creating space for God, embracing and harbouring the divine within her own body, as if saying that God is not to be found in another world but in the very middle of our own, human and physical, lives.

The matrimonial metaphor is appropriate also on structural and narrative levels of the spiritual autobiography since it resonates with understandings of the process of individual development in conversion as outlined in the psychology of religion. According to psychologists of religion (see e.g., Marcus Koskinen-Hagman), the self is not obliterated in the process of conversion, instead, it expands and reaches a point where it can identify with something much larger than the self, something holy whereby, as Inger Littberger puts it in her study of conversion in the Swedish novel (*Omvändelser: nedslag i svenska romaner under hundra år*), a conversion narrative is "a tension-filled synthesis of surrender of the self and expansion of the self" (27, my trans). Marriage, analogously, involves both a surrender of the self and an expansion of the self into something larger.

Interestingly, Winner herself writes that "Marriage has always been [her] synecdoche of choice, a wedding-cake part for the whole of [her] life" (*Girl Meets God* 218).⁹ Indeed, on a personal level, marriage is uppermost in Winner's life and in her imagination. In *Girl Meets God*, she gets "consumed with jealousy" in the company of happily married friends. For Winner, marriage is important in at least two major ways: firstly, the companionship, the togetherness, and the intimacy (*Girl Meets God* 279). But marriage and parenthood are also related to development. Being unmarried, Winner feels "stuck living like a college student" (*Girl Meets God* 279), and In *Real Sex*, she writes: "For many of my own single years, I cringed when Christians talked about marriage. I was sick of hearing about nuptial bliss, sick of feeling as if I wasn't participating in authentic Christian life because I wasn't married, sick of feeling inferior to everyone who happened to be a wife" (*Real Sex* 25).

Insofar as it concerns Winner's own process of learning how to practice chastity, *Real Sex: The Naked Truth about Chastity* could be regarded as partly autobiographical, although her primary aim with this book is to offer an argumentative essay on Christian marriage. Written by "a fellow pil-grim," *Real Sex* is, Winner tells us, "no more and no less than one person's reflections on the process of learning how to practice chastity" (*Real Sex* 10). Although initially intended as a supportive manual for Christian singles struggling with chastity, her book turned out to be about marriage, too, since, as she puts it, "the heart of the Christian story about sex is a vigorously positive statement: sex was created for marriage" (*Real Sex* 25). "Without a robust account of the Christian vision of sex within marriage, the Christian insistence that unmarried folks refrain from sex just doesn't make any sense" (*Real Sex* 25). "God created sex for marriage and that is where it belongs," Winner affirms, and "in Christianity's vocabulary the only real sex is the sex that happens in marriage" (*Real Sex* 15, 38). Sex outside marriage "is only a distorted imitation of sex," it is *ersatz* and not real sex (*Real Sex* 38). Winner continues: "The inflections of community are important because they get at the very meaning of marriage. Marriage is a gift God gives the church; He does not simply give it to the married people of the church, but to the whole church, as marriage is designed not only for the benefit of the married

⁹ Winner comments chiasmatically that "[i]f being a Christian might help a couple stay married ... being married might help a couple stay Christian, too" (GMG 219).

couple. It is also designed to tell a story to the entire church, a story about God's relationship with and saving work among us" (*Real Sex* 144).

In *Real Sex*, Winner remembers "that the Bible tells [her] over and over that marriage is like the relationship between God and His beloved" (*Real Sex* 144). Interestingly, however, at resurrection there will be no marriage at all: Winner points to Matthew 22:23–30, "in which a band of Sadducees comes to Jesus and asks him about a woman who had married, and survived, seven different men. At the resurrection, the Sadducees wanted to know, whose wife would she be? Would she have seven husbands in heaven? Jesus replies: 'At the resurrection people will neither marry nor be given in marriage'" (*Real Sex* 146). "Married people—as the frequent scriptural analogies between marriage and Christ's relationship with His church make clear—mirror God's relationship with His people eschatologically. At the end of time, when the kingdom of God is consummated, when Christ returns, there will be a huge wedding feast between Christ and His people.... Marriage, in this way, instructs the church in what to look for when the kingdom comes—eternal, intimate union" (147).

Narratives of arrival often lead up to or include conversion. One may think of conversion as a point of arrival, a happy ending after which the converted person lives blissfully enveloped by the love of God. Like other forms of passion, however, the passion of conversion can wear off and become stale. Towards the end of *Girl Meets God*, Winner admits that "a sort of sinking staleness" has made its appearance, making her think that it "*isn't working, [she doesn't] believe this Christian thing anymore, this is just some crazy fix [she's] been on, and now [she's] reached [her] toleration level, and it's not working*" (*Girl Meets God* 269, italics in original). In *Girl Meets God*, when Winner reflects on the passion of falling in love with a religion, the matrimonial metaphor returns, mixed with other metaphors. In *Still*, that stage of falling in love is behind her; now it is the long-term relationship that lies ahead of her. If conversion is flying high, life after conversion is a potentially more exhausting "long grind" closer to the ground: "How to fall in love is not, now, what [she needs] to learn. What [she needs] to learn, maybe what God wants [her] to learn, is the long grind after you've landed" (*Girl Meets God* 270). Having begun with Lauren Winner's orientation in a particular time and place (Oxford, Mississippi), the alternatively analeptic and proleptic narrative of *Girl Meets God* ends with Winner projecting herself into the future and to the thoughts she imagines that she is going to have of a story of a conversation between a rabbi and the prophet Elijah, a story that, given its placement as a forward-looking conclusion, has a particular significance as an exhortatory message both to Winner herself and to her readers to be open and listen to the voice of Jesus.

At the end of *Still: Notes on a Mid-Faith Crisis*, Winner's second autobiography, God reappears, God is heard again, and God speaks to Winner. The scene is not a dramatic one, rather, it is in the stillness after having received communion and returning to her seat that Winner hears a voice saying: "You can stay here now"; "Just five words, and I know that this voice is God and what God means is that there is ground beneath my feet again, that this is the beginning of sanity and steadiness; this is the beginning of a reshaped life" (*Still* 149). Winner is aware of the fact that many people might construe this as an instance of hearing one's own voice, it might be seen as "a bit of liturgical cliché, hearing this promise of revivification at the Easter Vigil" (*Still* 149), but she knows that she hears God's voice "naming a resurrection of sorts, telling [her] that she could stay" (*Still* 149).

While the first section of *Still: Notes of a Mid-Faith Crisis* depicts the experience of being stuck in front of a spiritual wall, in the second section there is a "wrestling with God," and in the third "a moment of presence" (*Still* xvii). Even though Winner is "still at the beginning of the middle," she understands that there is no way to go back. There is a shift: "you are looking for God and you are looking in ways you hadn't known before" (*Still* xviii). At this point, Winner is no longer in the wilderness but in "a place, a house, a room," understanding that "something will turn up in this room," that is, faith. Even though *she* may be "less certain," the *place* is certain and it is "sure." A *climb* recalling Jacob's ladder, the journey is vertical.

Still—the title of Winner's second autobiography—has several layers of meaning. The author tells us that her book is partly an answer to the question as to why she is *still* a Christian. But 'still' is also pointing to the idea of the spiritual journey itself a "process of distillation" [203]). 'Still', furthermore, is a word that carries associations ranging from a deathly state of spiritual lifelessness to the serenity and profound peace *also* inherent in the word, thus covering the entire spiritual journey Winner has traversed in her second autobiography. Settling for a three-part structure for *Still*, as she explains (in the final section of her book), has everything to do with the sense of movement from "depressed, intense crisis to pacific openness, from no sense of God to a new sense of God" (*Still* 202).

Despite her two conversions, Winner, in the end, does not see herself as having turned around completely. She doubts that she "will achieve a complete turning around here on Earth" (*Girl Meets God* 213), and she continues to need confession and the absolution given after confession. But at the end of the second autobiography, Winner has, in a spiritual sense, been transformed. Towards the end of the narrative, she is about to be ordained, and she concludes: "I am not a saint. I am, however, beginning to learn that I am a small character in a story that is always fundamentally about God" (*Still* 194).

Eating the Body of Christ:
Conversion and Social Activism
in Sara Miles' *Take This Bread*

Meanwhile the disciples were urging Him, saying, "Rabbi, eat." But He said to them, "I have food to eat that you do not know about."

(John 4:31–32)

Central metaphors in the autobiographical texts explored in this study resonate with theological concepts of oneness, unity, transcendence, and permanence. In material and symbolic ways, the body, firstly, is central in many of these self-narratives, as it is in religious thought as well. A Christian is united not only with Jesus, but with other Christians, who become one body: "For as in one body we have many members, and all the members do not have the same function, so we, though many, are one body in Christ, and individually members one of another" (Rom 12:4–5).[1] Understandings of incarnation, taking on flesh or being embodied in flesh, are linked to cultural concepts of the body. In as Sara Miles' *Take This Bread: A Radical Conversion* (2007), a sense of union and oneness is articulated through intricate extended metaphors of body, food, and communion. The journey is inwards, and the writer-protagonist has an experience of expansion and merging with a divine dimension as well as with humanity in a larger sense.

In her Introduction to the anthology *Religion, Food, and Eating in North America*, Marie W. Dallam observes that religious foodways (foodways being a subfield of food studies that "specifically examines cultural communities and group behavior in relation to food and eating") are "tied inherently, often dialectically, to concepts of identity and salvation and the nature of the divine" (xviii, xx). Even though there is a "burgeoning interest

---

[1] Paul speaks about the same idea also in 1 Corinthians 12:12, and 37.

in the area of food and religious history," in Dallam's view, "the connections among religion, food, and eating in America have not yet been studied widely and systematically" (xxi, xx). *Religion, Food, and Eating in North America* focuses on four major themes: theological foodways (concerned with religious mandates related to spiritual purity), identity foodways (related to both group and individual identity), negotiated foodways (aspects of lived religion), and activist foodways. Although Sara Miles' *Take This Bread: A Radical Conversion* could be related to all four aspects it is best understood as part of negotiated and activist foodways.

In *Take This Bread*, the experience and consequences of conversion are central. The starting point is non-religious—until "something outrageous and terrifying [happens]" to Sara Miles at St. Gregory's Episcopal Church in San Francisco: "Jesus [happens] to [her]" (58). The intellect is rudely pushed aside, unable to offer a rational explanation: as her experience is predominantly emotional and physical, it is "nonrational" and "desiring" (91): "I was eating a piece of bread; what I heard someone say was happening—the piece of bread was the 'body' of 'Christ,'—and what I *knew* was happening—God, named 'Christ' or 'Jesus,' was real, and in my mouth—utterly short-circuited my ability to do anything but cry" (58–59). Afterwards, her cognitive abilities fail her, while the physical and material take precedence as "that impossible word, *Jesus*, lodged in [her] like a crumb"; "it was as real as the actual taste of the bread and the wine. And the word was indisputably in my body now, as if I'd swallowed a radioactive pellet that would outlive my own flesh" (59). "Conversion isn't, after all, a moment: It's a process, and it keeps happening, with cycles of acceptance and resistance, epiphany and doubt" (97).

In the Bible, metaphors of food and drink, hunger and thirst, are ubiquitous. In Jeremiah (51:7), we learn that "Babylon was a gold cup in the Lord's hand; she made the whole earth drunk. The nations drank her wine; therefore they have now gone mad." Further, "Nebuchadnezzar king of Babylon has devoured us, he has thrown us into confusion, he has made us an empty jar. Like a serpent he has swallowed us and filled his stomach with our delicacies, and then has spewed us out" (51: 34). "Because of all your detestable idols, I will do to you what I have never done before and will never do again. Therefore in your midst parents will eat their children, and children will eat their parents" (Ezekiel 5:10). In Ezekiel 16, the Lord thunders against Jerusalem (metaphorized as a 'brazen prostitute' or an 'adulterous wife') for sacrificing her children: "'And you took your sons and daughters whom you bore to me and sacrificed them as food to the idols. Was your prostitution not enough? You slaughtered my children and sacrificed them to the idols'" (Ezekiel 16:20–21). In Psalm 107, on the other hand, the Lord "satisfies the thirsty/ and fills the hungry with good things." Images of bread are central when Jesus is tested in the wilderness in Matthew 4: "Then Jesus was led by the Spirit into the wilderness to be tempted[a] by the devil. After fasting forty days and forty nights, he was hungry. The tempter came to him and said, 'If you are the Son of God, tell these stones to become bread.'" Jesus answered, 'It is written: 'Man shall not live on bread alone, but on every word that comes from the mouth of God'" (Matthew 4:1–4). In 1 Corinthians 3, further, Paul tells his listeners: "I gave you milk, not solid food, for you were not yet ready for it." In Peter 2:2–3 we read: "Like newborn babies, crave pure spiritual milk, so that by it you may grow up in your salvation, now that you have tasted that the Lord is good."

In *Varieties of Religious Experience*, William James writes that "[l]anguage drawn from eating and drinking is probably as common in religious literature as is language drawn from the sexual life," that we "hunger and thirst' after righteousness," and we "find the Lord a sweet savor." James continues: "[s]piritual milk for American babes, drawn from the breasts of both testaments," is the sub-title of the once famous New England Primer, and Christian devotional literature indeed quite floats in milk, thought of from the point of view, not of the mother, but of the greedy babe" (14, fn 1).

Trudy Eden points out in her Introduction to *Food and Faith in Christian Culture* that even though "food and the act of eating, particularly group eating, are potent forces in human culture," the image of the Eucharist, "that of the table laid for a meal, has received little scholarly attention" (1). As Miles's title indicates, food metaphors are central in *Take This Bread*. In a "shocking moment of communion," Miles is "filled with a deep desire to reach for and become part of a body," something she defines as "a subversive practice" (xiii). Through this experience, her mission in life suddenly becomes crystal clear: it is to "feed people" (xi). This is what Miles will do: set up a food pantry in her church to help the marginalized and downtrodden survive in hard times. Miles states that "Food and bodies have always been wrapped up in meaning for [her]: They were [her] way of understanding the world" (xiv). Communion is "the heart of Christianity" (74), and at the heart of communion is food. The epiphany consists in "experiencing God in your flesh, in the complicated flesh of others" (97). Miles has the insight that communion is "Eating Jesus" as "actual food." The title and many chapters in the book point to the physical and metaphorical significance of food. The first chapter is called "The Family Table" and the last chapter "The Heavenly Feast." In between there are chapter titles with biblically inflected references to food such as "Manna," "Multiplying the Loaves," and "Sunday Dinner."

Considering the centrality of food as reality and metaphor in *Take This Bread* (even Miles' wish to be baptized is "almost a hunger" [122]), it may at first glance seem curious that the foods mentioned tend to range from the unappetizing to the disgusting. Although probably not chosen by Miles herself, firstly, the image on the book cover symbolically represents Communion by an unappealing, nutrition- and tasteless slice of white bread with a 'cut' where red jam oozes through, recalling a bleeding wound on a body.

Although they are not on par with the Bible (where some of the most appalling food images are found in Jeremiah, with God declaring: "I will make [Judah and Jerusalem] eat the flesh of their sons and daughters, and they will eat one another's flesh because their enemies will press the siege so hard against them to destroy them" [Jeremiah 18:9]), there are countless unappealing references to bread in *Take This Bread* such as "a simple chunk of wheat and yeast and water" (xiv), "ordinary yet mystical bread, so besmirched and exhausted and poisoned by centuries of religious practice" (xv), "the sappy, Jesus-and-cookies tone of mild-mannered Christianity" (xv), and "imported biscuits—dreadfully dry" (45). The descriptions range from neutral to unappetizing, and words like "besmirched and exhausted and poisoned" evoke toxic associations. Some liquid food images are equally unappetizing: "a five-gallon bucket full of broken eggs," "blue milk leaking from [Miles'] breasts" (72), references to "iguanas, squash blossoms, corn fungus, bright pink sweets speckled with flies" (11), "sugar and MSG sprinkled over impossibly thin shavings of beef" (27); "bar food: fat, protein, and salt" (28); "heavy, graying cheesecake; heavy, muddy chocolate cake; heavy chunks of canned brioche soaked in rum" (28); "a handful of bacon, a slab of cheese, a couple of shrimps" (28–29), "greasy Chinese noodles, steamed rice in banana leaves, Coca-Cola, and lumpia" (41), "grayish soupy rice, with cracked corn—animal feed—mix in, and little bits of salty, stiff dried fish" (43). In a restaurant the attention is drawn to the waste: "huge barrels of soft vegetables, half-eaten chickens, meat trimmings, stale bread, spoilt milk" (29). Then, there is "the food of peasants, which always tasted of dirt" and "the food of the urban poor, which always tasted of cheap grease" (49). Negative images of food are also used in mild putdowns (as when Miles asserts that *her* preferred kind of Christianity is *not* "the sappy, Jesus-and-cookies tone of mild-mannered liberal Christianity" (xv): Indisputably, the worst of all the negative food metaphors is when Miles, having taken Jesus into her body, finds that "the word was indisputably in [her] body now, as if [she'd] swallowed a radioactive pellet that would outlive [her] own flesh" (59).[2]

On closer consideration, however, the lumpy, gray, raw, or spoiled food stuff in *Take this Bread* makes sense. It is there to underline the tough-guy stance of the narrator-protagonist and her activist ideals. The worse it tastes, the better it is for Miles' image of herself, as when she recalls how "People gave food to [her], and [she] ate it all: roots, leaves, animal hearts; raw, canned, cooked, or spoiled" (49). These references signal Miles' stance of inclusivity and embrace of diversity, her openness to people and situations: although much of the food referred to is off-putting, Miles asserts: "whether it was a fake fast-food frozen chicken nugget or an unadorned chunk of carrot with the dark earth still clinging to it, what mattered to me was not what I ate" (49). What matters is sharing.

In emphasizing the connection between the food and divinity, Miles is drawing on a long tradition. In Milton's *Paradise Lost* and *Paradise Regained*, for example, food and eating are central. In *Paradise Lost*, the fruit is the most heavily charged symbol, and in *Paradise Regained* bread is a key symbol. Not only are fruit and bread satisfying to the taste and to the stomach, from a perspective of temptation they are held up as inroads to divinity. By eating the fruit, the serpent tells Eve, "ye shall be as Gods,/ Knowing both Good and Evil, as they know" (*Paradise Lost* Book IX 707–09). Similarly, in *Paradise Regained*, Jesus is tempted by Satan in ways modeled upon the temptation scenes in Luke 4:1–13 and Matthew.

Sara Miles' autobiographical narrative delineates her conversion and the development of her spirituality within the Episcopal Church in San Francisco from the first steps into the church: "One early, cloudy morning when I was forty-six, I walked into a church, ate a piece of bread, took a sip of wine. A routine Sunday activity for tens of millions of Americans—except

---

[2] In the Bible, food often represents clues, and Miles finds "clues about [her] deepest questions. Salt, grain, wine, and water; figs, pigs, fishermen, and farmers. There were psalms about hunger and thirst, about harvests and feasting. There were stories about manna in the wilderness and prophets fed by birds. There was God appearing in radiance to Ezekiel and handing him a scroll: 'Mortal,' he said, 'eat this scroll,' and Ezekiel swallowed the words, 'sweet as honey,' and knew God" (91). In Matthew, "Jesus was led by the Spirit into the wilderness to be tempted[a] by the devil. After fasting forty days and forty nights, he was hungry. The tempter came to him and said, 'If you are the Son of God, tell these stones to become bread.' Jesus answered, 'It is written: 'Man shall not live on bread alone, but on every word that comes from the mouth of God.'" (Matthew 4:1–11).

that up until that moment I'd led a thoroughly secular life, at best indifferent to religion, more often appalled by its fundamentalist crusades. This was my first communion. It changed everything" (xi). In and of itself, there is nothing surprising about being a Christian, at least not in America, where, as Miles herself points out, about 85 percent of the population see themselves as Christians and where "there has never been a non-Christian United States president" (66). Christians in America are hardly an "oppressed minority" (66).[3] For Sara Miles, however, conversion to Christianity is an overwhelming, explosive, and far-reaching experience strongly linked to outsiderhood, subversiveness, and radical politics. Christianity, then, should first of all be subversive. This is a Christianity that "commands" and "insists" and demands from others "a willingness to act" (xvi).

Stark, dramatic contrast is created by a counterpositioning of Miles' secularist point of departure and her 'Jesus Freak' point of arrival. The dramatic aspects are further emphasized as Miles states that "Mine is a personal story of an unexpected and terribly inconvenient Christian conversion," adding that as an intellectual, left-wing lesbian "with a habit of skepticism" she is "a very unlikely convert" (xii). But perhaps Miles' 'radical conversion' is not as surprising as the dramatizing narrative wants to represent it. Although she states that she is "unprepared and unreformed" (83), this is not completely the case. Even though it is only later on that she discovers "a cache of papers from [her] grandparents, whose interpretation of the Social Gospel turned out to be far more radical that [she has] ever suspected" (83), many spiritual threads prepare the ground for and may even lead the way to her conversion, albeit in unconscious ways. Miles' political stance might be the opposite of missionary Christianity, the "ambitions" of which, as Miles asserts, "were inextricably linked with those of empire" (3). Still, it could be argued that Miles follows in the footsteps of her grandparents who were missionaries, especially those of her maternal grandmother, who "was drawn by the Social Gospel of the time, seeking justice and an end to war through the teachings of Jesus," and her grandfather, who had "a burning desire to right wrong" (5). True, they were not

---

[3] To the contrary, in the view of Richard Dawkins, who asserts in *The God Delusion* that it is atheists who are an oppressed minority whose situation, he suggests, recalls that of homosexuals half a century ago (14). Dawkins is hoping to convince the world's atheists to come out of the closet, since according to him, *not* believing in God is a kind of liberation, a recipe for greater happiness and freedom (16, 27). Dawkins compares the kind of consciousness-raising necessary to become aware of the rationality of atheism to the consciousness-raising efforts of feminism (23).

missionaries of the kind that, as Miles quotes from William Hutchison, sees it as Christians' right and duty to "displace other religions and effect a spiritual conquest of other nations" (qtd. by Miles 8). Miles' parents, by contrast, after years of "the claustrophobic niceness of church ladies" and the "bland boiled dinners every Sunday" (8–9), became fervent atheists. For Miles' parents, Jesus was primarily a teacher. Throughout her narrative, Miles has a hands-on approach to social and political action. Looking back, she muses: "I'd also absorbed a confidence that was pretty overblown: I thought I could go anywhere, do anything, approach whatever work was at hand and take it on. Because I'd been encouraged to claim responsibility and to act, I didn't have a lot of respect for conventional credentials or the rigors of a discipline: I assumed I could learn whatever was necessary as I went along" (15).

Whereas spiritual autobiographies such as Karen Armstrong's *The Spiral Staircase* and Elizabeth Gilbert's *Eat Pray Love* depict a slow and painstaking progression toward conversion, enlightenment, or illumination, Sara Miles plunges herself and her readers headlong into the drama of (as the title of her book announces) a *radical* conversion, a conversion of the kind that changes everything. Having arrived at spiritual transformation, Miles identifies with Paul, who was "knocked upside down by the conviction that Jesus, whom he had never met, was blazingly alive in him" (83). Aware of the prototypical conversion story, Miles asserts that her own story deviates completely from conventional patterns. She comments: "While the classic conversion story involves desperation, hitting bottom, and a plea for help, I think now that it was gratitude, as well as *the suffering I'd seen*, that made room for me to open my heart to something new" (57, my italics). Given her emphasis on direct, hands-on experience, however, it is particularly noteworthy that her conversion is said not to have come not from her *own* suffering, but from the suffering she *has seen*.

In a chapter entitled "First Communion," Miles' conversion is recounted in an old-fashioned, fairy tale manner: without any conscious plan to go to church, one winter morning she finds herself drawn to a particular church, St. Gregory's Episcopal Church in San Francisco. The sense of drama is heightened by the use of striking contrasts: although Miles has "no earthly reason to be there," there she is; although her attitude is cavalier (she has no desire to become "a religious nut"), she is drawn by the beauty of sacred space. From the wintry morning she enters an interior of a beautiful wooden building and comes into a rotunda that is "flooded with morning light" (57). Since she is not a church-goer, Miles does not realize that St. Gregory's is 'different' in its conception of architectural space and in its liturgy, but these are aspects that will come to matter a great deal. Had it been a 'conventional' church with parishioners who, unlike the congregation at St. Gregory's, come from "conventional, tradition-bound churches" (80), her conversion might never have taken place. Still, even in this 'radical' church, Miles has to "struggle" with what she sees as "the prejudices and traditions of [her] newfound church" (xii). It is the determination behind the mission of St. Gregory's "to reform the ossified Episcopal liturgy by reclaiming the ancient Middle Eastern roots of Christian worship" that appeals to her (57): "there was no organ, no choir, no pulpit: just the unadorned voices of the people, and long silences framed by the ringing of deep Tibetan bowls" (58). In St. Gregory's there may be "fervent hugging and kissing" and "quasi-Quaker 'sharings,'" and preachers might sit "in a wooden chair" instead of "proclaiming from a pulpit" (63). Other churches are regarded as conventional and boring, one example being a Lutheran church Miles 'tries' that offers "dead white disks of wafers" and "fussy little shots glasses full of grape juice," a fare that leaves Miles "unmoved" (63). These are churches of a kind where "the traditional authority of the clergy went unquestioned, and the body of God was draped decorously in an ironed white napkin" (63–64). By contrast, St. Gregory's, in Miles' view, offers something different:

> There [is] the immediacy of communion at St. Gregory's, unmediated by altar rails, the raw physicality of that mystical meal. There [is] an invitation to jump in rather than official entrance requirements. There was the suggestion that God could be located in experience, sensed through bodies, tasted through food; that [her] body [is] connected literally and mysteriously to other bodies and loved without reason. (64)

The Christocentric theology embraced by Miles has less to do with a perception of, as she puts it, "God as an abstract 'Trinity' or trying to 'prove' divine existence philosophically" (71). She continues: "It was the materiality of Christianity that fascinated me, the compelling story of incarnation in its grungiest details, the promise that words and flesh were deeply, deeply connected" (71). She is not bothered by "the gory physicality of the language," the language of "eating body and drinking blood" (59). To the contrary, as already emphasized, Miles is familiar with the gory: having worked in restaurants she has "been fascinated to cut open the side of a pig or the heart of a cow, revealing the chambers and the fat, the muscles and shimmering lines of tendon" (60). Despite her confusion, she craves the bread and the blood, again and again: "It was a sensation as urgent as physical hunger, pulling me back to the table at St. Gregory's through my fear and confusion" (60).

A touch of competition and condescension creeps into the tone when Miles describes other, in her view less 'real' or 'radical' forms of religious conversion. "Conversion [is] turning out to be quite far from the greeting-card moment promised by televangelists, when Jesus steps into your life, personally saves you, and becomes your lucky charm forever" (70). Obviously, Miles is not attracted to such simplistic forms of salvation. With her celebration of a willingness to dwell in dangerous zones inhabited by those who are down and out or in areas marked by war, Miles emphasizes, rather, the confusion, awkwardness, and destabilization of her own conversion process. Similarly, a condescending tone colours the portrait of a fellow Christian woman who approaches Miles in an airport. Although both of them are wearing crosses, this woman "was wearing some kind of sexless denim jumper that reeked of piety" (89). From this, Miles apparently makes the assumption that this woman is a conservative Christian who dislikes homosexuality, feminism, and moral relativism, and who would regard St. Gregory's as "a dirty joke" (90). Since the anecdote stops at the woman's 'frozen' reaction, and, since we are invited to see the episode from the narrator's perspective only, we cannot be sure what the 'sexlessly' clad woman really thinks or what kind of Christianity she embraces.

There is no hegemonic strategy behind the organization of Miles' food pantry and no hidden intention to dominate over the 'whores' and the 'outcasts.' And yet, since the organizer assumes the power to decide what is best for others and to make decisions on their behalf, a hierarchy is nonetheless created that places the givers of gifts in a position of strength and the receivers of gifts in the position of thankful victims.

Miles relishes the stance of the rebel. When a seminarian at St. Gregory's is wondering if her practice of praying and laying on hands in connection with the food pantry is authorized in the Episcopal Book of Common Prayer, Miles' reply is that people make up the priests they need (132). Some people assume that Miles is an ordained priest. But in her view, "looking to official rule books and clerics to tell you how to act—this was what was wrong with religious life" (134). Perceiving herself as a "misfit" and "a lesbian mother" who has "never gone through official channels" but "stayed on the edges of things" (134–35), she has no patience with formal credentials and established rules if they contradict her own "handmade and activist project" (138).

The God Miles has found, or the aspect of the Trinity that she is focused on, then, is Jesus: the "God who lived on earth, who knew what it was like to walk around in a body, fight with religious authorities, hurt his mother's feelings" (264). But God cannot be summed up: "It made me even more of a believer to accept that none of us, fundamentalist or radical or orthodox, Muslim or Jew or Christian, could adequately sum God up. If you believed that God had created all life—protozoa and bears, coral and eels, mold and kingfishers and roses—wasn't it reasonable to assume that there wasn't one single template for human belief, one single way to get it right?" (265). Miles seems to suggest that because of the plurality of nature, belief in God, too, lends itself to a plurality of interpretations, which would make religion into a make-your-own-rules enterprise. Miles congratulates herself that she and her congregation are *different* and that *they* have an appropriately relaxed and dynamic attitude to religion. Although God is 'unmanageable,' God somehow has intentions, for example regarding the qualities in Miles that he 'intends' to use (222). For Miles, "the hunger that had drawn us here was so that we could see what the kingdom of heaven looked like" is a message from God (222). The food pantry thus gives a sneak preview of heaven, one that would seem to be denied to "aging congregations in proper Gothic stone buildings" (84), to the "worshippers sitting rigid in pews" (86), and to the "gray-haired parishioners in sensible shoes" (88). In contradistinction to the bland, aging, and gray-haired folks in sensible shoes, Miles does think that she has the right idea about what heaven is like (perhaps echoing Jesus' words in Luke): "Some Christians thought the kingdom was about afterlife, but I believed that it was *this* world .... The kingdom was the same old earth, populated by the same clueless humans, transformed wherever you could glimpse God shining through it" (222).

Towards the end of the book, Miles thinks about communion: "Communion. I chewed and swallowed it. It was the absolute center of my faith: wheat and water and yeast and heat: grape and sun and time: bread and wine, transformed into life. I ate it up. I kept coming back for more. And yet, even though church was where I found communion, church couldn't, finally, contain it" (267). Although, as Miles writes, "only ordained priests were supposed to preside over the Eucharist" (267–68), in her view "because of tradition: power, institutional arrangements, politics" (268), none of which are valid reasons in Miles' eyes, she decides to offer communion (brought from Sunday communion at her church) to a dying friend. It is at this point that a divine presence seems to be with her: "Something was in the kitchen with me, like the sunlight falling on the braided rug, like the piece of bread in my hands, warm and uncompromisingly alive" (272). She offers the sacrament to her friend, and later, driving home, Miles is "stunned and blinking and saying aloud to [herself], 'Oh my god, it's real'" (272). Next week, she repeats the act, and thinks: "it was like time out of time, each earthly detail incredibly vivid, with the eternal hovering right there in the middle of it, side by side with the suffering, and a huge peace beating slowly like the heartbeat of God" (273).

Miles' physical hunger for communion and her bodily attraction to spirituality resemble sexual and romantic passion. Her state of mind is described thus: "I went through my days excited beyond words, frequently on the verge of tears, then confused and scared. My throat was tight as if facing danger or intense sexual excitement; I'd be ravenously hungry, then unable to eat, as you are when you're heartbroken or newly in love" (61).

In *The God Delusion*, Richard Dawkins points to the anthropologist, Helen Fisher, whose study *Why We Love* Dawkins regards as an incisive analysis of the madness of romantic love. Falling in love, as Fisher has shown, generates particular brain states. Dawkins also points to other researchers who have posited what Dawkins terms the 'irrationality of religion' as a particular 'mechanism of irrationality' in our brains that is linked to or a byproduct of love—since falling in love must have evolutionary advantages (202). Dawkins asks: "Could the irrational religion be a by-product of the irrationality mechanisms in the brain?" Religious faith resembles being in love—and both have dependency-producing aspects (203). In this view, the intense love and worship of another human being resembles the intense worship of God.

On spiritual, psychological and political levels there is a struggle between different forces that recalls both the classic Apollonian-Dionysian polarities and a conservative-radical divide, and it is clear that Miles likes to position herself at the Dionysian and 'radical' side of the spectrum. The binary opposetions on which Miles builds her structure of values makes this clear. Old age tends to be described in negative terms with references to aging congregations and gray-haired parishioners on the one hand, and "dull prayers and dreary sermons," on the other. At the negative end, we find "the hack routine of mainstream churches" (81), "preachers ranting about Sodom and 'family values' and baby-killing" (84), "Aging congregations in proper Gothic stone buildings" (84), "suburban megachurches" (85), "worshippers sitting rigid in pews" (86), "shopping-mall fellowships" (85), and a "culturally conservative" Episcopalianism with "dull prayers and dreary sermons, and "gray-haired parishioners in sensible shoes" (88). Further, there are the "believers who [crave] certainty" (88). There are "those who insisted Scripture was inerrant and unchanging, given once and for all time" (88), who think that religion should be pure. Miles quotes Andrew Linzey, an English priest, who asserts that: "The logic of all purity movements is to exclude" (88). Miles dismisses "anxious formulas of religion" (93) and "codified religious law" (192) and remains deeply suspicious of "the unquestioned center of Establishment power in the United States" (89).

Religious power, then, is connected with young, energetic, and unconventional 'radical' people, in particular, and not with 'conventional' congregations that are seen as uninteresting at best and half-dead at worst. "It was as if the very habits of churchgoing had stripped away people's capacity to take authority and do things on their own," Miles reflects after visiting one such church (204). Parishes where "three pleasant and worn-out white people would offer [her] stale cookies" (204) are not to her taste. Neither are churches "where you sit obediently and listen to someone tell you how to behave" (214), or churches offering "limp pastries and weak coffee" (218).

When Miles first has her 'vision' of the food pantry, she thinks: "This is it ... what I'm supposed to do: *Feed my sheep*" (104). The sheep are the poor and marginalized people, and Miles is the one who feels that she has been anointed by God to feed them. Casting herself as the hero and saviour of the poor and downtrodden, she becomes a saintly woman who, like Jesus, eats with whores. Between the lines one detects a certain amount of self-righteousness, as when she begins her crusade for a food pantry at St. Gregory's (against the wishes of almost everyone), and she comments on her 'surprise' that this congregation, "so innovative liturgically, so liberal theologically, and so committed to welcoming strangers would be so lackluster when it came to activism" (109). Unlike the "perennially overwhelmed" or "frazzled, depressive" people (on a community outreach committee), Miles prefers a "jump-in, personalized, occasionally dictatorial method of organizing" (114). Initially, no one from the congregation goes along with Miles' ideas (or methods of organizing), except for a "hip young graphic artist" who is impatient with the "blather" of committees and wants to ask them (but doesn't?), "What the fuck would Jesus do?" (118). Miles acts, she "[explains]" and she "[tells]"; she "[assures]" and "[argues]" and "[quotes]" (112–13)—like someone who is sure that those who oppose her are wrong. When objections are raised to her project, she sees them as "scolding" (118). Replying to the resistance, she formulates a letter addressing the whole congregation, a letter, she later admits, in which she is "being disingenuous" in the way she depicts the process (116). Power plays a part here: "No matter how idealistic I might seem to others," she writes, "I was almost always determined to get my way. 'When I first met you,' an old New York friend of mind admitted once, 'I remember thinking, Damn, this is the bossiest white woman I've ever seen'" (116–17). "I *was* manipulative," Miles admits. "I felt as shrewd and self-important as any smooth-talking, right-wing evangelist with a political agenda" (118).[4]

At a certain point, Miles reflects: "I had no clue that I was crossing the line from self-righteous do-gooder to crusading zealot" (251). Convinced that she is right, she "[starts] to fight fiercely with the people [she is] supposed to be in communion with, [struggles] to institutionalize [her] own dogma, and generally [hounds] people in the name of the lord"; when other people yearn for "space for art or music or their own peaceful services" Miles asks herself if St. Gregory's had not "proclaimed that God's Table was open to everyone?" (254). She fervently wants her congregation "to see and recognize the food pantry as communion" and "to be transformed by what was happening among us on Fridays, to accept the Gospel of the pantry and make it part of its official theology" (260). She wants to get other people "walking, without the safety net of ritual correctness, along the path that Jesus blazed and to share the feast of their lives with others" (266). For Miles, a radical spirituality is a religion focused on social and political power relations. She states:

> The Christianity that called to me, through the stories I read in the Bible, scattered the proud and rebuked the powerful. It was a religion in which divinity was revealed by scars on flesh. It was an upside-down world in which treasure, as the prophet said, was found in darkness; in which the hungry was filled with good things, and the rich sent out empty; in which new life was manifested through a humiliated, hungry woman and an empty, tortured man. (68)

Miles' transformation into a 'radical' Christian is not without crises. Although she quotes the Bible saying that one has to give up one's home, wife and children and leave one's own self behind for the sake of salvation, a crisis ensues when she realizes that she has focused on her mission at the

---

[4] In "A Conversation with Sara Miles" at the end of *Take This Bread*, Miles admits that the biggest challenge she is facing is her own "bossy nature, [her] impatience, and [her] desire to be right," even though she wants "to be less controlling and more open to change and to seeing God in the most unexpected places and in the most unlikely people" (288–29).

expense of her partner and her daughter, both of whom feel a certain resentment because of this.

In a clear inversion of hierarchies in *Take This Bread* all outsiders and 'sinners' are to be embraced, but only if they are colorful rather than bland old ladies, active rather than hesitating and 'liberal' and 'innovative' rather than 'conservative' or 'conventional.' There may not be a separation between sinners and saved in Miles' thinking, but there is certainly a separation between 'sinners' and 'conventional Christians,' a separation that makes the bland and boring appear damned while the unorthodox remain 'righteous.' Miles revels in her own radicalism and emblazons the image of herself as 'deviant' and provocative. It is her young daughter who craves a more conventional setting and who urges her mother and her partner to marry on Valentine's Day in 2004, the day when civil marriages were offered to homosexuals in San Francisco. After the ritual, Miles understands the significance of marriage, "a rite binding people into community and, beyond that, pointing to the union of all humanity with God" (234). She believes that "a marriage such as [theirs] prophesied the politically inconvenient but spiritually resonant truth that the unlikely and outcast were part of God's creation, in all ways" (234).

Although the marginalized "[throw] light ... on how the whole system [works] (216), and Miles argues that there is "no separation of sinners from saved, righteous from damned" (222), and although she at one point states that there is no "clear line between the public and [them]" (213) (the public in this case being the beneficiaries of the food pantry), the presence or absence of such a line is never problematized in Miles' story, and one cannot disregard aspects of social hierarchy and power relations. The practice of the food pantry is premised upon a social hierarchy that depends on boundaries and classifications. Since the implicit assumptions concerning the divide between different social groups are never fully examined, certain power dynamics may, contrary to the best intentions, be perpetuated and institutionalized.

Since Miles' conversion does not lead to "a set of easy answers and certainties," she has to "wrestle" with Christianity (xv). Her new life after her conversion leads to "something huger and wilder than [she has] expected: the suffering, fractious, and unboundaried body of Christ" (xv). Being knocked upside down, relentlessly challenged, wrestling in the huge and the wild, she finds that, for her, faith has everything to do with action and very little to do with words, doctrine, or catechism. Instead, religion is primarily action-oriented and instrumental. First and foremost, Miles wants Christianity to "be a force for connection, for healing, for love" (xv). She wants it to be an almost surgically envisioned "voice that can crack religious and political convictions open" and that "advocates for the least qualified, least official, least likely; that upsets the established order and makes a joke of certainty" (xi). Christianity, then, in the view of *Take This Bread: A Radical Conversion*, should first of all be subversive.

Walking the Camino:
Journeys on the Route of the Stars

Pilgrim: one who journeys in foreign lands; one who travels to a shrine or holy place as a devotee; one of the English colonists settling at Plymouth in 1620.

(From Latin *peregrinum*, foreigner, stranger)

Once, on being asked by the Pharisees when the kingdom of God would come, Jesus replied, The coming of the kingdom of God is not something that can be observed, nor will people say, 'Here it is,' or 'There it is,' because the kingdom of God is in your midst.

(Luke 7:20–21)

Pilgrimage has a long history in most religious traditions. Abraham's journey to Canaan in obedience to God's command as described in *Genesis* 12 could be seen as one of the first pilgrimage narratives. Countless ancient stories explore the significance of pilgrimage in spiritual autobiographies. Historically, such autobiographies were often written by dissenters whose journeys took them from states of sin to blissful grace. In English literature, John Bunyan's allegory, *Pilgrim's Progress* (1678), could be seen as a model pilgrimage narrative depicting a journey from the City of Destruction to the Celestial City (through stages such as "Christian's deplorable condition," the "Slough of Despond," the "Valley of Humiliation," "The Devil's garden," and to "the way to glory"). Interestingly, in "THE AUTHOR'S APOLOGY FOR HIS BOOK," John Bunyan makes his purpose very clear to the reader: "This book will make a traveler of thee, If by its counsel thou wilt ruled be; It will direct thee to the Holy Land." *Pilgrim's Progress*, then, is a kind of a spiritual travel guide.

For the autobiographical accounts of pilgrimages examined in this chapter, a way to approach key concepts is to pay particular attention to points of departure, turning points, milestones, and arrivals. In pilgrimages, definite points of departure are given and definite points of arrival are visualized, points that are often as concrete and material as they are symbolic and spiritual. In pilgrim narratives, inter-personal and intra-personal aspects are important. Yet another level concerns the relationship to or experience of a transcendent dimension. Oftentimes, the first two levels are subordinate to this third level, as may also be the case with the narrative itself in its focus on spirituality and religion while downplaying other aspects. In these stories, the relationship to God or a transcendent dimension is more important than anything else. It suffuses the first two levels and determines how authors see themselves and how they interact with others. The relationship with a trans-cendent dimension may be precarious, it may appear in sudden glimpses or in unexpected mystic experiences, or it may be an imagined future point of arrival. A pilgrimage narrative, then, may be an account of a journey towards a real or a utopian future point. Although it is an outward, physical pilgrimage, it is always and primarily also an inner voyage.

Pilgrimage has been defined by Luigi Tomasi as "a journey undertaken for religious purposes that culminates in a visit to a place considered to be a site or manifestation of the supernatural—a place where it is easier to obtain divine help" (3). According to Erik Cohen in "Pilgrimage and Tourism: Convergence and Divergence," pilgrimage is "a movement toward the Center," while travel is "a movement in the opposite direction, toward the Other" (50). Tourism is associated with inauthenticity, and pilgrimage with authenticity, writes Nancy Frey in *Pilgrim Stories On and Off the Road to Santiago: Journeys along an Ancient Way in Modern Spain* (129). In "Spiritual Tourism: Religion and Spirituality in Contemporary Travel," further, Alex Norman separates out a category he calls spiritual tourists: "Where both religious (including implicitly religious) and secular pilgrims travel towards an acknowledged sacred 'centre', spiritual tourists are often moving towards novelty, or are experimenting with concepts and practices.... The contrast, both between 'regular' tourists and spiritual tourists, and pilgrims and spiritual tourists comes when the fundamental reasons behind the journeys, and the understandings of why they are travelling are examined" (47).

In William S. Schmidt's definition in "Transformative Pilgrimage" pil-grimage is a journey that "is consciously chosen as an intentional movement on a sacred path" (65). A wider definition would be that of Alan Morinis in "Introduction: The Territory of the Anthropology of Pilgrimages": pilgrimage is "a journey undertaken by a person in quest of a place or a state that he or she believes to embody a valued ideal" (4). "When faced with the complexity of the contemporary Camino," writes Nancy Frey, "the categories 'pilgrimage' and 'pilgrim' seem to lose meaning" (4). And yet, pilgrims "believe they will find 'something'—God, friendship, themselves, others—while on the road" (Frey 87). A definition more oriented toward narrative is that of Sarah Bill Schott in "Pilgrims, Seekers, and History Buffs: Identity Creation through Religious Tourism in Late Modernity," where she points to the importance of telling and interpretation in the stories of pilgrims and asks: "in what kinds of identity speech and action are they participating?" (323).

Pilgrimage could also be discussed as an aspect of population mobility that has economic and political implications. Whereas migration has become a widely studied and theorized phenomenon, up to recently, travel and movement with spiritual and religious implications has been much less so. With the realization of the numbers of people globally who go on pilgrimage every year it becomes clear that it is an area that deserves more attention. One need only think of the millions who make the Hajj every year, or those who go to Lourdes, or Hindus that travel to the River Ganges.

In "Creating Sacred Space by Walking in Silence: Pilgrimage in a Late Modern Lutheran Context," Anna Davidsson Bremborg presents and theorizes field data from 2005–8 from twenty-five Swedish pilgrimages. Although there are points in common, there are many striking differences compared to other European pilgrimages, such as the Camino.[1] Forbidden in Sweden in 1544, pilgrimages have been looked upon with suspicion until fairly recently. Only in 1930 was the concept of pilgrimage reintroduced in Swedish theology by Nathan Söderblom, and in the mid-1980s, a Swedish branch of the Franciscan pilgrim movement was started. In Denmark, pilgrimages were seen as vaguely Catholic expressions of narcissistic piety until 2009 when the first pilgrim priest was appointed. In Sweden, pilgrimages have tended to be defined through seven key words originally formulated by Hans Lindström in 2005: slowness, freedom, simplicity, silence, carefreeness, sharing, and spirituality. These are key words that could be seen as a counter-cultural response to what is regarded as a greedy, materialist, and overwhelming late modern society. Taking these keywords to indicate a lifestyle theology or lifestyle populism, Anna Davidsson Bremborg (with a reference to the ethnologist Orvar Löf-

---

[1] The average age of Swedish pilgrims is older than those who walk the Camino. They are between 50 and 70, whereas most pilgrims to Santiago are under 45 and a big group are under 35 (Davidsson Bremborg 2010 45). Swedish pilgrims also tend to be highly educated and active in their own parishes.

gren), underlines that the polarizations upon which the key words build tend to be simplifications that could be regarded as culturally constructed polarities (2010 120).

Today, ancient and contemporary forms of spirituality and visions of the sacred merge in an avalanche of books about the route to Santiago de Compostela. In pursuit of spiritual illumination and personal insight, thousands of people walk this route every year in challenging conditions. Countless contemporary spiritual autobiographies focus on the inner and outer journeys involved in this pilgrimage. In this chapter, I will explore a constellation of themes in a selection of pilgrimage narratives, such as Conrad Rudolph's *Pilgrimage to the End of the World: The Road to Santiago de Compostela* (2004), Arthur Paul Boers' *The Way Is Made by Walking: A Pilgrimage Along the Camino de Santiago* (2007), Tony Kevin's *Walking the Camino: A Modern Pilgrimage to Santiago* (2007), Linda C. Magno's *Bliss: My Pilgrimage to Santiago de Compostela* (2011), and Lee Hoinacki's *El Camino: Walking to Santiago de Compostela* (1996).

Walkers of the Camino—in pre-Christian times called the Route of the Stars—may be propelled by vexing personal problems, or their pilgrimages may be understood as a form of purification in the hopes for profound emotional and spiritual renewal. Although the Camino is fundamentally a Christian pilgrimage, one finds many other spiritual perspectives, including esoteric ones: "Some pilgrims are sensitive not only to signs but also to tellurian points, or sites believed to possess accumulated energies" (Frey 34). Nancy Frey points to the multiple motivations for undertaking the pilgrimage to Santiago. The Camino might have "a religious foundation based in Catholic doctrine regarding sin, its remission and salvation," but there is also "transcendent spirituality, tourism, physical adventure, nostalgia" and much more, even "esoteric initiation" (Frey 4).

Pilgrims are of course a heterogeneous group with a variety of conceptions and motivations. "When pilgrims speak of the Camino as a spiritual journey there is no shared definition," as Nancy Frey explains in *Pilgrim Stories On and Off the Road to Santiago*, "but it is generally related to this idea of the uncontained, nonstructural, personalized, individual, and direct relationship one has to ultimate reality" (31). And yet, delving into these pilgrimage narratives one finds that they have many things in common. Firstly, on the level of structure, although they are autobiographies, they are rarely purely autobiographical. Instead, many of them are a *mélange* of personal reflection, historical background, and guidebook. Secondly, there is often an important teaching dimension that explains things to the reader, ranging from the history of pilgrimage to geographic routes undertaken, biblical references to exile and wandering or mythical aspects such as the frequently occurring projections of transformative dimensions onto the Camino itself, making it into a personified entity possessing remarkable agency and an ability to affect pilgrims in astonishing ways (see e.g. Boers 104–06). The teaching aspect may also include musings upon 'our' materialistic modes of living and philosophic thoughts about ecology. In *The Way Is Made By Walking*, for example, Arthur Paul Boers introduces thoughts (from Sigurd Olson) about 'focal living,' the idea of keeping a focus on objects or activities (such as gardening, cooking, hiking) that need effort and concentration as well as discipline and that involve a connection to other people and to nature. Structured around points along the way as well as around certain themes, another book, Tony Kevin's *Walking the Camino: A Modern Pilgrimage to Santiago*, offers an education in history, includes snippets from Kevin's diary, and gives information about walking techniques and sound nutrition for prospective pilgrims (Kevin loses eight kilos and finds that with this weight loss it is "as if a fog [is] clearing from [his] brain" after it has been "clogged and dulled by the work of digesting so much food and drink" (165).

Narrative structure and organization may carry deep significance. Elizabeth Gilbert's *Eat Pray Love*, to take an example that concerns a more global pilgrimage, has an intricate tripartite structure that not only holds the story together but that infuses the whole narrative with deeper dimensions of meaning in pointing to a conceptual framework relating the spiritual search to Christian and other religious traditions, a framework within which inner and outer journeys can move forward geographically and spiritually while affording backward glances on levels of memory. Lacking a clear a chronological movement, Arthur Paul Boers' *The Way Is Made By Walking*, on the other hand, consists of a collage of recollections organized around different themes or important points along the journey. Similarly, in *Pilgrimage to the End of the World: The Road to Santiago de Compostela* (2004), Conrad Rudolph organizes his narrative in four sections that are "not a day-by-day description of the journey but a series of reflections on a number of different levels": a historical account of pilgrimage in the Middle Ages, his own internal experience of the pilgrimage, a presentation of the external experience of the route itself, and finally a section on practical perspectives on how to do a pilgrimage (x).

Although the pilgrimage narrative is a capacious category, this mixing of subgenres is not always felicitous, as the differences in style and tone between the different sections can be jarring. Some pilgrimage narratives range rather awkwardly between lyrical landscape descriptions and practical advice to presumptive pilgrims. Generally, however, despite the sense of narrative assemblage, there is a movement from a point of departure to a point of arrival via a terrain of movement and discovery. There may be an 'outer,' geographic movement whereby chapters are organized around stops on the road, or there may be an inner, psychological and spiritual move-ment, whereby the narrative is organized around key themes.

The first chapter in Tony Kevin's *Walking the Camino*, for example, begins with a question: "What Am I Doing Here?" 'Here' is both a specific geographic place, it is "the middle of Extremadura, the hottest and driest region of Spain" (1), and the physical space of a tired and sweating body. Walking from Granada to Santiago, Kevin wonders: "Why am I sitting in the blazing sun, in the middle of this harsh, god-forsaken landscape?" (3). Trying to locate the real point of departure, Kevin asks himself: "Where did it start, this middle-aged folly?" (6). This experience is rather typical, and one finds it across different types of pilgrimage narratives. In *El Camino: Walking to Santiago de Compostela*, Lee Hoinacki, at the beginning of his trip, "[shudders] … with fright": he is sixty-five, and he wonders if he is "acting like some kind of kid, attempting a rash, foolhardy adventure": "Why am I here? How did I get myself into this?" (3, 7). In Linda C. Magno's *Bliss: My Pilgrimage to Santiago de Compostela*, the same question pops up. "Why am I doing this walk?" she asks herself: "Is it for the experience? Is it for the sake of just doing it? I am fifty-seven years old" (42). But, as Frey points out,

> The pilgrimage does not begin with the first step or ride down the trail. Pilgrims begin to shape their journeys well before they leave the front door. The physical movement of arriving at the Camino is anticipated by some kind of internal movement—a decision, an impulse, an unexplained prompting, a long-held desire finally realized, a promise seeking fulfillment, a hope for change. (47)

Other recurring features in pilgrimage narratives are found on thematic levels. One such recurring feature is the experience of a sense of timeless-ness. "When pilgrims begin to walk several things usually begin to happen to their perceptions of the world which continue over the course of the journey," notes Nancy Frey; "they develop a changing sense of time, a heightening of their senses, and a new awareness of their bodies and the landscape" and "linear time often gives way to circular time" (72). In *Walk-ing the Camino: A Modern Pilgrimage to Santiago*, Tony Kevin experiences the present differently. His walk becomes "a different kind of observed reality" where he can let his "mind slide into a different rhythm of existence"—"a rare and lovely feeling" that is "an intensely spiritual experience of extended and focused meditation on [his] life" (171). Kevin writes about "the most wonderful quality of pilgrimage—how it slows down and separates time into discrete bundles" (11). Describing the "magically suspended state of being" (238), he suggests that, during a pilgrimage, time may 'expand.' For Conrad Rudolph in *Pilgrimage to the End of the World: The Road to Santiago de Compostela*, a key aspect of pilgrimage is the silence and solitude that lead to a sense of timelessness. Approaching Finisterre, Rudolph finds himself "in a countryside so beautiful that there [is] a palpable sense of enchantment, a place far from anywhere, a land that [seems] to have been wholly untouched by time" (41).

This sense of timelessness and of being in landscapes untouched by time is the opposite of everyday life marked by work and duties dictated by one's calendar. Pilgrimages, as Victor Turner and Edith Turner note in *Image and Pilgrimage in Christian Culture: Anthropological Perspectives,* "have several time dimensions" (23). At the same time, the pilgrimage is not eternal. It does have an end, and one must return to the nitty-gritty of everyday life. The Camino often leads to existential reflections on the transience of life and the Camino itself is a seen as a metaphor for life by many writers. Since the Camino has a beginning and an end, just like life, Kevin, for example, sees pilgrimage as a metaphor for life itself. While the experience of the journey "takes you so completely out of your 'real' life back home that you enter an altered state of perception of being" (Kevin 172), a pilgrim looks forward to arrival in Santiago with mixed feelings, because arriving, the end of the journey, is a point in time that resembles death.

Another recurring aspect in modern pilgrimage narratives is a sense of serendipity and synchronicity. Writers marvel at what they see as instances of the miraculous. This might be unexpectedly meeting someone again along the route. It is often described like this: if I had arrived two minutes earlier or later, this person would not have emerged from that shop across the street and we would never have bumped into each other again. Or it may be the sense of magic at the end of the trip of running into someone that you had met at the very beginning and thought you would never see again. Perhaps not quite as surprised at such encounters as the writers themselves, the reader might not be convinced of the high degree of serendipity or synchronicity of some of these encounters.

From a postmodernist perspective, there are no intrinsically sacred places but only places that are sacralized by humans. By contrast, in most pilgrimage narratives a sense of continuity and connection with past and present pilgrims is uppermost. A search for such a connection and continuity may be one of the main motivations to undertake a pilgrimage in a postmodern society where such aspects appear to have been irretrievably lost. Walking in the footsteps of pilgrims who took the same path in the twelfth century or even of those who walked here in pre-Roman times leads to a profound sense of connection and continuity for many writers. This sense of connection with fellow pilgrims has been described by Victor Turner and Edith Turner as *communitas*. Conrad Rudolph describes the "great camaraderie on the road that creates a special feeling among pilgrims, a feeling that often extends to those who come into regular contact with pilgrims and that, to a large extent, comes about from the closeness of the pilgrim's way of life" (27). For Rudolph, it is the people that make the journey. Tony Kevin, too, writes about the "human solidarity, and generosity of spirit" (13) he encounters among fellow pilgrims, how even among strangers, there can be "an immediate intimacy of a shared profound experience" (290). A sense of being special, almost like part of a chosen people, may also be present in the awareness of doing "what so many others will only dream about: the Great Journey" (Rudolph 47). Such a feeling is certainly present at the end of the 'great journey,' when pilgrims are welcomed at the Mass in the Cathedral at Santiago de Compostela, "congratulated and thanked for our courage, our fortitude, our endurance, and our sacrifice in completing our arduous journeys, which were testament to our sincere love of God"—like a welcome home for Olympic athletes or "soldiers home from the wars" (Kevin 284–85).

Considering the meltdown level of exhaustion many pilgrims experience on a daily basis, one wonders if walking the Camino is sometimes also a modern flagellation and purification process. Do some pilgrims feel that modern life has become too comfortable? In *The Way Is Made by Walking*, Arthur Paul Boers describes himself as a rich Christian and go-getter who has embraced a competitive lifestyle of struggle and performance to the point where he regularly drives himself to burnout and has to go away on retreats in order to recuperate and find the time for reflection, prayer, and paying attention to dreams that his busy life gives too little room for. "Pilgrimage is often an occasion to review one's life and confess one's sins," as he puts it (75). In *Pilgrimage to the End of the World*, people Conrad Rudolph meets on the way even "jokingly [ask] what great sin [he has] committed that [has forced him] to undertake such a grueling penance" (32). This penitentiary aspect goes back to the middle ages. In *Pilgrimage to the End of the World*, Rudolph tells us that pilgrims at that time might be forced to undertake a pilgrimage "to expiate some great crime, wearing nothing but a loincloth" (4), that a "murderer might perform it as a punishment with the murder weapon chained to his body for all to see," and that the pilgrimage might be a penance for heresy, which could be "a simple difference of opinion on religious beliefs" (5).[2]

Is strenuous pilgrimage a way to revel in one's sufferings because "we know that suffering produces perseverance; perseverance, character; and character, hope" (Romans 5:3–4)? At the same time, when making a TV series on pilgrimage for BBC in 2013, Simon Reeve found that "around half of those walking the Camino are no longer religious pilgrims, at least in the medieval sense of penance and suffering. It [seems] to [Reeve] they're often well off adventure hikers seeking an experience they'll remember forever." It is clear that pilgrimage represents a break with routine. Already in the Middle Ages, a wish to escape from dull and difficult lives of drudgery was an important motivating factor along with a desire for salvation and a need for healing. In many modern pilgrimage narratives, a sense of stepping out of the ordinary is conveyed. For Tony Kevin, for example, walking the Camino is "the strangest adventure of [his] life" (34).

Since pilgrimage is not a form of pointless meandering or even organized tourism but a journey with a clear direction toward a specific point of arrival, it may seem odd that arrival itself takes up so little space in Camino narratives. "Curiously," as Boers writers, "many Camino books say little—sometimes nothing—about the apostle James or the city and the cathedral of Santiago de Compostela itself" (188). Nancy Frey also comments that the goal "is often the road itself" (45).[3]

---

[2] Spiritual autobiographies written in the Middle Ages, moreover, were "typically structured less by the experience of becoming a Christian—or even becoming a monk—than by the pursuit of compunction and final beatitude itself" (Hindmarsh 24).

[3] This is true also for Swedish pilgrims. Anna Davidsson Bremborg found that destination was less important for the Swedish pilgrims in her study. For them, walking itself was primary. It was important to reach the goal, but more in the sense of having reached it than having arrived at a special or holy place. Among Swedish pilgrims there is the notion that one's inner stance is more important than the goal or even to walk along a particular trail. Davidsson Bremborg suggests that this minimization of the historical importance of a particular trail or the geographic place itself may be a typically Swedish feature (2010 62).

Of course, 'real' points of arrival may or may not coincide with the geographic destination. Nancy Frey suggests something along those lines in her study of Santiago pilgrims: "endings and arrivals may or may not be place- or space-specific. Depending on the pilgrim's goal and motivation different internal endings or resolutions can come at any moment and may not be linked to the physical arrival in Santiago" (Frey 137). If, on the deepest level, the real destination is God, this kind of arrival is rarely elaborated in detail in contemporary pilgrimage narratives. While Boers, in an Appendix entitled "Planning a Christian Pilgrimage," invites pilgrims to ponder questions such as: "How did this experience change or affect your understanding of God? Your relationship to God?" (190), he doesn't go into this question himself except to suggest that walking the Camino has enabled him to understand God's ways in a larger sense and to feel that God is leading him.

If the real goal of the journey is an encounter with God, this will certainly be visualized differently due to different theological or denominational backgrounds, which will also colour the descriptions of such encounters if and when they occur. For some, there might be mystical overtones, whereas for Arthur Paul Boers in *The Way Is Made By Walking*, despite his deep and fervent theology, the journey appears to be undertaken with a practical and rational approach. Nancy Frey's study shows "that depending on one's orientation toward a Catholic tradition, the importance of the path as led by Jesus or God is fundamental. Often in French and German reflections the connection to God is made more directly, whereas in Spanish instances or evangelical orientations Jesus often mediates the spiritual connection" (122). The images of God, consequently, may be very different.

Arthur Paul Boers distances himself from what he sees as pantheistic heresy, and he takes exception to the views of a woman who 'contends' that God is in all of us. 'Contends' is Boers' choice of a verb, one that indicates an evaluation of the woman's statement and an analysis leading to the conclusion that it is a question of pantheistic heresy. But even if her statement is not theologically sophisticated, the view that God is in human beings is not absent in the Bible. In 2 Corinthians (6:16), for example, God says: "I will live in them and walk among them, and I will be their God, and they shall be my people."

In Boers, God is imagined in sporting or hunting terms: "God is a moving target" (39). Such metaphors could be seen as an indication of an apophatic theology. "Deity is not easily tied down," Boers says, "Biblical faith is wary of confining divine presence too closely to one place or building or sanctuary, race or nation" (39).[4] The main point Boers wishes to make with his movement metaphors, I would like to suggest, is that we are all marked by a fundamental inner restlessness, one that makes us pilgrims who constantly search for God. "We are all homeless," Boers says, "ever since our eviction from Eden. And pilgrimage is an inevitable consequence. We need to constantly look for—and stay on the move for—God" (39). Thus, Boers visualizes a "God of movement," a God you cannot pin down, a God we must always be searching for or hunting down (resembling the God in 1 Chronicles who, after bringing Israel out of Egypt, "moved from one tent site to another, from one dwelling place to another"). To some extent, however, the divinity metaphors in Boers' account are contradictory, since Boers also has a chapter entitled "Seeking God's homeland." There is a sense of homecoming in Boers' narrative: "Because of the Camino, I grew in my ability to see God's larger purposes at work," he writes. "I can embrace a quote from Meister Eckhart that I heard at a low point years ago: 'Whatever happens to you is the best possible thing for your salvation.' Yes, God led and leads me into life" (177). More precisely *how* Boers feels that God leads him into life is not elaborated. The lack of an elaboration of what the sense of arrival in "God's homeland" is all about is an absence that may seem curious in spiritual autobiographies in general and in pilgrimage narratives in particular.

In Conrad Rudolph's *Pilgrimage to the End of the World: The Road to Santiago de Compostela* (2004), on the other hand, the divine aspects of pilgrimage are deemphasized. Not in any way believing in miracles himself, Rudolph strains to understand the fervor for miracles of the middle ages: "in an age when a direct relationship with the divine was felt to be beyond the average person's capacity and worth, the pilgrimage was a way to address, persuade, and even experience the divine more immediately than was possible at home" (5). When it comes to contemporary reasons for pilgrimage, Rudolph presumes that pilgrims today are "still looking for their own little miracles, though these may be nothing more than antidotes for the stress and strain of modern life" (16). Satisfying one's curiosity and finding stress relief, then, are the main aims of modern pilgrims, as far as Rudolph is

---

[4] While many passages in the Old Testament do locate divine presence in specific places, in Solomon's Prayer of Dedication in the Book of Kings, Salomon asks: "But will God really dwell on earth? The heavens, even the highest heaven, cannot contain you. How much less this temple I have built!" (1 Kings 8:27–28).

concerned, curiosity being his own motivation for undertaking the pilgrimage. Although undeniably the journey does have a deeper purpose, in Rudolph's view, "the undertaking is spiritual not in the sense of being religious but in the sense of having to do with the spirit" (39).

Nonetheless, Rudolph's lyrical landscapes are bathed in a sense of magic and almost surreal mystery. In the southern French landscapes, for example, it is "almost as if a spell had been cast" (22); a chapel like Saint Michel d'Aiguilhe has "a spiritual intensity so extreme that it's completely irreconcilable with the world that surrounds it" (20); the sound of tinkling sheep bells is "almost magical, timeless" (22), and a waterfall just before dawn "almost otherworldly" (23). Thus, in Rudolph's *Pilgrimage to the End of the World*, it is nature that elicits a profound sense of spiritual intensity and magic.[5]

For Lee Hoinacki, a sense of *communitas* is the central aspect in focus when he arrives in Santiago in the final chapter of *El Camino: Walking to Santiago de Compostela* and he thinks about how "[his] shoes fit directly into the footsteps of thousands, maybe millions, who came here before [him] and who walked exactly to the place where [he] now [goes]" (270). Breathing in the atmosphere in Santiago on arriving early in the morning, "twenty centuries of prayer and hope," he tries to "hear the sighs of a million pilgrims" (271). Thinking about those who precede him on the Camino, he muses: "Do I walk in their footsteps? Do I know anything of the Interior Castle of their spirit? Am I truly one of them? Am I moving in the sacred time where they dwell?" (272). These pilgrims of the past, he feels, brought him here, without them he would not have walked here, nor would he "have been able to endure the pain and exhaustion" of walking the Camino (272). Having no desire to see any relics, Hoinacki finds that what he has learned from the Camino is that he is not alone, and he is not an autonomous self. Perhaps this is because the deepest level of spiritual 'arrival' is impossible to convey. As Hoinacki comments: "each of us is very different; each seeks his or her own grace, an intimate, incommunicable secret in each soul" (270).

---

[5] In Alex Norman's interpretation in "Spiritual Tourism: Religion and Spirituality in Contemporary Travel," "Rudolph is in essence positing that the tourist experience is essentially like the pilgrim experience, for he does in fact count himself as one of the 'curious,' and in certain passages "Rudolph is articulating the spiritual aspect of his touristic experience (29, 30). Norman concludes that Rudolph's book belongs to a category of writing about "accounts of journeys made for ostensibly secular reasons, at least to begin with," written by writers who, "at some stage of their journeys, crossed into the mode of spiritual tourist" (32). Spiritual tourists, in Norman's definition, are "individuals who either search for or have significant spiritual experiences whilst being tourists" (33).

Like many other pilgrim narratives, Tony Kevin's *Walking the Camino* is rich in external detail, painting a vivid and engaging picture of the country, the landscape, and the stops along the way. Kevin, a former diplomat, gives a knowledgeable account of Spanish civil and religious history and culture. While he mentions initially that his impulse to leave his wife and young children at home in Australia and set out on a nine-week pilgrimage stems from a need for healing of his "bruised beliefs in [his] society's continuing worth" (267), the first half of his book does not go into spiritual aspects at all (apart from a mere mention that Kevin is Catholic). It is only in the middle of the book, and the middle of his journey from Granada to Santiago, that a turning point comes. Walking through "the harsh dry plains of Extremadura [starts] to unblock [Kevin's] memories and [his] spirituality" and his soul starts to open (149): "Though I did not recognise it at the time, these were probably the most life-changing days of my walk, days that re-shaped it as a real pilgrimage and something more than just an interesting, long walk through Spain. Spiritual growth can steal up on you: it does not have to be a moment of blinding, dramatic revelation, of Saul becoming Paul on the road to Damascus; it can also take the form of a slow recognition of good things, the slow spreading of a sense of peace, and the inner healing of an unsettled soul" (149). Around this point, Kevin succumbs to a terrible diarrhoea brought on by exhaustion and "the cumulative impact of the pilgrimage so far" (164). At the middle point of his pilgrimage, then, Kevin reaches a new meditative and spiritual level. At this point, he has left all the worries and concerns of his daily life behind, and entered into a steady pace of walking whereby his soul enters "a gloriously private and peaceful world" and he finds himself "free-wheeling through a benign, ambient space," feeling "safe, untroubled, joyous" (170). In a startling and evocative image, he sees himself as "a little capsule of life crawling forward across a vast landscape" (170). Such an experience of being a small creature held in the vastness of the universe is typical for many pilgrimage narratives.

Having time to ponder his own life and contemporary society, Kevin arrives at a determination to live a more caring and compassionate life both in taking better care of his family as a good, Christian patriarch and in taking better care of the planet. It is only towards the end of Tony Kevin's book that one comes upon a more specifically spiritual and religious chapter entitled "Walking with God." While sex, politics, and religion, in Kevin's view, have been subjects to avoid in conversation in Anglophone societies, this is changing, and he feels that his book would be incomplete without a chapter on religion. This chapter tells us about Kevin's family, parents, marriages, and schooling. He is "not a fervent or doctrinaire Catholic, and [has] never experienced any dramatic 'born again' experience of rekindling of [his] religion" (258). Instead, it is a "more gradual thing, a gentle re-orientation" leading to a greater conviction and faith in God (258). Nonetheless, it appears that he did return to the practice of Catholicism during the crisis ensuing after the death of his second wife. Kevin is comfortable with the Catholic Church because it is the church he has grown up with and because he appreciates its central, all-embracing ethos. During his pilgrimage he ponders the doctrine of the Holy Trinity and finds that for him, God is like a Father, "a safe refuge and a strong patriarch who lays down the rules for a good life," Jesus is "our hero and friend" and the Holy Spirit "the quiet voice of our conscience, the cool, soothing breath that steals into our hurt souls"; Mary, the Virgin Mother of God is "not a goddess" but a saint who "satisfies our widespread human yearning for a spiritual mother figure" (266). For Kevin, the art, music, and culture generated by Christianity are also important. His chapter on religion reads more like a biography than a religious confession—perhaps because Kevin is not terribly keen on confession as such: "The notion that one should regularly confess one's sins to God through the intermediation of a listening priest, another human person, strikes me as burdensome on both confessor and auditor. It seems to me that, just as one prays to God privately, one may properly confess to God privately" (259).

Similarly, even though Linda C. Magno would give a short answer in *Bliss: My Pilgrimage to Santiago de Compostela* to questions as to what she did during her pilgrimage—"Eat, Sleep, and Walk"—she does arrive at a wish to become a better and more forgiving person. On the sixteenth day of her pilgrimage, described in a chapter entitled "Enlightened," Magno experiences a conversion she compares to that of Paul on the road to Damascus. Due to lightning during a storm she actually loses eyesight temporarily. When this is happening, she thinks of the passage (in Acts 9:3–6) where the conversion of Saul and his becoming the Apostle Paul is described. She comments: "On this journey, we do not know what lies ahead. We can only have faith and trust in one another and our God" (151).

For as gruelling an undertaking as a walk to Santiago there has to be a culmination. For many pilgrims, the climax of the journey is the arrival in Santiago de Compostela. For Conrad Rudolph, it is Finisterre, about one-hundred kilometres further on from Santiago, that represents such a culmination: "it was the end of the journey, the End of the World, something was happening, everyone knew, but just what is better sensed than defined, as Sophocles knew" (44–45). As Nancy Frey underlines:

> the idea of the journey's goal is often flexible and variously situated. While Santiago is an obvious geographical goal, it is not necessarily the end of the interior journey. Journey's end and the pilgrim's goal should not be conflated. The multitextured quality of endings is visible in the closure of the physical journey and the turn toward home. The pilgrimage does not simply end with the pilgrim's arrival in Santiago but is a process that often begins well before the pilgrim reaches the city's gates and is prolonged indefinitely as the pilgrim continues to interpret in daily life the experiences he or she lived while making the way. (138)

Most of the pilgrimage narratives lead to positive results. For Tony Kevin, "there was no magic, revelatory moment in Spain; rather, it was a series of little steps forward, towards a slowly opening door" (267). He says: "My pilgrimage opened my heart wider to God; it washed away my emotional constrictions and defence mechanisms; it enabled me to pray more frequently and unforcedly than ever before in my life. It gently but insistently urged me to confront my life, warts and all" (267). During the pilgrimage, he has been able to "[live] his religion rather than [think] about it at an intellectual level. The pilgrimage wasn't a mental exercise in theology on the move" (269).

As already emphasized, the autobiographical act of narration itself is central in pilgrimage narratives. How experiences are interpreted in pilgrim narratives, then, is crucial. "The Camino, which begins as an abstract space, comes to be an accumulation of internalized spaces made up of stories, sensations, and changes in perception" (Frey 87). "Retelling," as Nancy Frey points out, "plays an important part in the return, whereby one is able to reinterpret, process the experiences, and create oneself as a pilgrim at the same time" (186). However, it may be impossible to adequately convey what one has experienced on deeper levels. Tony Kevin, in the end, doesn't know if he should even try: "Can I sum it up? Can I share it? Should I even try, or should I just leave off here, letting my readers draw whatever they want from what I have set down in this book so far?" (291). Whereas initially some pilgrims may have a hero's welcome back, people's interest in their pilgrimage may center on material and superficial details of the journey such as hostels and food, leaving pilgrims with a sense of alienation, disorientation, and loss of directionality.

With pilgrimages and spiritual tourism, there are often expectations as to where it will lead, metaphorically speaking, and as to what kind of answers to existential questions such journeys will provide. But are the answers otherwise unobtainable? How necessary is travel for spiritual transformation? How necessary are pilgrimages? As Boers writes: "Pilgrimage sites are not merely an end in themselves. They are not strictly speaking even necessary. They richly symbolize the fact that our lives are to be a journey with and to God" (42). Boers reminds us that the word for parish, with its roots in the Greek word *paroikia* (sojourn), means congregation of pilgrims. Thus, going to church for worship is already a pilgrimage.

Paradoxically, then, after all the effort, pilgrimage may not be necessary. We can think of the words in Luke: "Once, on being asked by the Pharisees when the kingdom of God would come, Jesus replied, The coming of the kingdom of God is not something that can be observed, nor will people say, 'Here it is,' or 'There it is,' because the kingdom of God is in your midst" (Luke 17:20–21). If the kingdom of God is found within ourselves and amongst ourselves, it means that one does not have to travel very far.

Shedding Stones, Reaching Peace:
William Schmidt's Spiritual Odyssey to Santiago

William Schmidt's *Walking with Stones* is an account of a strenuous, physical and bodily journey to the Pilgrim city of Santiago de Compostela in Spain. Emphasizing the remarkable achievement of walking eight-hundred kilometres (five-hundred miles) across northern Spain, William Schmidt's narrative begins with arrival at the spiritual goal, placing the point of departure in a solidly physical and geographical realm where the wildest dreams can and will be realized. Having thus at the outset established that this spiritual journey will be amazingly and successfully accomplished, Schmidt then returns to his real-life point of departure, the unimaginable event of his divorce, and goes on to interweave an account of this traumatic loss with the story of a both difficult and uplifting, material and spiritual journey traversing mountains and plains on foot. Gradually forming an unanticipated whole that constitutes a movement toward transformation and transcendence, the two levels of the pilgrimage mirror and intersect with each other.

The narrative paths of pilgrims are often studded with symbols, and William Schmidt's *Walking with Stones* is no exception. In Acts in the New Testament we read about Peter's miraculous escape from prison. He was "guarded by four squads of four soldiers each." An angel came to Peter and conducted him out of the prison, through an "iron gate leading to the city," and thus "rescued [him] from Herod's clutches" (Acts 12:4, 12:10, 12:11). Analogously, we could read William Schmidt's pilgrimage narrative in *Walking with Stones: A Spiritual Odyssey on the Pilgrimage to Santiago* as a passage through a literal and symbolic gate leading to a spiritual city, where Schmidt is rescued from the clutches of grief and confusion that imprison him at the beginning of his journey. There are four squads of four soldiers each in the passage about Peter in prison. Certain numbers in the Bible have extra significance, and one of the most common is the number four. We can think of the four Gospels, the four rivers in Paradise, the four cherubim guarding the tree of life, and the "living creatures" in Revelation. In Revelation, there are "four angels standing at the four corners of the earth, holding back the four winds of the earth" (Revelation 7). Ezekiel (1: 5–8) sees "what looked like four living creatures. In appearance their form was human, but each of them had four faces and four wings.... Under their wings on their four sides they had human hands." In Daniel we read: "Daniel said: 'In my vision at night I looked, and there before me were the four winds of heaven churning up the great sea. Four great beasts, each different from the others, came up out of the sea" (Daniel 7:2).

The number four also figures in the cross, as any cross per definition has four end points. A central theological and psychological symbol in *Walking with Stones*, the four points of the cross, pointing in four different directions, could be related to the four cardinal compass directions, which will here be related to the four elements of fire, water, earth, and air, whose significance for the transformative spiritual path depicted in *Walking with Stones* is profound. Fundamental for our physical survival, the four classical elements, dating back to Empedocles' four 'roots' and regarded as irreducible universal components, have been cornerstones in structures of abstract, metaphysical, and spiritual systems of all-encompassing spatio-temporal classification of material and spiritual phenomena not only in ancient Greek thought but in Eastern spirituality and in medieval philosophy.

Although fire is not the first of the classical elements, and although the elements as related to phases of pilgrimage are not only sequential but overlapping and interconnecting, here, fire will be a starting point. Fire propels the outward journey, pushing the pilgrim forward on his path.[1] In the Bible, in the first book of Kings, fire (and water) are prominent symbols that prove that God is God and the only God worth believing in (1 Kings 18:16–40). Setting out on his journey, William Schmidt knows he is "heading into the sacred fire of God's purifying furnace." Perhaps the solitude he encounters on the Camino is "God's cauldron, to burn off what is impure and untrue in [his] life" (6). There is also the "the emotional furnace inside" that Schmidt experiences before "the burial moment of [his] marriage" (130). Fire represents purification, change, and transformative power.

---

[1] Fire can also be negative: "Consider what a great forest is set on fire by a small spark," we read in James: "The tongue also is a fire, a world of evil among the parts of the body. It corrupts the whole body, sets the whole course of one's life on fire, and is itself set on fire by hell" (James 3:6).

If numbers are important the Bible, so are the cardinal directions. Abraham was told by God to leave Canaan and go west. The pilgrimage to Santiago, the Way of St. James, is also a journey west. Orienting oneself in space and mapping out directions is the first logical step of any journey. Nonetheless, despite Schmidt's meticulous preparations, confusion is a frequent fellow passenger on his journey. Comparable to the dilemma of choosing the right path delineated in Guillaume de Deguileville's *Le Pèlerinage de la Vie Humaine*, confusion arises at the start of the pilgrimage in *Walking with Stones* when Schmidt finds two different scallop shells, the markers along the Camino that pilgrims follow, pointing in two different directions. Even before that, on his stopover in Paris, confusion as to directions make Schmidt lost in the airport and later along the Seine, where, unwittingly, he points another tourist in the wrong direction and sets out in the wrong direction himself. Similarly, confusion envelops Schmidt as he exits from Mass in a spiritual fog at Notre Dame in Paris. Later on, confusion is caused by the fog in which Schmidt finds himself, which makes him "run the risk of losing all bearings and either going in circles, or walking off a cliff" (20), recalling the passage through the Valley of the Shadow of Death in Bunyan's *Pilgrim's Progress*. Danger and stagnation seem to be the dual menaces on the spiritual road, as is also letting oneself be led astray and then forced to retrace one's steps. A sense of direction and reliance upon the cardinal points are very important in *Walking with Stones*. At the outset, on a psychological level, Schmidt, facing divorce and experiencing "a sense of existential aloneness in the universe" (6), feels as if he is jumping "into the great unknown" (4).

All this confusion seems to be there to point to the emotional confusion and turmoil arising from the trauma of divorce and the sense of loss of directions to God. While directions are clear in *Walking with Stones* in walking west, spiritually speaking, the directions sought are divine, and they involve losing oneself in order to find oneself, that is, letting go of one's own strong but perhaps misguided will and submitting to divine guidance in a surrender that is often prefaced by humiliation and suffering. If the starting point of the pilgrimage in *Walking with Stones* is fire, then, the cardinal directions for the route that follows could be understood as both outward in a physical and geographical sense, and inward, where it is, rather, a matter of height and depth. "I am being driven deep down into myself," Schmidt muses (5). This self is as physical as it is spiritual. Even though this is a spiritual journey, the body has a dominant place in Schmidt's day-to-day, detailed, nitty-gritty narrative. The physical pains caused by walking the

Camino, the thorny bushes, and the simple pleasures of the body such as the bliss of a meal of bread, salami, and fountain water that makes Schmidt feel he has feasted, all contribute to this.

Walking on the earth in a literal and concrete sense, the body, inescapably immersed in the local and the immanent, is linked to the element of earth. One of the central symbols linked both to the element of earth and to the cardinal directions is that of the doorway. Doorways allow transitions into different spaces. Symbolically, they allow transitions into transformed mental and spiritual states. At the beginning of the pilgrimage, there is an actual medieval city gate that Schmidt walks through. Structurally, Schmidt provides his book with a metaphorical doorway in an initial chapter, "A Brief History of the Pilgrimage to Santiago," inviting the reader to step into the pilgrimage along with the author and to understand the purpose of a pilgrimage such as this. As doorways on the Camino are often made out of stone, they could be seen as related to the element of earth. The earth is the element associated with stability and fertility. In the Bible, the stability and eternity of God is likened to a rock. As Schmidt points out, "Christian scripture abounds with references to stones as foundational markers for life" (213), the cornerstone being one example with Jesus as the "living Stone—rejected by humans, but chosen by God and precious to him" (1 Peter 2: 4–5).

Like cornerstones, milestones can be real or metaphorical. In *Walking with Stones*, the most important milestone is the Cross of Ferro. As a pilgrim, you are supposed to bring something to the journey that you leave behind. Schmidt has brought "a heart-shaped stone given to [him] by [his wife] many years ago" (xi). At the Cross of Ferro, Schmidt will place the cherished heart stone once given to him by his soon-to-be ex-wife. Placed virtually at the middle of the book, the chapter on the Cross of Ferro constitutes a narrative and symbolic climax. Stone, cross, and water symbolism come together when Schmidt, in tears over the loss of his marriage and with the rain blowing into his face, approaches the Cross of Ferro, a high point topographically and structurally and a low point emotionally in being "the burial moment of [Schmidt's] marriage" (130). Coming down from the mound after his "ritual of release" (132), Schmidt is able to continue onto the second stage of his journey of purification and healing.

Connected to the element of earth, stones are central in Schmidt's pilgrimage narrative on literal and concrete as well as figurative and symbolic levels. The Camino itself, as he explains in an epilogue entitled "A Meditation on Stones," consists of stones of all sorts and shapes. Remembering also that the Ten Commandments were written on stone, and re-membering the passage in Exodus (33:22) where Moses is protected in the cleft of a rock from seeing God's face, Schmidt regards "stones as symbols of hope" (213). Rocks and stones are part of the earth, the element associated with stability and fertility. In the Bible, the stability and eternity of God is likened to a rock. The first acts of creation involved the containment of formlessness and void through stone. Stone gives form and substance to our Earth, and ultimately to our very own being" (209).

An element often associated with emotion and the unconscious as well as with baptism and rebirth, water is endowed with strong symbolism in *Walking with Stones*. There are the icy waters of the many streams and rivers that revive Schmidt's feet, swollen from walking, and all the lyrically described restorative showers enjoyed to the hilt after full days of walking. In one place, the Albergue of San Bol, water is a poetically described cleansing and soothing element. Here, "[t]he sound of the stream babbling away adds to the effect of washing away care, hardness, and brittleness" (92). In this healing oasis where Schmidt can soak his feet in ice cold water and sleep under the trees, the flow of the water seems to have spiritual qualities, and he thinks: "let the eternal flow of God, who brings us into balance and sustains our truth-seeking, do God's sacred works" (92–93). The water symbolism is continued in the description of foot-washing in the church of San Nicholas where the feet of the pilgrims are washed and kissed in "a profound act of grace" and one is "embraced in one's vulnerability and woundedness," something that brings tears to Schmidt's eyes (104). Although initially he resists this act out of a sense of unworthiness, it brings "a profound sense of unity with the countless pilgrims who have found rest in this sanctuary," and makes Schmidt ponder the pains pilgrims preceding him might have carried and wonder if "the Spirit of God [met] them as the Sacred Spirit found [him]" (104).

Diving into the cold water of the Atlantic at Finisterre at the end of the journey is purification and baptism. Euphoric, with "a soft warm breeze wrapping itself around [him]," Schmidt takes in the "panorama of deep blue water matched by an equally blue sky" (197) where "blue upon blue reveals the deepening depths of the ocean" (200):

> I dive deep and feel the strength of my stroke and the renewal of healing waters. I feel myself to be undergoing a true baptism, with an old life being washed away. I have no illusions that pain is permanently washed away, but I also know that the new is coming.... I am not magically 'healed' in the sense that my physical or emotional pain is gone. The painful scenarios of my life are as real as they were

before I began the Camino, but I have been birthed into new life by God's grace. These waters enveloping me at this moment represent that new birth (202).

While three of the four classical elements are present in the description at the end of *Walking with Stones* when "the sun sinks lower into the sky [creating] a wide river of light dancing on the ocean below" (200), the element of earth soon makes itself felt, too, as Schmidt muses, rather humorously: "We have also discovered that, while we may have experienced moments of heightened awareness, sand can still get into one's cheese. Enlightenment always runs into our earthly reality, and reminders of our dust nature are never far away" (201).

At the end of his pilgrimage, Schmidt makes an observation regarding the effect of the Camino on consciousness. Walking the Camino, he says, "there emerged a quality of consciousness that is akin to what [he] will call the 'observer self,' that is neither the 'normal consciousness' of focusing on data outside ourselves nor a focus inward but a 'deeper consciousness that is able to observe us both in our inner and outer preoccupations. In this third form of consciousness I hover over both my body and my inner life, as well as my surroundings. This state is not dissociative, but detached and engaged" (211).

This third form of consciousness occurring when Schmidt enters into a "visionary state" "as if the eternal has broken into [his] awareness" (200), resembles what some thinkers have called unity consciousness. For Ken Wilber, for example, unity consciousness is a term used to denote the transcendence of our two modes of knowing, one a nondual mode and the other a dualistic mode that makes divisions between subject and object, seer and seen. Unity consciousness is a recognition of what Wilber calls primal experience, where "knowing and the Real coalesce" (86). In the West, we have been trained in a dualistic mode of knowing even though "the nondual mode alone is capable of giving the 'knowledge of Reality'" (82). This is "nothing less than a state of awareness wherein the observer *is* the observed, wherein the universe is *not* severed into one state which sees and another state which is seen" (87). Schmidt's description of a third form of consciousness resembles unity consciousness, but we might also relate it to the element of air, remembering that air, in classical Greek thought and in alchemy, could be understood both as the 'air' of a lower atmosphere and as 'ether' (or quintessence), a higher, timeless and translucent aspect of the atmosphere.

During the pilgrimage to Santiago it is as though the Camino itself takes on life and agency, becoming a subject in its own right, almost like a tough personal trainer or a tyrant exercising his rule and imposing intolerable rigors in unpredictable ways and thus holding his subjects, the pilgrims, in a cruel and exacting grip. As if equipped with hands, the Camino can squeeze tears and "gut-splitting laughter" out of its walkers (Schmidt 1). Or, like a gut-wrenching therapist, the Camino can "dredge up ... buried memories" (17). Towards the end of his journey, Schmidt concludes: "The Camino has done its work in dismembering me" (186). So what is the real reason for walking eight-hundred kilometres in difficult terrain, embracing "an ascetic Camino discipline of medieval proportions" (49)? This question is posed in the first chapter and then again, many times, in the pages that follow. At one point, Schmidt asks himself if this pilgrimage is a spiritual or a sporting event. The description of the hardships endured and the primitive conditions suffered certainly makes the journey seem exceedingly sporting.

For Schmidt, the scallop shell, a marker on the road pointing pilgrims in the direction of Santiago, becomes a symbol of directions and distances to God. The scallop shell is the supreme symbol of the Camino, one that predates the Christian era and connects with the times when Finisterre was the goal of the original Camino. Traditionally, Schmidt tells us, scallop shells were picked up by the pilgrims who had reached Finisterre and the Atlantic "as a ritual object to symbolize the completion of their journey" (2). Metaphorically speaking, the grooves of the scallop shell resemble the many routes travelled by pilgrims toward the destination shared by all of them: Santiago, and the tomb of St. James. But there is more to the scallop shell. It "reveals something about the path itself" (2). Here, we are no longer talking about cardinal directions *outward* in a geographic sense but about cardinal directions *inward* in a spiritual and theological sense: "Its many grooves all point to the centre and every groove reaches the centre, but the spiritual mystery of the scallop is that the grooves at the centre of the shell are longer and thus further away from its end, therefore covering more distance than those grooves at the perimeter" (2). This means that even though he is "living close to [his] spiritual centre," a "spiritual fat cat" like Schmidt might actually be further away from his spiritual goal and may not get to the destination any faster than seekers on the margins of spirituality. Those who "begin the search for God from the perimeter, from a more painful place of searching" might get there more quickly since they are "perhaps hungrier for the Sacred" and have "less accumulated spiritual clutter to cut through" (3). And Schmidt reminds us that "Jesus noted how the first often arrive last, while the last seem to arrive first" (3). "I believe we all seek our spiritual home," Schmidt concludes, "and for me this is particularly strong in a mystical sense. Santiago beckons to me as a surrogate spiritual destination, a kind of practice run for the real thing" (33).

Through the Wormhole of the Absolute:
Mystic Experience in
Elizabeth Gilbert's *Eat, Pray, Love*

Written from the perspective of a *teologia cordis* rather than a *teologia mentis* and focusing on, as the telling subtitle reveals, *One Woman's Search for Everything*, Elizabeth Gilbert's autobiography *Eat Pray Love* (2006) describes the journey of a modern pilgrim exploring material and spiritual roads to God. Building on William James's *The Varieties of Religious Experience* (1902) and Andrew Newberg's *Why God Won't Go Away: Brain Science and The Biology of Belief* (2002), this chapter will focus on Gilbert's pilgrimage narrative whose high point is an encounter with God that, as will be argued, could be understood as a mystic experience comparable to the transcendent experiences of saints and sages throughout the ages.

In her more recent book, *Big Magic: Creative Living Beyond Fear* (2015), Gilbert looks back on her earlier bestseller:

> I once wrote a book in order to save myself. I wrote a travel memoir in order to make sense of my own journey and my own emotional confusion. All I was trying to do with that book was figure myself out. In the process, though, I wrote a story that apparently helped a lot of other people figure themselves out—but that was never my intention. If I'd sat down to write *Eat Pray Love* with the sole aim of helping others, I would've produced an entirely different book, I might have even produced a book that was insufferably unreadable. (99)

At the beginning of *Eat Pray Love*, "a state of hopeless and life-threatening despair" (15) reigns. Gilbert is down on the floor in her bathroom, "[s]obbing so hard … that a great lake of tears and snot [is] spreading before [her] on the bathroom tiles, a veritable Lake Inferior (if you will) of all [her] shame and fear and confusion and grief" (10). Desperately unhappy about the direction her life is taking, Gilbert has come to the realization that she does not want to be married any more. Nor does she want to have a baby even though she is 'supposed' to want this. Instead, she wants to be free to go out into the world on journalistic trips. The realization alone of not wanting a baby would perhaps not in and of itself lead to a "great lake of tears and snot." Whereas one reads between the lines that the husband places certain expectations on Gilbert, that she is the main breadwinner, and that she is tired of their pleasant but conventional life, the marriage dynamics are not delved into, and the reasons for the "great lake of tears and snot" are only hinted at. The full reasons for Gilbert's great despair are not disclosed.[1]

Nonetheless, it may be sufficient to know that, whatever the exact parameters of the "great lake of tears and snot," Gilbert has actively participated in building a life she now desperately wants to get out of and she has now ended up in supplication on the bathroom floor, where she has an unusual and startling experience:

> something was about to occur on that bathroom floor that would change forever the progression of my life—almost like one of those crazy astronomical super-events when a planet flips over in outer space for no reason whatsoever, and its molten core shifts, relocating its poles and altering its shape radically, such that the whole mass of the planet suddenly becomes oblong instead of spherical. Something like that.
> What happened was that I started to pray.
> You know—like, to *God*. (13)

To Gilbert's surprise, God responds. He speaks to her, "from within [her] own self" (16), an episode that "[has] all the hallmarks of a typical Christian conversion experience—the dark night of the soul, the call for help, the responding voice, the sense of transformation" (17). If, at the outset (on the

---

[1] In a review of *Eat Pray Love* Jennifer Egan comments that while she is "willing to believe that Gilbert despaired over having failed at a more conventional life even as she sought out its opposite—complications like these are what make us human," she finds that Gilbert "doesn't tell that story here, or even acknowledge the paradox. As a result, her crisis remains a shadowy thing, a mere platform for the actions she takes to alleviate it." Katie Roiphe sums up the pattern thus: "*Eat, Pray, Love* begins with Gilbert in her early 30s, crying on the floor of a bathroom of a big suburban house because she realizes that she does not want to have a child; she divorces her husband, falls dramatically to pieces, and then travels around the world. Along the way, she finds god in an ashram in India, big plates of pasta in Italy, and triumphs over her severe depression." Commenting on the pattern, Roiphe adds: "Admittedly, the memoir is constructed with a certain amount of artifice. As one gathers from her catchy title, Gilbert orchestrates her recovery in three parts: She goes to Italy to experience pleasure, India to explore spirituality, and Indonesia to find something she calls balance. In real life, of course, one doesn't often get to structure one's emergence from a black period quite so neatly."

bathroom floor), Gilbert feels enveloped in a "pocket of silence" and hears God's voice, she knows that it is her own voice, even though it is her own voice as she "has never heard it before" (16). "I would not say that this was a religious *conversion* for me," she goes on to say, "not in that traditional manner of being born again and saved. I would call what happened that night the beginning of a religious *conversation*. The first words of an open and exploratory dialogue that would, ultimately, bring me very close to God, indeed" (17). While Gilbert wants "to have a lasting experience of God" (27), she doesn't "want to be a monk" or "totally give up worldly pleasures"; instead, her desire is to learn "how to live in this world and enjoy its delights, but also devote [herself] to God" (28).

Some critics have dismissed *Eat Pray Love: One Woman's Search for Everything* as a banal bestseller (it was on *The New York Times* Best Seller list for 187 weeks). Suspicious of the genre of the spiritual journey and of books that have an "inevitable arc of recovery built into the story," Katie Roiphe writes: "The memoir lacks the ambiguity we associate with a more literary effort. It feels like there is something inherently trashy about reading for that redemption, for a happyish ending in a tropical place."[2] Disparagingly, Maureen Callahan of the *New York Post* describes the narrative pattern in *Eat Pray Love* thus: "She got divorced, then went looking for answers, spending four months in Italy to eat, four months in India to find God (she says she did, even sat in his palm), then four months in Bali to pull it all together and maybe find love." Callahan sees the "the most disturbing aspect of Gilbert's book" as "narcissistic New Age reading," and judges it to be "the worst in Western fetishization of Eastern thought and culture, assured in its answers to existential dilemmas that have confounded intellects greater than hers."

This chapter will argue instead that *Eat Pray Love* could be seen as a modern pilgrimage narrative the high point of which, an encounter with God, is described in ways that recall classical spiritual autobiographies and the writings of mystics.[3] The moment on the bathroom floor could be identi-

---

[2] Other critics were positive, such as Jennifer Egan of *The New York Times* who wrote that "Gilbert's prose is fuelled by a mix of intelligence, wit and colloquial exuberance that is close to irresistible."

[3] Callahan, who prefers books like "God is Not Great: How Religion Poisons Everything," comments condescendingly: "You may be a well-off white woman, but if you are depressed, the answer can be found in the East, where the poor brown people are sages." In Callahan's view, further, it is mainly women who are such gullible suckers as to fall for "this silliness." Her fear is that, as "anecdotal evidence suggests," "readers are using *Eat,*

fied as the starting point of Gilbert's spiritual journey. "[Responding] to the transcendent mystics of all religions" (14), Gilbert sets out on a one-year journey to Italy, India, and Indonesia to find God. While she does not wish to discuss God's existence, she comments on this appellation: 'God', she says, is the word she uses because it feels "the most warm" (14): "I could just as easily use the words *Jehovah*, *Allah*, *Shiva*, *Vishnu* or *Zeus*. Alternatively, I could call God 'That,' which is how the ancient Sanskrit scriptures say it, and which I think comes close to the all-inclusive and unspeakable entity I have sometimes experienced" (13). Other terms—"The Universe, The Great Void, The Force, The Supreme Self, The Whole, The Creator, The Light, The Higher Power, or even the most poetic manifestation of God's name, taken … from the Gnostic gospels: 'The Shadow of the Turning'" (14)—seem equal to Gilbert in being "equally adequate and inadequate descriptions of the indescribable" (14).[4] Culturally if not theologically a Christian, Elizabeth Gilbert "was born a Protestant of the white Anglo-Saxon persuasion," but she "can't swallow that one fixed rule of Christianity insisting that Christ is the *only* way to God" (14). Jesus is mentioned in *Eat Pray Love* but he remains marginal, and the narrative focuses almost entirely on God.

On her journey, Gilbert follows in the footsteps of mystics from Buddhist, Taoist, and Christian traditions whose rituals attempt to clear the everyday mind of its ceaseless chatter in order to move beyond the ego. Adhering to a strict spiritual discipline and practicing yoga and meditation at an ashram in India, Gilbert has the experience of being suddenly "transported through the portal of the universe and taken to the center of God's palm" (208). She arrives at "the wormhole of the Absolute" (209).

Mystical experiences are states that may be sporadic and spontaneous, or they may be arrived at after the discipline of religious ritual or meditation.[5]

Pray, Love as a shortcut to finding a spiritual 'truth' (one that is not even theirs, but Gilbert's), as an excuse to have that extra glass of wine, and as a license to abandon all critical thinking."

[4] Commenting in *Circuitous Journeys* on the "inevitable gap between the human signifier and the divine signified" (22), David Leigh recalls how St. Augustine "begins his *Confessions* with four paragraphs of speculation and prayer about the difficulty of shaping any finite language to express experiences of the Infinite: 'Can any man say enough when he speaks of you? Yet woe betide those who are silent about you! For even those who are most gifted with speech cannot find words to describe you'" (1.4, p. 23, quoted in Leigh 21).

[5] In Walt Whitman one finds "a classical expression" of the "sporadic type of mystical experience," according to William James (306). James writes that the other way to reach a mystical experience is to follow the discipline of Christian or Muslim meditation or the philosophies such as the Buddhism. Yoga, practiced by Buddhists or Hindus, is one way, and yoga, meaning "the experimental union of the individual with the divine," leads to a

Looking at studies of mysticism, we will find that Gilbert's experience described here has much in common with transcendent experiences throughout the ages. Although she is aware of her own frequent frustration when reading about "this moment in somebody else's spiritual memoirs—that moment in which the soul excuses itself from time and place and merges with the infinite" (208), Gilbert nonetheless attempts to describe her own 'indescribable' experience:

> Simply put, I got pulled through the wormhole of the Absolute, and in that rush I suddenly understood the workings of the universe completely. I left my body, I left the room, I left the planet, I stepped through time and I entered the void. I was inside the void, but I also *was* the void, all at the same time. The void was a place of limitless peace and wisdom. The void was conscious and it was intelligent. The void was God, which means I was inside God. But not in a gross, physical way—not like I was Liz Gilbert stuck inside a chunk of God's thigh muscle. I was just part of God. In addition to being God, I was both a tiny piece of the universe and exactly the same size as the universe. (209)

Experiences such as this are described in William James' chapter on mysticism in *Varieties of Religious Experience* (1902). Proposing that "personal religious experience has its root and centre in mystical states of consciousness" (294), James suggests that "[o]ur normal waking consciousness, rational consciousness as we call it, is but one special type of consciousness, whilst all about it … there lie potential forms of consciousness entirely different" (300). James makes a distinction between two types of religiosity. On the one hand there is the "ordinary religious believer" whose "religion has been made for him by others, communicated to him by tradition, determined to fixed forms by imitation, and retained by habit" (11). On the other hand there are the "pattern-setters" who have "original experiences" and "for whom religion exists not as a dull habit, but as an acute fever rather" and who are "'geniuses' in the religious line" (11).[6]

"superconscious state" or *samâdhi* (310). Similarly, the Persian theologian Al-Ghazzali writes in his (eleventh-century) autobiography: "During [a] solitary state things were revealed to me which it is impossible either to describe or to point out" (quoted by James 313).

[6] With George Fox (and his vision of Litchfield) as a prime example, James suggests that the pattern-setters are often "creatures of exalted emotional sensibility" who suffer from melancholy and tend to have visions (11). In James's view, Fox "was a psychopath or *détraqué* of the deepest dye" (12). There is a great divide in the field of religion, according to James, one side being what he calls institutional and the other personal. Whereas religion in the institutional field is "an external art, the art of winning the favor of the gods" (28), in the personal field, we encounter religion as "more fundamental than either

For James, the mystic experience is at the center of religion, and he outlines four central aspects. As we shall see, these aspects could be brought to bear on Gilbert's description of her transcendent experience. According to James, firstly, the mystic experience is *ineffable*, since it "defies expression": "no adequate report of its contents can be given in words. It follows from this that its quality must be directly experienced; it cannot be imparted or transferred to others. In this peculiarity mystical states are more like states of feeling than like states of intellect" (295). Secondly, there is a *noetic quality* involving "states of knowledge," "states of insights into depths of truth unplumbed by the discursive intellect. They are illuminations, revelations" (James 295). Thirdly, mystical states are transient, lasting no more than an hour at most, and fourthly, they are marked by *passivity*: "Although the oncoming of mystical states may be, [sic] facilitated by preliminary voluntary operations, as by fixing the attention, or going through certain bodily performances, or in other ways which manuals of mysticism prescribe; yet when the characteristic sort of consciousness once has set in, the mystic feels as if his own will were in abeyance, and indeed sometimes as if he were grasped and held by a superior power" (James 295). In James's view, then, the mystic experience is central in religious life, and in an often quoted passage he sums it up thus:

> The overcoming of all the usual barriers between the individual and the Absolute is the great mystic achievement. In mystic states we become one with the Absolute and we become aware of our oneness. This is the everlasting and triumphant mystical tradition, hardly altered by differences of clime and creed. In Hinduism, in Neoplatonism, in Sufism, in Christian mysticism, in Whitmanism, we find the same recurring note, so that there is about mystical utterances an eternal unanimity which ought to make a critic stop and think, and which brings it about that the mystical classics have, as has been said, neither birthday nor native land. Perpetually telling of the unity of man with God, their speech antedates languages, and they do not grow old. (325)

James does modify his all-inclusive statement somewhat and admits that "religious mysticism ... is much less unanimous than I have allowed.[7] He

---

theology or ecclesiasticism" (29). James reserves the term 'religion' "for the fully organized system of feeling, thought, and institution, for the Church" (28).

[7] "It has been both ascetic and antinomianly self-indulgent within the Christian church. It is dualistic in Sankhya, and monistic in Vedanta philosophy. I called it pantheistic; but the great Spanish mystics are anything but pantheists. ... How different again, apart from the happiness common to all, is the mysticism of Walt Whitman, Edward Carpenter,

continues: "The fact is that the mystical feeling of enlargement, union, and emancipation has no specific intellectual content whatever of its own. It is capable of forming matrimonial alliances with material furnished by the most diverse philosophies and theologies, provided only they can find a place in their framework for its peculiar emotional mood" (329).

The profound insight reached in states of mystic experience is, according to James, first and foremost a sense of reconciliation—"as if the opposites of the world, whose contradictoriness and conflict make all our difficulties and troubles, were melted into unity" (301).[8]

Those who have had mystical experiences "have been 'there,' and know" according to James, and it is useless for skeptics to question these experiences.[9] The result of the mystic experience is as important as the experience itself. According to James, many mystical experiences lead to optimism and monism: "We pass into mystical states from out of ordinary consciousness as from a less into a more, as from a smallness into a vastness, and at the same time as from an unrest to a rest. We feel them as reconciling, unifying states. They appeal to the yes-function more than to the no-function in us" (322).

Richard Jefferies, and other naturalistic pantheists, from the more distinctively Christian sort" (329).

[8] James gives a number of examples of this. In his experience of cosmic consciousness, Dr R. M. Bucke, a Canadian psychiatrist, firstly, "saw that the universe is not composed of dead matter, but is, on the contrary, a living Presence" (quoted by James 309). Saint Ignatius, another example, felt that one "single hour of meditation at Manresa had taught him more truths about heavenly things than all the teachings of all the doctors put together could have taught him" (Bartoli-Michel, *Vie do Saint Ignace de Loyola*, quoted by James 318). Saint Teresa, further, expresses herself along similar lines: "One day, being in orison … it was granted me to perceive in one instant how all things are seen and contained in God" (quoted by James 318). Perhaps less well-known, Jacob Boehme writes: "In one quarter of an hour I saw and knew more than if I had been many years at a university. For I saw and knew the being of all things, the Byss and the Abyss, and the eternal generation of the holy Trinity, the descent and original of the world and of all creatures through the divine wisdom" (quoted by James 318). George Fox, to take another example, felt that he had returned back to "the state of Adam in which he was before he fell. The creation was opened to [him]; and it was shown [him], how all things had their names given to them, according to their nature and virtue" (quoted by James 318). Angelus Silesius, finally, wrote about his experience: "Ich bin so gross als Gott. Er ist als ich so klein; Er kann nicht über mich, ich unter ihm nicht sein" (quoted by James 325).

[9] James points out, further, that "our own more 'rational' beliefs are based on evidence exactly similar in nature to that which the mystic quote for theirs. Our senses, namely, have assured us of certain states of fact; but mystical experiences are as direct perceptions of fact for those who have them as any sensations ever were for us" (328). As James asserts: "The mystic is, in short, *invulnerable*, and must be left, whether we relish it or not, in undisturbed enjoyment of his creed" (328).

A closer look at Elizabeth Gilbert's transcendent experience in *Eat Pray Love* shows that it includes the four aspects posited by James: ineffability, a noetic quality, transiency, and passivity. It is indescribable, it conveys knowledge ("I suddenly understood the workings of the universe completely"), it is transient (when she tries to hang onto the experience she falls out of it), and she is passive while it lasts. Gilbert describes her experience thus: "The place in which I was standing can't be described as an earthly location. It was neither dark nor light, neither big nor small. Nor was it a place, nor was I technically standing there, nor was I exactly 'I' anymore" (209). Actually, identity becomes completely irrelevant: "Imagine cramming yourself into such a puny box of identity when you could experience your infinitude instead" (210).

Many other thinkers in the field of theology and psychology have attempted to understand mystic experiences. A hundred years after James's *Varieties of Religious Experience*, Andrew Newberg published *Why God Won't Go Away: Brain Science and The Biology of Belief* (2002). Newberg explores precisely this melting into unity and delves into what he calls the biology of transcendence. According to Newberg, "[v]irtually all mystical traditions identify some sense of union with the absolute as the ultimate spiritual goal" even though mystical experiences of union with God remain difficult or impossible to describe (103). Echoing James, Newberg states: "while the mystics of different times and traditions have used many techniques to attain this lofty union, from the pious self-denial of medieval Christian saints to the ritual sexuality of some tantric Buddhists, the mystical states they describe sound very much the same" (102).[10] Making brain scans of people in meditation or prayer, Newberg discovered a brain state of oneness that involves a sense of connection with everything beyond the usual barriers, where one's sense of being a separate being disappears. He suggests that this state of 'unitary being' is what some would call heaven, nirvana, paradise, or, in other words, the ultimate form of bliss one might

---

[10] As Newberg comments: "James rightly understands that the essential mechanics of the mystical experience—that is, the attainment of spiritual union through detachment from the self—is rooted in something deeper and more primal than theology or scriptural revelation" (106–07), and he adds: "Neurogically, and philosophically, there cannot be two versions of this absolute unitary state. It may look different, in retrospect, according to cultural beliefs and personal interpretations—a Catholic nun, for whom God is the ultimate reality, might interpret any mystical experience as a melting into Christ, while a Buddhist, who does not believe in a personalized God, might interpret mystical union as a melting into nothingness" (122–23).

experience in life.[11] Newberg's findings indicate that the "mechanics" for "the attainment of spiritual union through detachment from the self" "are wired into the human brain" (106–07). When neural input is blocked, as in meditation or religious ritual, a process leading to an experience of transcendent spiritual unity may follow. Newberg proposes that there is a continuum from the light sort of trance one may experience in everyday relaxation rituals to the profound states of transcendence experienced by mystics. In other words, "all mystical experiences, from the mildest to the most intense, have their biological roots in the mind's machinery of transcendence": "if the brain were not assembled as it is, we would not be able to experience a higher reality, even if it [does] exist" (123).[12]

The goal of mystical striving, then, would seem to be a dissolution of the limits of the self and a return to an original condition of wholeness and unity with God, much like the fourteenth-century German nun Margareta Ebner, who had an experience of being "surrounded by a grace beyond measure" and "grasped by an inner divine power of God" in an "immeasurable sweetness" (Newberg 98). Newberg observes that many scientists regard such states as delusional or as "indications of brain dysfunction or any number of psychological stresses" (99). Looking back to Freud, moreover, many psychiatrists "have believed that mystical experiences are illusions triggered by the neurotic, regressive urge to reject an unfulfilling reality, and recapture the bliss we knew as infants, bathed in the safe and all-encompassing unity of a mother's love" (Newberg 99).[13]

---

[11] Further, there is evidence that mystical experiences are signs of health rather than disturbance. Newberg mentions a sociological study by Andrew Greeley from 1975 that indicates that "people who experience genuine mystical states enjoy much higher levels of psychological health than the public at large" (Newberg 108).

[12] Proposing that "neurology could explain the Unio Mystica—the Mysterious Union with God that characterizes the spiritual experience of so many Christian mystics," Newberg adds that "this state of mystical union is not the same as the ultimate transcendent state, Absolute Unitary Being, in which no sense of self is possible, and no specific images of God or even of reality can exist. It's likely, though, that if active meditation carries a mystic as far as the Unio Mystica, it may carry him or her even further, to the ultimate unitary state. This would occur as the mystic tires, and willed intention of the attention association weakens" (122).

[13] In *Major Trends in Jewish Mysticism*, Gershom Sholem argues along similar lines but from a phylogenetic perspective that mysticism appears at a certain point in the development of religion. In the earliest times, when no abyss had opened up between the human and the divine, mysticism as such did not exist, because, at that time, as Sholem puts it, you were able to meet God and petition him directly. There was an immediate consciousness of universal unity, something that is different from mysticism. It is the arrival of religion in its classical forms that opens up an absolute divide between the

Elizabeth Gilbert's experience in *Eat Pray Love* resembles the 'intro-vertive' experiences described by Walter T. Stace in *Mysticism and Philo-sophy* (1960) which "occur predominantly in advanced stages of the mystic vocation" and which "are clearly regarded as the higher type by persons such as Meister Eckhart who have experienced both," as Edward F. Kelly and Michael Grosso write in "Mystical Experience" (505–06). According to Kelly and Grosso, "[i]n these experiences one's perceptual world is not merely transfigured but abolished, along with all other contents of ordinary consciousness such as specific thoughts, images, memories, and the like" (506). Kelly and Grosso regard Walter Stace as a member of the 'peren-nialist' school "which seeks out and emphasizes *commonalities* in religion generally and in the mystical and primordial wisdom tradition in particu-lar," in polemical contrast to radical constructivists such as Steven Katz. For Katz *"[t]here are NO pure (i.e. unmediated experiences. ... That is to say, all* experience is processed through, organized by, and makes itself available to us in extremely complex epistemological ways. ... the experience itself as well as the form in which it is reported is shaped by concepts which the mys-tic brings to, and which shape, his experience" (qtd. by Kelly and Grosso 511, italics in original). In other words, for Katz, the experiences are "*completely* determined by cultural conditionings" (Kelly and Grosso 512, italics in original). But "[t]he radical constructivist position," as Kelly and Grosso point out," "becomes increasingly strained as we progress toward the deeper regions of mystical experience," since "[t]he central objective of mystical teachings and practices everywhere is essentially the same—speci-fically, to overcome conditionings and attachments of everyday life that get in the way of a mystical receptivity which is presumed to exist in all of us" (513). Examples are the Yogic practices of Patanjali "specifically to overcome the conditionings that keep us culturally and psychologically bound," and practices in Buddhism of "progressively and systematically deconditioning the beliefs and assumptions of one's working epistemology, leading to a state of pure consciousness called the Middle Way or Emptiness" (Kelly and Grosso 513). Kelly and Grosso go on to state that "[t]he same sort of

infinity of God and the finiteness of humanity. In what Sholem calls the romantic period of religion, mystics would take this great abyss as their point of departure from which they attempt to bridge the gap and restore the lost unity. One may wonder how something that per definition is indescribable can be expressed in language. And yet, as Sholem writes, mystics have had a great desire to express their experiences in words, and the experiences described by mystics may be valuable both for the knowledge they contribute and for their literary qualities.

disciplined effort to overcome ordinary conditionings is also central to the practices of Plotinus and many Christian mystics," such as Dionysius the Areopagite, who emphasized the idea of the *via negativa*," "a way of not doing, forgetting, letting go" (514).

Elizabeth Gilbert's experience recalls, further, the descriptions of the Neoplatonist philosopher Plotinus, who wrote in *Ennead* (tractate 9, section 10): "The man is changed, no longer himself nor self-belonging; he is merged with the Supreme, sunken into it, one with it: centre coincides with centre, for centres of circles" (qtd. by Kelly and Grosso 508). Plotinus, according to James, finds that the person subject to a mystic experience "changes, he ceases to be himself, preserves nothing of himself. Absorbed in God, he makes but one with him, like a centre of a circle coinciding with another centre" (qtd. by James 325). It also resembles the experiences of Arthur Koestler: "The 'I' ceases to exist because it has, by a kind of mental osmosis, established communication with, and been dissolved in, the universal pool. It is this process of dissolution and limitless expansion which is sensed as the 'oceanic feeling', as the draining of all tension, the absolute catharsis, the peace that passeth all understanding" (qtd. by Kelly and Grosso 510).

Gilbert's experience could also be compared to what Ken Wilber has called unity consciousness, a paradoxical state, since it is "of the timeless moment, it is entirely present now," and "there is no way to reach now. There is no way to *arrive* at that which already is" (Wilber 558). Unity consciousness is radically all-inclusive since it is not different from other states "but the condition and true nature of *all* states" (558): "If it were different from any state (for example, if it were different from your awareness right now), then that would imply it had a boundary, that it had something to separate it from your present awareness. But unity consciousness has no boundaries, so there is nothing to separate it from anything. Enlightenment flashes clear in this moment, and this moment, and this" (559). Unity consciousness, then, "is the simple awareness of the real territory of no-boundary" or "no-boundary awareness"—something that is very hard to catch and even more so because of the boundary-creating effects of language (Wilber 474). Although, in Wilber's view, we ceaselessly create boundaries that do not exist, the first or "primary boundary" is the one we establish between ourselves and the rest of the world:

> In unity consciousness, in no-boundary awareness, the sense of self expands to totally include everything once thought to be not-self. One's sense of identity ·
> shifts to the entire universe, to all worlds, high and low, manifest or unmanifest,

sacred or profane. And obviously this cannot occur as long as the primary boundary, which *separates* the self from the universe, is mistaken as real. But once the primary boundary is understood to be illusory, one's sense of self envelops the All—there is then no longer anything outside of oneself, and so nowhere to draw any sort of boundary. Thus, if we can begin to see through the primary boundary, the sense of unity consciousness will not be far from us. (476)

During her transcendent experience, Gilbert is *inside* the void but she *is* also the void, she is a 'tiny piece.' Her self envelops everything so that there is no longer anything that is 'outside' of herself. Hers is a no-boundary awareness. William James remarks that there is often in the mystical experience "a monistic insight, in which the *other* in its various forms appears absorbed into the One" (301). Along such lines, after her transcendental experience, Gilbert feels that she can "personally attest" the truth of the sage Kabir's words: "All know that the drop merges into the ocean, but few know that the ocean merges into the drop" (209).[14] Elizabeth Gilbert's union with God, further, recalls descriptions in the Christian tradition, where God is described as all beginnings and all endings. Irenaeus, one of the Church fathers, to take one example, wrote that God alone contains all things and that there is nothing above or after God. Gilbert's experience is in harmony with the Christian doctrine of creation that sees God as the source and container of all things. As the comparisons to the transcendental experiences described in the literature of mysticism suggest, then, Elizabeth Gilbert's experience in *Eat Pray Love* could be understood as a mystic experience. Her one-year journey to Italy, India, and Indonesia is a pilgrimage in a search for God and inner peace, a search placed within a universal mystical tradition.

---

[14] This also recalls the experience of John Tauler, a fourteenth-century German mystic whose soul becomes "sunk and lost in the Abyss of Deity, and loses the consciousness of all creature distinctions. All things are gathered together in one with the divine sweetness, and man's being is so penetrated with the divine substance that he loses himself therein, as a drop of water in a cask of strong wine" (quoted by Newberg 101).

Paradise Lost and Reclaimed:
Tentative Homecoming
in Anne Rice's *Called Out of Darkness*

And lead us not into temptation, but deliver us from evil.

(Matthew 6–13)

For spiritual autobiographies, as Bruce Hindmarsh observes in *The Evangelical Conversion Narrative*, "the Bible's account of fall from innocence and return provided a structure and many topoi" (8). David J. Leigh suggests in *Circuitous Journeys: Modern Spiritual Autobiography* that the journey of the autobiographical narrative "[parallels] several biblical narratives with circular patterns" (4). Looking at ten modern spiritual autobiographies in the light of Augustine's *Confessions*, Leigh finds that there is "a remarkable similarity in their narrative form and literacy patterns" (x, xi). "More important than a mere convenience of plot, the circular journey pattern provided Augustine with a structural metaphor for several doctrines important to his theological understanding of his conversion story" (Leigh 4).

The story told by Anne Rice in her autobiography, *Called Out of Darkness: A Spiritual Confession* (2008), could be understood along such lines. It could also be analyzed with the help of typological patterns employed in biblical exegesis. Historically, Christian theology and biblical exegesis have departed from a doctrine of typology or correspondences between the Old and the New Testaments, whereby stories in the Old Testament are seen as pointing forward to and prefiguring events in the New Testament. A typological pattern is articulated in Chapter IV in *Dei Verbum* where it is stated that "God, the inspirer and author of both Testaments, wisely arranged that the New Testament be hidden in the Old and the Old be made manifest in the New" (*Dogmatic Constitution on Divine Revelation Dei Verbum*). Typological patterns involve events or characters in the Old Testament, then, that in crucial and charged ways point forward to events or characters in the New

Testament. From a typological perspective, original sin and the fall prefigure the redemption offered by Christ. One example of this can be seen in the painting by Fra Angelico, *The Annunciation* (1430), showing Adam and Eve in Paradise on the left side, and the Angel Gabriel with Maria (who in obedience to God bows to Gabriel) to the right. A typological exegesis could in itself be seen as a symbol of oneness or unity, too, since metaphorically speaking it achieves a union between the Old Testament and the New.

As this chapter will argue, in Anne Rice's *Called Out of Darkness*, a 'fall' into atheism prefigures a redemption through Christ, who is symbolically present in the narrative through haunting Christ statues that figure prominently as material markers and symbolic turning-points on Rice's journey. Anne Rice's story subtly parallels the biblical story of the fall, loss of paradise, and the hope for redemption through Christ. After dwelling in an Eden of a Catholic childhood, Rice goes to a non-Catholic college, where she tastes forbidden fruits from the tree of knowledge of good and evil and ends up transgressing the codes she has grown up with. Her eyes are opened and she understands good and evil in new ways—but at the price of being cast out from the Garden of Eden of her religious childhood. Losing her faith in the process, she becomes an atheist for almost four decades. Then, after a series of significant spiritual turning points, paradise is regained as Rice returns to faith. In the end, in *Called Out of Darkness*, there is a return to faith at a deeper level and a sense of certainty about God—a homecoming, although a tentative one due to the unexpected post-narrative twist related to the contemporary social and political American context when Rice, while affirming that she will remain committed to Christ, steps away from organized religion in 2010.[1]

Unlike many other spiritual autobiographies, *Called Out of Darkness*, "the story of one path to God" (4), does not begin in darkness or despair, even though there are such stages on the way (such as the death of Rice's daughter before the age of six and the death of Rice's husband). Instead, Rice's autobiography begins with a long flashback to an enchanted Catholic childhood (Chapters 1–5). Although there are sad and difficult events in

---

[1] In 2010, Rice marked her distance to the Catholic Church largely because of the Church's stance on homosexual weddings. Still, as she puts it: "Certainly I will never go back to being that atheist and that pessimist that I was"; "I live now in a world that I feel God created, and I feel I live in a world where God witnesses everything that happens. "Writer Anne Rice: 'Today I Quit Being A Christian.'" NPR. By NPR STAFF. August 02, 2010. http://www.npr.org/templates/story/story.php?storyId=128930526. Accessed March 14, 2016.

Rice's childhood, the overall impression is of a deeply spiritual, secure and stimulating, sometimes almost magic childhood such that few children experience. Fostered and educated by brilliant and loving parents, immersed in a vast, extended religious universe, moving between the wealthy garden district and the working-class Irish channel in New Orleans, Rice imbibes it all and develops an unusual personal and intellectual independence. The first half of the book is filled with descriptions of stunningly beautiful church interiors and the peaceful solemnity of Mass. Indeed, constituting the first half of the book, this flashback is so long that the reader begins to wonder about the spiritual journey that, according to the title, is going to take the author-protagonist out of darkness. But after a childhood immersed in religion, adolescence brings an inner turmoil and a loss of the "intimate conversation with God" that Rice has enjoyed up to then (116).

In *Genesis*, temptation, the fall, and the consequences of our first parents' disobedience against God are described. Two trees are mentioned, the tree of life and the tree of knowledge of good and evil (*Genesis* 2:9). It is the last-mentioned tree whose fruit is forbidden, the fruit that Eve is seduced to eat and then give to Adam to taste. In order to stop them from eating the fruit from the Tree of Life, too, and have eternal life, God casts Adam and Eve out of the Garden of Eden. "More subtil than any beast of the field which the LORD God had made," in *Genesis*, the serpent enters into dialogue with the woman and questions God's words: "Yea, hath God said, Ye shall not eat of every tree of the garden?" and continues: "Ye shall surely not die: For God doth know that in the day ye eat thereof, then your eyes shall be opened, and ye shall be as gods, knowing good and evil (*Genesis* 3:1–4).

Going to college in a Protestant area of the country, Rice is no longer surrounded by practicing Catholics. Instead, the codes and perspectives she has been brought up with collide with other codes, and she now comes to feel a strong impetus to go beyond what she comes to see as the limitations of Catholic dogma. One of the teaching sisters in school, for example, tells Rice and her classmates that "it [is] better for a Catholic not to go to college at all than to go to a non-Catholic college," something that both Rice and her forward-looking father dismiss (120). Other aspects that Rice comes to question include the Index of Forbidden Books and the idea that it is inappropriate to read writers such as Hemingway, and "[she cannot] understand why so much vital information [is] beyond [her] Catholic reach (122)." In college, Rice meets "interesting people," "essentially good people, people with ethics, direction, goals, values—and these people [aren't] Catholic (121)." Somewhat to her own surprise, Rice finds that "outside the

Catholic Church, one did not find a sinkhole of depravity" (127). The attitudes of her new friends toward sexuality, surprisingly, "[seem] wholesome and natural (122)." Clearly, it is the strict and forbidding codes of the Catholic Church at that time, codes that Rice feels unable to live up to, that cause her to walk away from anything to do with religion:

> I could not separate my personal relationship with God, and with Jesus Christ, from my relationship with the church. As I mentioned, I'd stopped really talking to God a long time ago. I hadn't felt entitled to talk to Him in a long while. I'd felt far too demoralized to talk to Him. I just wasn't the Catholic girl who had a right to talk to Him. I harbored too many profane thoughts. (124)

The entire edifice of what Rice comes to see as "the utter falsity of Catholicism" becomes, as she puts it, "a pack of lies—and it had to be a lie that one could burn in hell for all eternity for masturbating or kissing a boy, or reading a novel by Alexandre Dumas, or an essay by Sartre" (125). Rice begins to think that the edifice of Catholicism must be very fragile if it is "so vulnerable to information" (125). In college, she develops "a great desire to read forbidden authors" (128). The natural desire for knowledge in someone who has all her life been a deeply spiritual person (and who in her youth wanted to be a nun) clashes with the prevailing dogma and leads to an entirely unmerited sense of unworthiness in this enormously capable and talented young woman, who ends up thinking that "[t]he church, with all its rules about sex, the modern world, and books and matters of dogma, had become absolute proof to [her] that God didn't exist" (125).

Rice begins to reflect on what she now sees as a string of lies, such as "[glossing] over the failings or corruption of the church" in order to "bring the subject of discussion back to the church's perfection," or blaming the secular state for the Inquisition (126). Moving away from these 'lies,' Rice has a strong sense of moving toward the truth, a realistic truth that does not need to gloss things over but that prefers instead to face them straight-on. Whereas Rice in her childhood was completely immersed in Catholicism, unaware of anything else, at college in the 1960s she wakes up to the realization that "millions were born and grew up and died without ever knowing anything of Christianity," something that makes her think that "Christianity was only one man-made sect making grandiose claims that could not be true" (126).

It is her spiritual director's well-intended attempts to define Rice (when she comes to him with her doubts) as a through-and-through Catholic who would be miserable outside the Catholic Church that "[pushes] Rice over the edge," stripping her of the Catholic identity that has fitted so well in her childhood (123). Hungry for knowledge and experience, Rice finds that for her, the Church has become "anti-art and anti-mind" (124), and she becomes desperate to seek "to escape the sense of sin that seemed to dominate every choice facing [her]" (124). It is when she finds herself at a non-Catholic college, then, that Rice, metaphorically speaking, tastes the forbidden fruit from the tree of knowledge of good and evil of the modern world, at the price of being cast out of the garden of Eden of her Catholic childhood. For a long time, Rice "[suffers] such an aversion to Catholicism that [she avoids] any mention of it anywhere, including contact with anyone who [is] Catholic (150)." Rice stops her dialogue with God. Losing her faith, she becomes an atheist for almost four decades.

Certainly, there is "dismal grieving for [her] faith" and "a certain bitter darkness" on stepping away from God and the church (127). Looking back, Rice sees that her first novel, *Interview with the Vampire*, was "an obvious lament for [her] lost faith" (137).[2] There is a loss of a sense of security, as a "world without God was a world in which anything might happen" (127), but as Rice concludes, at the time: "One couldn't run an outmoded idea of God for comfort. One had to be strong, one had to construct meaning in the silence in the wake of the departure of God" (127).[3]

Rice does not step away from religion into sexual licentiousness.[4] Nor does she entirely embrace feminism. With a great deal of integrity and independence, Rice moves through the decades of hippie revolution (whose sexism and surprisingly antiquated views of women (or 'chicks') Rice outlines in revealing and amusing ways), the Vietnam War, and changes in family constellations along with transformations in views of race and gender.

Despite Rice's 'aversion' to Catholicism during her decades of atheism, there is one story to which she keeps returning, *The Nun's Story* from 1959, a

[2] Rice comments: "I wrote twenty-one books before faith returned to me. And in almost all these books, creatures shut out of life, doomed to marginality or darkness, seek for lives of value, even when the world tells them they cannot have such lives" (140). Rice continues: "I poured out the darkness and despair of an atheist struggling to establish bonds and hopes in a godless world where anything might, and could, happen, where happiness could be torn away from one in an instant, a world in which the condemned and the despised raised their voices in protest and song" (141).

[3] "In fact, being an atheist required discipline very like that of being Catholic. One could never yield to the idea of a supernatural authority, no matter how one might be tempted" (129).

[4] Later, she does, however, become "a nationally famous pornographer for a series of fairytale erotic books written under the pen name A. N. Roquelaure" (128).

film she watches "sometimes crying, grieving for [her] lost Catholic faith" (151). As she sums up the content of the film: "It is entirely about the inner struggle for this one person, and her failure to become the religious she had hoped to become" (151). Because the protagonist in *The Nun's Story*, Sister Luke, "could not be perfect according to the system, she left the system" (151)—a spiritual impasse Rice understands "completely" (151). "I never watched this film without realizing that it could have been my own story," Rice comments, "and that perhaps it should have been my own story, that I should have tried to be a nun as I had once dreamed of doing" (152). While this story does not lead to an immediate return to the church, it is, for Rice, a "way of visiting [her] old church, her] magnificent and timeless church, and being there, in sorrow, for a little while," feeling "a special refuge in the film" (152).

Then, gradually, there are some turning points, transformative moments that are almost imperceptible at the time, but clear in retrospect. Some of these moments occur during trips abroad to Brazil and to Italy. The journey metaphor is central in Rice's invocation of exterior and interior geographies. In her travels in Europe visits to churches are paramount, even though Rice tells herself that this is for her interest in art, as religious faith still seems "inaccessible and unrecoverable" (161). Traveling to Israel, she is "secretly obsessed with Jesus Christ, but [she does not] tell anyone, and [she does not] tell [herself]" (161). Thus, Rice's return to faith happens through both conscious and unconscious stages. Collecting books on the life of Jesus while telling herself that she is interested in Jesus as an interesting character, Rice continues to regard atheism as a reality that one must simply accept instead of turning to religion for comfort and spiritual sustenance: "I held out against God and I held out against the church because I thought I was holding out for bitter truth" (173).

In what could in retrospect be seen as a pilgrimage to the statue of Jesus in Rio in Brazil, Rice has what appears to be a mystic experience as the clouds surrounding the huge statue break up and reveal the gigantic Christ: "The moment was beyond any rational description. It didn't matter to [her] what anyone else felt or wanted from this journey. [She] had come thousands of miles to stand here. And here was the Lord" (163). At the foot of the statue of Jesus on the Corcovado Rice experiences "a kind of delirium, a kind of joy" (163). After this transcendent experience, another curious thing happens, also in Brazil. Entering a church, Rice comes upon a statue whose twin, amazingly, she knows extremely well. Years ago, she has purchased a "hyperrealistic," "outrageous" statue in San Francisco, a double statue showing "Christ nailed to His cross, and beside Him the figure of St. Francis of Assisi, reaching up to embrace the Crucified Lord. But what makes the statue unique is that Our Lord is also reaching down from the cross to embrace Francis" (165). "Never," writes Rice, "had [she] seen a statue that so reflected the disparate elements of [her] earlier faith. Here was the sensuality and excess and the spirituality which [she] had so loved" (166). Having purchased this double statue, Rice has kept it in her office even though some visitors are "understandably shocked by it, by its lurid embodiment of the suffering of the two figures" (166). Francis has the marks of the Stigmata, signs of "a mystical union with the Lord" that "must be offered by God," something Rice herself has prayed for (167).

To her amazement, Rice finds the exact same "potent double image of the love of God" in Salvador da Bahia in Brazil, "a figure of the love of Jesus Christ that is waiting for you," an image of "the mystery of the Incarnation" and of "the Lord bridging the gulf between God and humankind" (167). In the concluding lines of Rice's narrative, surprisingly, this statue turns up a third time, this time in the St. Francis of Assisi church in Coachella Valley in California.

Very gradually, then, Rice is drawn back to faith, through her own research and pilgrimages and through art and cinema with religious themes: "The creation was talking to [her] of God" (174). Rice realizes that she is not alone in this: even though "a host of modern thinkers [has] declared that religion [has] no validity" and that God is "dead," America is as obsessed with Jesus as she is herself. Her spiritual search has led her to the story of Incarnation, and she begins to perceive this "as something unique in the history of the ancient religions [she] constantly [studies]" (175). Even though there are ancient mystery cults that include stories of vegetation gods who die, for Rice, incarnation goes beyond everything else in its unicity.

Rice "[begins] to sense that [she is] being blinded day in and day out by an inexplicable light," and she starts to feel "Christ haunted," hearing "a deafening chorus of voices singing the songs of God to [her] as [she struggles] with myriad doubts, myriad fears, and, seemingly, alone"—even though, for a long time, she is "[clinging] to [her] atheism with a martyr's determination," thinking that atheism represents the sad, but unavoidable truth (176, 177, 178). Then—and here we are given an exact time and date, "the afternoon of Sunday, the sixth" of December, 1998, when Rice goes to Mass and Holy Communion—everything changes. Here, extracts from Rice's diary are included, placed in italics as if to testify to the strong emotion, nervousness, and gratefulness she experiences in her return and surrender to faith. While it is a spiritual home-coming, her conversion is certainly far from "a collapsing into consolation and happiness" (190):

> It seems to me that many people think a Christian conversion is exactly that—a falling into simplicity; a falling from intellect into an emotional refuge; an attempt to feel good. There are even writers today who see Christian conversion as a form of empowerment, and books are written that promise born-again Christians not only complete peace of mind, but even monetary gain. (190–91)

It is primarily the sense of reality of Christ, his "Real Presence," and not Catholic doctrine of the Transubstantiation that brings Rice to church.[5] All these things are miracles for Rice, as is the terrifying event of her going into a life-threatening diabetic coma (not knowing that she has developed diabetes) and surviving. She experiences a complete surrender: "I let go of all the theological or social questions which had kept me from Him for countless years. I simply let them go" (183). In equal measure, she surrenders to a need to be in control of knowledge, to understand the workings of God, or to have opinions about them: "I didn't have to know how He was going to save the unlettered and the unbaptized, or how He would redeem the conscientious heathen who had never spoken His name" (183).

As if to underline a surprising sense of discovery on the part of Rice, the final pages of *Called Out of Darkness* are dotted with exclamation marks: "God became a Baby. God became a child!" (213). "*Why did he do it this way!*" (213, italics in original). "*Sweet little Jesus Boy!*" (214, italics in original). "This is The Redemption! This is The Atonement!" (215). "I am conservative when it comes to doctrine because this is what I see!" (222).

While an autobiography may be an attempt on the part of the author to clarify and compose her life story into a comprehensive and comprehensible whole, in Rice's spiritual autobiography, there is an additional and equally important purpose. After her conversion, Rice shifts her literary efforts toward writing for God. With her spiritual autobiography, one aspect of this larger purpose is to draw the reader into her tale: "If this path to God is an

---

[5] She comments: "Only dimly did I care about the doctrine of the Transsubstantiation, the Catholic teaching as to how Our Blessed Lord is present Body and Blood in the small wafers kept in the Catholic tabernacle. Only dimly did I reflect on it, because truly I had a sense of something so much greater than the verbal expression of any doctrine that it didn't matter to me how superstitious such a belief might seem to a skeptical mind. And my mind was still, to some extent, a skeptical mind" (182).

illusion, then the story is worthless. If the path is real, then we have something here that may matter to you as well as to me" (4).

Many spiritual autobiographies begin from a post-Eden point of view and progress to a recapturing of a modified Eden. Although it might not be immediately obvious, *Called Out of Darkness: A Spiritual Confession* is an autobiography that follows a pattern moving from innocence to a 'fall' and then to a return, to faith if not to innocence. In Rice's case, the spiritual journey goes from light to darkness and back to light again. The "darkness" alluded to in the title, then, is primarily the darkness of the middle period of non-religion. As suggested in this chapter, the story told by Anne Rice could be understood along typological lines, whereby the 'fall' into atheism prefigures redemption through Christ. In the end, Rice arrives at a sense of union with God. The arrival at the end of the narrative to faith in God brings immense happiness and inner peace. Having "come home to something of incalculable power," Rice is "a grappling with the Absolute" (194, 195).

Climbing Out of Darkness:
Karen Armstrong's *Spiral Staircase*

Enter through the narrow gate. For wide is the gate and broad is the road that leads to destruction, and many enter through it. But small is the gate and narrow the road that leads to life, and only a few find it.

(Matthew 7: 13)

Karen Armstrong has written three spiritual autobiographies. The first, *Through the Narrow Gate* (2005), is an account of her years in a Roman Catholic convent. The second, *Beginning the World* (1983), an account of her life just after leaving the convent, is "a mistake" in her own view: since it is "not a truthful account," she "can hardly bear to look at it" (xviii, xix). This oeuvre will not be dealt with in this chapter. Instead, the main focus will be on Armstrong's third autobiography, *The Spiral Staircase: My Climb Out of Darkness* (2005), since it is this memoir that most exhaustively covers Armstrong's entire spiritual journey. *The Spiral Staircase* is an account of Armstrong's life after leaving the Roman Catholic convent where she spent seven years in the search for God—without finding him. In *A History of God: The 4000-Year Quest of Judaism, Christianity, and Islam* (2007), she looks back to that period of her life:

The more I read about the raptures of the saints, the more of a failure I felt. I was unhappily aware that what little religious experience I had, had somehow been manufactured by myself as I worked upon my own feelings and imagination. Sometimes a sense of devotion was an aesthetic response to the beauty of the Gregorian chant and the liturgy. But nothing had *happened* to me from a source beyond myself. I never glimpsed the God described by prophets and mystics. Jesus Christ, about whom we talked far more about than about 'God', seemed a purely historical figure, inextricably embedded in late antiquity. (2)

While it is true that a life crisis provokes a quest in *The Spiral Staircase*, at first glance it might seem that Armstrong's narrative is an inversion of religious conversion following a sequential stage model. Rather, *The Spiral Staircase* would seem to be the opposite, that is, a narrative that conveys the ways in which a *deconversion* is taking place over a period of time.

As Heinz Streib points out in "Deconversion," there is a long tradition of research on conversion, whereas studies of deconversion is a relatively young field, presumably because "a growing number of people choose to convert more than once in their lifetime" (274, 271). Defining deconversion as loss of faith in *Versions of Deconversion: Autobiography and the Loss of Faith*, John D. Barbour perceives four aspects that are generally present in deconversion. First, there is doubt regarding the beliefs one has held. This may be followed by moral criticism directed at the practices one has embraced. Third, there may be grief and despair and considerable emotional turbulence. Fourth, one may come to completely reject the religious community to which one has belonged: "Deconversion encompasses, then, intellectual doubt, moral criticism, emotional suffering, and disaffiliation from a community (2). At the same time, as Barbour points out, "every conversion is a deconversion, and every deconversion a conversion" (1994 3).[1]

The result of Armstrong's inner journey, as described in *The Spiral Staircase*, is a deeper and more compassionate spirituality. *Spiral Staircase* has a tripartite structure starting with Armstrong's initial sense of having "finished with religion forever" (xx) via several social, professional, and spiritual stages leading up to, at the end of the narrative, a sense of deep inner transformation.

The darkness alluded to in the title refers to, among other things, Armstrong's attacks of epilepsy, her spiritual confusion arising from the time in the convent, and her sense of a loss of God. The difficulties Armstrong struggles with over a period of time lead to a massive spiritual burnout. Her inexplicable and apparently unconscious suicide attempt in the third year of her studies represents a milestone. At that time, nothing has changed in Armstrong's life situation, but after this experience, she feels that it is pointless to resist the (so far) undiagnosed epileptic attacks she takes to be panic attacks and amnesia.

---

[1] Heinz Streib regards Barbour's work as significant and departs from Barbour's four categories, but he wants to add one aspect. Among Streib's "deconversion trajectories" are listed secularizing exits, oppositional exits, religious switching, integrating exits, privatizing exits, and heretical exits (272).

Instead, she decides simply to "ride with them" (135), since there seems to be no hope of treating these problems.

In spiritual development, complete acceptance and surrender is often a way forward. Since, as Kurt H. Wolff points out in "Surrender and Religion," surrender stands in "opposition to our official contemporary Western, and potentially worldwide, consciousness, in which the relation to the world is not surrender but mastery, control, efficiency, handling, manipulation," surrender can open the door to unforeseen development in new directions (44). It is during a stage of letting-go and acceptance of reality such as it seems to be that Armstrong comes across T. S. Eliot's "Ash Wednesday" and "the experience of spiritual progress and illumination ... represented by the symbol of a spiral staircase" (140). As James Olney has suggested, "Ash Wednesday" could be seen as Eliot's spiritual autobiography (5). Identifying with the spiritual journey delineated in Eliot's poem, Armstrong underlines that "in mythology, stairs frequently symbolize a breakthrough to a new level of consciousness" (xx). That is precisely what happens to Armstrong during a tortuous and difficult, spiralling, spiritual process. Eliot's poem holds out hope.

Armstrong's leaving the convent and waking up to the emotional limitations of that environment could be seen as a loss of innocence. While it would be wrong to say that it is a brutal awakening to real life, life in the convent having been real and brutal enough, it does involve a rude collision with bustling, secular, academic life in Oxford.

As a teenager, Karen Armstrong "wanted to find God" and "lose the confusions of [her] adolescent self in the infinite and ultimately satisfying mystery that we call God" (vii). There are complex reasons behind her decision to enter a convent in 1962 at the age of 17. While her search for God is primary, there may also be social reasons, since she feels that she is "awkward, plain, bookish, and unpopular with boys" (ix), and since marriage, in her view, does "not look particularly appealing" (x). The nuns seem to be leading a serene life, a life Armstrong prefers. She stays in the convent for seven difficult and (in positive and negative ways) transformative years, until she suffers a breakdown and comes to the decision that she must leave. Although there is no criticism of convent life as such and there are nuns who make a positive difference, the seven years in the convent nearly break Karen's spirit, passion, and the natural inclination of this highly intelligent young woman to learn, question, and develop intellectually. Even though there is an "emotional frigidity" in the convent and an atmosphere that is often "cold and sometimes unkind," she sees her breakdown as "nobody's fault" and takes most of the blame upon herself (xvi): "I left the convent ... because I had failed to find God and had never come within shouting distance of that complete self-surrender which, the great spiritual leaders declared, was essential for those who wished to enter into the divine presence" (9). One cannot help but think that, despite the lack of denunciation on the part of Armstrong herself and despite the presence of positive images of the spiritual life of the convent—which Karen Armstrong misses and mourns after leaving—that the obedience and submission that demand a near-obliteration of individuality, curiosity, questioning, joy and high spirits, have done an almost irreparable damage that it takes Armstrong many years to heal.

After her breakdown, Armstrong is released by the Vatican from her vows of poverty, chastity, and obedience. As a student in Oxford, far from her disciplined life of the convent, she thinks that "God [is] no longer calling her to anything at all—if he ever had" (4). Nonetheless, her conditioning from the convent is still in place, and occasionally, she lapses back into convent rule: in the convent "[they] always kissed the floor when [they] entered a room late and disturbed a community duty" (6), so in Oxford, on one occasion when Armstrong is late for dinner, she automatically kisses the floor in front of the principal at her college. Armstrong gives a colourful and convincing account of the social and political transformation in Great Britain during the 1960s, with student demonstrations, demands for mixed-sex colleges, and the music of the Beatles that stand in stark contrast to the previous years of silence and seclusion, "physical restraint" and "religious modesty" (22). In the convent, the nuns are forbidden to have special friendships, since all love should be for God only. It was because of such views and because of the "arcane rituals" that "the reforms of the Second Vatican Council were so necessary," Armstrong thinks (8).

There are many blessings in disguise on Armstrong's spiritual path that could almost be seen as divine interventions that change the course of her life and make her autobiography as exciting as a mystery novel. The repeated references to the absence or indifference of God in Armstrong's life create suspense: will God turn up before the book is over? Will Armstrong experience the transformation she yearns for?

Looking back at her years in the convent, Armstrong compares them to the initiation rituals in indigenous societies that are set up like a "process of death and resurrection: initiates die to their childhood and rise again to an entirely different life as mature human beings" (27). This is also what happens within the narrative framework of *The Spiral Staircase*. Significantly, the subtitle of Armstrong's memoir is *My Climb Out of Darkness*. Whereas the young people undergoing initiation rituals may be "forced to lie alone in a cave or a tomb" or be "buried alive" since it is thought that "in these extreme circumstances, the young discover inner resources that will enable them to serve their people as fully functioning adults" (27), Karen Armstrong, analogously, is 'buried alive' in the frightening experiences of blackouts and hallucinations that later prove to be symptoms of epilepsy, and she has to confront a series of difficult experiences before she becomes a 'fully functioning adult' who comes to serve her people. Thus, while she herself draws a parallel to life in the convent aimed "to die to our old selves and to our worldly, secular way of looking at things," it is the hard and exhilarating years that follow after the convent that bring about a profound spiritual transformation in Armstrong. At the beginning of *The Spiral Staircase*, she comments: "[n]ow it seemed to me that I had indeed died, but I was certainly not bringing forth much fruit" (28). "The training was designed to make us transcend ourselves, and to go beyond the egotism and selfishness that holds us back from God," she thinks (28). For Armstrong, however, the training in the convent, in its denial of the body, the emotions, and independent thinking, does not lead to spiritual transformation but to a collapse, even though she later finds that the idea of the necessity for self-transcendence is correct. The same thing could be said about the Ignatian exercises of the convent: "Prayer, Ignatius thought, was an act of will. It had nothing to do with pious thoughts or feelings, these were simply a preparation for the moment of decision. Ignatian spirituality was never an end in itself, but was directed toward action and efficiency. He wanted his Jesuits to be effective in the world, and their daily meditation ensured that their activities would proceed from God" (40).

While Armstrong has the ability to focus on her studies, to her "immense distress," although she "would kneel as intent on God as [her] sisters," she "[finds] that [she] could not keep her mind on God for two minutes" (40). She continues: "In other ways my mind was capable and even gifted, but it seemed allergic to God" (42). "I never had what seemed to be an encounter with anything supernatural, with a being the existed outside myself. I never felt caught up in something greater, never felt personally transfigured by a presence that I encountered in the depths of my being" (42): "I don't know quite what I thought should be happening. Certainly I didn't expect visions and voices. These, we were told [in the convent], were only for the greatest saints and could be delusions, sent by the devil to make us proud" (42). Armstrong learns that "periods of dryness" are "inevitable," and then God might "comfort the soul, make it feel that he was near, and enable it to experience his presence and love" in a "periodic breakthrough" offered "as a carrot, until the soul outgrew this need and could progress to the next stage of its journey. Gradually the soul would be drawn into the higher states of prayer, into further reaches of silence, and into a mysterious state that lay beyond the reach of thoughts and feelings" (42).

After leaving the convent, Armstrong's doubts surface: "I could not stop wondering whether the Virgin Mary really had been conceived without original sin and been taken up body and soul into heaven after her death. How did anybody know that Jesus was God? And was there even a God out there at all?" (44). A focus on God in the convent comes at the cost of a suppression of the body and the emotions. The anorexia of Karen's friend, Rebecca, becomes "a symbol of a deeper discontent" (66). "The nuns who gathered together around the altar seemed an image of prayerful com-munity, and yet they were allowing one of their members to waste away before their very eyes" (68). Armstrong's factual statement that Rebecca will die if nothing is done is dismissed as "nonsense" and "childish displays," and it is laughed off by the Reverend Mother as an exaggeration. (Later, Rebecca decides to leave the order, telling Armstrong that the nuns had been unable to forgive her anorexia). Similarly, the psychological difficulties Armstrong experiences in going from life in the convent to a secular life, and her pleas for support and advice, are of no particular interest to the Mother Superior. If Armstrong has "been somehow disabled by the regime" in the convent, this is something that cannot be admitted.

While there are moments when Armstrong's "path ahead [seems] clear and secure" (77) (as, for example, when she receives a congratulatory first at Oxford), there are plenty of losses and disappointments. During such times Armstrong finds solace in literature. Firstly, as already mentioned, T. S. Eliot's poetry, especially Ash Wednesday, six poems on "the process of spiritual recovery" is central in Spiral Staircase (xix). Secondly, Tennyson's poetry brings a sense of recognition and identification. "The Lady of Shallott" seems to hold up parallels to Armstrong's own life, being im-prisoned in a tower as she feels she is: "When [Lady Shallot] finally did fall in love and ventured into the outside world, it killed her immediately" (91). Analogously, when Armstrong leaves the 'tower' of the convent it almost kills her, and the reader is held in suspense as to the outcome even while being aware of the successful life as a writer in the field of religious studies that lies ahead. Indeed, Tennyson's poem "[resonates] with the hallucinatory visitations that [keeps Armstrong] imprisoned in [her] own inner world"

(91). Not only does it resonate with the experience of transition between sacred and secular worlds, it continues to mirror Armstrong's life after the convent, when she "[longs] to joins the vibrant life that was going on all around [her], but [finds herself] compelled to withdraw by forces that [she does] not understand" (91).

Autobiographies often balance on a fine line between reticence and revelation. If an account is too reticent, the reader loses interest, and if it is too revealing (particularly of the lives of others), the story may be seen as too explicit. Further, autobiographies may balance between being too self-critical and too self-congratulatory. Selections of incidents are as crucial as the omissions. In Armstrong's memoir, many things are left out, and not all mysteries are cleared up. As regards romance, during the summer before accepting a teaching position in London, Armstrong seems to have had some brief relationships, but these are left entirely outside the narrative. The problems with Armstrong's second TV production (among other things leading to the demise and fall into alcoholism of her Israeli collaborator) are never explained, and perhaps Armstrong herself never learns the full truth. There are many setbacks that seem to be blessings in disguise that propel Armstrong in the right direction and many milestones that are deeply significant, such as the intervention of her 'landlady,' Jenifer Hart, who saves Armstrong from being committed to mental hospital. Like Eliot, Armstrong has "given up hope—and yet, Eliot seemed to be saying, that could be a way forward" (140). She reflects: "When I had embarked upon the religious life, I had been certain that if only I tried hard enough, I would see the world transfigured by the presence of God and that I would, as the Bible promised, soar like an eagle" (141). At this later stage, however, her "hope of discovering eternity [has] died" (141). Coming upon T. S. Eliot's poem is like a gift, it is "a moment of grace" (142).

About halfway through *The Spiral Staircase*, Karen Armstrong's sense of alienation vis-à-vis anything to do with religion seems to be at its greatest. She writes:

> Indeed, I now felt a distaste for the whole churchy enterprise. It seemed not only a colossal waste of time and energy, but positively harmful too. If I saw somebody reading a theological or devotional book on the underground, I felt an involuntary twinge of disgust, and would even turn away as though I had seem something abhorrent. The word 'God' or 'Jesus' or 'church' filled me with a lassitude akin to nausea. Conventional religion had worn me out and I wanted nothing more to do with it. If possible, I would have liked to forget that it existed. (165)

What is noteworthy here is the almost physical revulsion Armstrong experiences vis-à-vis religion. Significantly, it is conventional religion that she feels increasingly distanced to. At this point, she is not looking for any unconventional or ecumenical forms of spirituality, but finds the solace she needs in literature: "If an unbeliever could experience the same kind of ecstasy as a Christian mystic, it seemed that transcendence was just something that human beings experienced and that there was nothing supernatural about it" (165). Her delight in literature is immense: "It was a kind of ekstasis, an ecstasy that was not an exotic, tranced state of the word, a going beyond the self" (177).

Two milestones are crucial in Armstrong's spiritual process. One is the decision to write her first memoir, *Through the Narrow Gate*. Writing becomes a way of processing her experience of life in the convent, remembering not only the difficulties but also the "beauty of the liturgy" and "the kindness of some of [her] superiors" (213). In autobiographical expression she is reclaiming her past and realizing how profoundly and permanently the experience has changed her, and that a spiritual yearning is still there. After the publication of *Through the Narrow Gate*, another turning point comes in the early 1980s when Armstrong gets a chance to create a television series on Paul for British Channel 4, *The First Christian*. For a year and a half, Armstrong immerses herself in the life and thought of the first Christian, Paul, and travels in his footsteps. For her, the result of her research is a complete reversal of her earlier, rather negative view of Paul. Having been "convinced that many if not all of the failings of Christianity could be traced back to this pugnacious apostle"—repressive orthodoxy, the oppression of women, and corruption—and that Paul "had perverted the simple, loving message of Jesus," Armstrong makes "some startling discoveries": "A disturbing number of eminent scholars agreed that Jesus had no intention of founding a new religion. He had preached only to his fellow Jews, and there was nothing strikingly original about his teaching, which was in line with other strands of first-century Judaism" (231). Thus, "the early Christians still regarded themselves as forming an exclusively Jewish sect. It was Saint Paul, who had never known the historical Jesus, who had first marketed the faith for the non-Jewish world of the Roman Empire" (232). Thus the founder of Christianity was Paul and not Jesus, and "the gospels, all written after Paul's own death, were penned by men who adopted Paul's version of Christianity" (232). Armstrong discovers, further, that the misogynist writings attributed to Paul may have been written sixty years after his death (232).[2]

Karen Armstrong's attempt to understand Paul, further, evokes a desire to learn more about Judaism, something that leads to radical revisions and constitutes yet another step toward a spiritual transformation. Up to this point, Armstrong "[has] simply regarded [Judaism] as a mere prelude to Christianity, superannuated and superseded by the later, more inspiring faith. [She has] accepted without question the portrait of Judaism in the New Testament, derived in large part ([she] now realizes) from Paul's early polemic with Jesus' disciples, who had wanted Christianity to remain a strictly Jewish sect" (234). Now, she is "beginning to learn that many of Jesus' teachings about charity and loving-kindness were almost identical with those of the leading rabbis of his day" (234). Armstrong realizes that notions inculcated in her childhood "that Judaism had become an empty faith, wedded to external observances and with no spiritual dimension" (234) need to be dismantled. In her discussions with a Jewish spiritual guide or mentor, Armstrong learns about certain differences such as the valorization of orthopraxy rather than orthodoxy in Judaism. Her mentor tells her that Jesus, in fact, might "have belonged to the school of Rabbi Hillel, one of the leading Pharisees" since Jesus had "taught a version of Hillel's Golden Rule" (235): "do not do unto others as you would not have done to you." Judaism, then, is "a religion of doing rather than believing" (243). She thinks: "I would never again be able to think about Christianity as a separate religion. I would have to develop a form of double vision. Increasingly, Judaism and Christianity seemed to be one faith tradition which [has] gone in two different directions" (244). As her insights into Judaism deepen, she sees how the role of study in Judaism is "not a barren cerebral exercise. It brought Jews into the presence of God" (244). The intensity of this kind of religious study appeals strongly to Armstrong.

[2] In another book, *The Gospel According to Woman: Christianity's Creation of the Sex War in the West*, Armstrong "[traces] the misogyny that had been the Achilles heel of Christianity.... In the crazed excesses of such theologians as Tertullian, Saint Jerome, or Luther, and the lamentable neurosis of some of the women saints, Christianity appeared as unhealthy, unkind, and unnatural in its rejection of women and sexuality. As I finished the book, I felt profoundly relieved to have shaken off the toils of religion once and for all" (255). Armstrong's film, *The First Christian*, is "iconoclastic": "It demolished the assumptions of many Christians and was ruthless in its denunciation of what the churches had done with Paul's teaching." And still after her delving into the life and thought of Paul, Armstrong finds that she is "very close to Paul"; that [she] could almost share his convictions. Almost—but not quite" (252, 253).

During the production of "The First Christian," Karen Armstrong sees how far she has moved from her original beliefs. Realizing that Judaism is a parent faith of Christianity, she feels ashamed of her earlier ignorance. In Catholicism, Jews have been marginalized figures who had taunted Jesus. Armstrong now realizes that many of her earlier conceptions have been preconceived and ill-conceived notions about Jews and Judaism. In Jerusalem, she has a clear sense of homecoming. Here are all the places and symbols that have been part of her inner landscape for so long. She is deeply affected, intellectually as well as emotionally, by her encounter with Judaism. Jewish spirituality and orthopraxy become crucially important for Armstrong. But there is a third factor that needs to be taken into account. Contemplating "the rock from which the prophet Muhammad was said to have ascended to heaven" at the Dome of the Rock, Armstrong feels ashamed of her ignorance while also feeling immediately at home in the Mosque of al-Aqsa (245). She is deeply impressed with the Muslims studying the Qur'an and realizes that this, "like the Jews studying Torah in the yeshiva … was a form of communion. By repeating words that God had in some sense spoken to Muhammad, Muslims were taking God into their very being" (245). In Jerusalem, Karen Armstrong is finding it "impossible to ignore this third member of the Abrahamic family" (245). As if echoing Edward Said's theses in *Orientalism*, she concludes that "Westerners had needed to hate Islam; in the fantasies they created, it became everything they hoped that they were not, and was made to epitomize everything that they feared that they were. Islam had become the shadow self of the West" (257). Armstrong realizes how lacking in "fairness and objectivity" the West's image of Islam is: "The stereotypical view of Islam, first developed at the time of the Crusades, was in some profound sense essential to our Western identity" (257).

Although Armstrong is deeply affected by these encounters, she remains at variance with religion in general, or, more particularly, with 'conventional' or 'traditional' religion. This is apparent in her book *The Gospel According to Woman*, and in her next book, *Holy War: The Crusades and Their Impact on Today's World*, the research for and writing of which book confirms Armstrong's "determination to keep as far away from [religion] as possible" (256). Armstrong's confrontation with "the darkness of the human heart" while studying the brutality of the Crusades, along with the improvement in her health, leads to a kind of 'thaw' of her defenses. She is coming out of a "frozen condition" (262). Even though her spiritual journey has been long underway, in Armstrong's own view, it is only at this particular point that her "spiritual quest [can] begin" (263). This is, she says, "because the ability to experience pain and sorrow is the sine qua non of enlightenment" (263). Significantly, it is also at this point, in 1989, that the idea for a new book comes to her, the focus of which is inseparable from her own next step on her spiritual journey. Deploring "the deadly hostility that had separated Jews, Christians, and Muslims," in *A History of God: The 4000-Year Quest of Judaism, Christianity, and Islam* (2007), Armstrong turns instead to what the Abrahamic faiths have in common: God.

Although it may not be the illumination or transformation sought by Armstrong initially, there is an epiphany of sorts at the end of *The Spiral Staircase*. Nonetheless, writing *A History of God* "[changes] her life so radically that, if [she] were a traditional believer, [she] might be tempted to call it an inspiration" (264). It is at this point that the spiritual journey she has actually undertaken becomes visible, as does the evolution she has undergone while also giving intimations of what is to come.

Karen Armstrong's journey has gone from her being a 'traditional' believer to being alienated from God and institutionalized religion to the discovery that she is not completely through with God, after all. As she sets out to write her memoir, she muses: "God, of course, did not exist, but I would show that each generation of believers was driven to invent him anew. God was simply a projection of human need; 'he' mirrored the fears and yearnings of society at each stage of its development" (265). At the same time, "despite all the evidence, [she] has so painfully amassed to the contrary, at some inchoate, unconscious level, [she] felt that God and [she] had some unfinished business—even though [she] didn't believe that he existed" (267). Faith, in Armstrong's view, is still a chimera, and yet, "maybe, like the mariner, [she is] moving toward salvation of sorts 'unaware,' [her] unconscious mind reaching out for what it [knows she needs]" (267). Further, her understanding of key precepts in religion also influences her approach to writing, and her understanding of God has changed dramatically during her spiritual journey:

> To my very great surprise, I was discovering that some of the most eminent Jewish, Christian, and Muslim theologians and mystics insisted that God was not an objective fact, was not another being, and was not an unseen reality like the atom, whose existence could be empirically demonstrated. Some went so far as to say that it was better to say that God did not exist, because our notion of existence was too limited to apply to God. Many of them preferred to say that God was Nothing, because this was not the kind of reality that we normally encountered. It was even misleading to call God the Supreme Being, because that simply suggested a being like us, but bigger and better, with likes and dislikes similar to

our own. For centuries, Jews, Christians, and Muslims had devised audacious new theologies to bring this point home to the faithful. The doctrine of the Trinity, for example, was crafted in part to show that you could not think about God as a simple personality. The reality that we call God is transcendent—that is, it goes beyond any human orthodoxy—and yet God is also the ground of all being and can be experienced almost as a presence in the depths of the psyche. (291–92)

The ego stands in the way of enlightenment and transcendence: "Self, after all, is our basic problem" (298). Here, Armstrong would seem to be espousing views that closely parallel those of contemporary spiritual teachers such as Eckhart Tolle in *The Power of Now: A Guide to Spiritual Enlightenment* (1999), and *A New Earth: Awakening to Your Life's Purpose* (2005). At the same time, this is part of the teaching she received in the convent, too, when the ego was seen as a hindrance to contact with God. The methods applied in the convent included a total denial of the desires of the body. One might force oneself to eat things one abhors, in Armstrong's case macaroni cheese (which makes her vomit), in an attempt to govern the body instead of letting it govern itself, a method meant to make one oriented towards God's will instead of towards one's own.

Toward the end of the book Armstrong appears to have outgrown the need for 'carrots' and to have has progressed to what could be called a "higher state of prayer" and "further reaches of silence." At that point, she has travelled a great distance, geographically and theologically. While her "mind, heart, and faculties remained scattered" during her time in the convent, so that "there was no way God could get through to [her]," at the end of her trajectory she has arrived at a blissful concentration that is almost a communion with her religious sources and an ability to listen to the silence. Thus, in one way, her climb up *The Spiral Staircase* of spiritual development has brought her back to the beginning, to the spiritual place she wished to inhabit in her youth but felt barred from.

Even if Armstrong does not re-join a particular religious community, the light at the end of her story is a return to spirituality and to an immersion in religious studies leading to maturity, inner peace, and serenity as well as to an orientation toward interfaith and what Armstrong regards as the core of the Abrahamic religions: compassion and the golden rule.

At the end of the narrative, then, Armstrong has definitely moved from darkness 'into the ambit of what we call the divine" (280). There are significant changes in her understanding of God and the meaning of religious life. Her mature approach has everything to do with compassion—an insight the importance of which Armstrong has since continued to emphasize. A long distance has been covered from the initial 'darkness' of the title to the final word in the book: 'light' (306).

Spiritual Autobiographies of Nonbelievers: Barbara Ehrenreich's *Living with a Wild God* and Kim Chernin's *In My Father's Garden*

> The God of religion, the enforcer of ethics, is one thing, the 'Wholly Other' revealed in mystical experiences quite another.
>
> (Ehrenreich 227)

> A spiritual awakening may be the most revolutionary experience possible in our time.
>
> (Chernin 176)

This chapter will discuss two spiritual autobiographers written by non-believers: Barbara Ehrenreich's *Living with a Wild God: A Non-Believer's Search for the Truth About Everything* (2014) and Kim Chernin's auto-biography, *In My Father's Garden: A Daughter's Search for a Spiritual Life* (1996), two books in which images of divinity are found beyond the creeds of organized religion and beyond any made-made images, rituals, and stipulations. Ehrenreich and Chernin both come from atheist families whose atheism has marked them profoundly. Barbara Ehrenreich experiences inexplicable epiphanies she wishes to understand (and her book has the subtitle "a nonbeliever's search for the truth about everything"[1]), while Kim Chernin sees herself as a "mystic" who wants to "give [her] life in service to the world" (130).

Brought up in an atheist family, the young Ehrenreich seems to have held a youthfully condescending attitude toward religion (her young self-commenting critically on 'superannuated' Baptists who are only interested

---

[1] This can be compared to the even more all-encompassing under title of Elizabeth Gilbert's autobiography: 'one woman's search for everything.'

in discussing sermons, on adolescent 'insights' that Catholicism and its rituals rest on cannibalism, and on Protestant church activities that appear to focus mainly on sports and fashion shows). Ehrenreich's youthful self takes a sarcastic distance to the ideas she thinks a religious friend subscribes to such as the belief that this friend "was at all times accompanied by an invisible person or personage. A person whose sole attribute was perfection—all goodness, all love, and all reason? Was I supposed to lie and say, 'Oh yes, I know who you're talking about—I can see him there, right over your shoulder, or at least the gleam of an impossible radiance'?" (56).

Ehrenreich's father's influence is very important, as is the story of how his mother, Ehrenreich's grandmother, on her deathbed, throws a crucifix at the priest who, in the past when her father was dying, had requested a small sum of money to come to her father's deathbed. The story of the grandmother's unforgivingness toward the priest and toward religion itself comes to constitute a spiritual backbone, a heritage that becomes all the more important since young Ehrenreich is keen on winning appreciation and approval from her father (something that also makes her want to excel at school).[2] Her grandmother's story is central, and the grandmother's gesture is mentioned on three different occasions in Ehrenreich's autobiography. Ehrenreich muses: "She understood that the great, unforgivable crime of the monotheistic religions has been to encourage the conflation of authority and benevolence, of hierarchy and justice" (214). Instead, the working-class atheism Ehrenreich has grown up with regards "priests as cynical parasites" (214).

The impetus for Ehrenreich's autobiography comes when she is sorting papers to give away to library archives and comes across a journal from 1956–66 she had started as typing practice in her youth and later continued in longhand. Ehrenreich's diary is remarkable both for what it reveals about the ideals and development of a supremely intelligent, talented, and precociously reflecting young girl and for narratologically providing an interest-raising book-within-the-book cameo that creates a dialogue between two writers, Ehrenreich as a mature fifty-nine-year-old woman who fears that her life might be foreshortened due to illness and Ehrenreich as an searching adolescent, a self that, in fact, implores her future self to take the journal notes seriously, which Ehrenreich does in building her autobiographical narrative

---

[2] Striving for her father's approval means that she has to be "smart and sarcastic, focused on science, and above all a winner" (96).

around them (even though her attitude towards her own younger self tends to be impatient, critical, condescending, and patronizing).[3] In surprisingly mature and insightful ways, her younger self, confronting the most complex and challenging existential questions, turns to Descartes and other philosophers to ponder issues of subjectivity, divinity, cosmos, and God. Early on, she also develops the sharp scientific perspective that becomes an integral part of her 'search for the truth about everything': "I was looking at the job of condensing the universe into a form compact enough to fit in my head, maybe as some kind of equation or—who knows?—an unforgettable melody or gorgeously intricate mandala" (108)—while also asking herself: "What made me imagine that I might ever know the hidden truth behind all things or that such a truth even existed?" (111).

For young Ehrenreich, freedom is uppermost, and if she has to choose between the authority of a paternal God and being on her own, the choice is easy, she thinks. Being an atheist from childhood places Ehrenreich in the margins of a society where for all intents and purposes religious affiliation is compulsory: "At school, I tried to blend in by mouthing the Lord's Prayer along with everyone else, which was mandatory in those days in the public schools, only sometimes permitting myself to slip into inaudible mocking gibberish" (4)—the 'mocking gibberish' of course indicating her fiercely independent and derogatory attitude. "Belief is intellectual surrender," she thinks, and "'faith' a state of willed self-delusion" (232). Ehrenreich goes so far as to regard "[t]he idea of a cosmic loving-kindness perfusing the universe" as "a serious, even potentially dangerous error" (173):

> If there was one thing I understood about God, it was that he was not *good*, and if he was good, he was too powerless to deserve our attention. In fact, the idea of a God who is both all-powerful and all good is a logical impossibility—possibly a trap set by ancient polytheists to ensnare weak-minded monotheists like Philo and Augustine, and certainly not worth my time (143).

In her youth, seeing a group of young nuns every morning on their way to what she imagines must be some "dark ritual," Ehrenreich thanks "God or fate or whatever spirits arrange these things, for giving [her] the parents [she] had, who ... would never dream of offering a child up to God" (29).

---

[3] For example, Ehrenreich finds that her journal "is full of brief, embarrassing reports on what I was reading," "dimwitted" judgments (21); "The early entries are adolescent in the full derogatory sense of the word" (22).

Condescendingly, she regards Christianity "as a kind of prefab metaphysics requiring no intellectual effort on the part of the user" (40). In "aiming for the transcendent," the Catholic Church, in Ehrenreich's eyes, manages "to achieve only the weird," and she finds that this is "a religion whose central ritual was an enactment of cannibalism" (41). Perceiving God as "a sort of parental supervision," Ehrenreich "formally [renounces] Christianity" in 1956 (41) and turns instead to Hinduism, a religion that seems to have "no single grand monotheistic god" but seems instead to offer an idea of "one infinite substance, the Brahman, from whom we are temporarily separated by the thinnest veil of illusion"; it appears to give the answer her youthful self seeks. Converting to Hinduism, she practices it "in perfect secrecy, silently repeating 'Om,' struggling to squelch the desiring self and lift [herself] beyond the limits of 'I'" (42, 43).

The main interest of the journal of young Ehrenreich is her attempt to articulate and describe the first instances of experiences out of the ordinary that might be seen as mystic experiences. The first instance occurs at a horse show. Suddenly, Ehrenreich registers reality in a completely unfamiliar way. The rational, logical world grasped through language vanishes and in its place there is another dimension that has no identity but indescribable depth, clarity, and aliveness. Possibly, she registers a different reality normally not accessible. Another important event of this kind occurs during a car trip with friends when Ehrenreich goes for a walk by herself and the unfathomable dimension descends upon and envelops her again. "Something unspeakable" happens, and she experiences "uncanny events" (45): "Often I have sudden jolts when the realness of things is lost. Then things are as if I was just born and had never seen them before" (76). This leads to the experience of "a world drained of references and connotation—the world as it is" (115). When all habitual, human-constructed categories are gone, what is left? *Something* remains, in Ehrenreich's experience, even though she thinks it must be an aberration caused, perhaps, by a lack of sleep. Aberration or not, the experience keeps occurring also when Ehrenreich is not tired at all. On one occasion, in school, she looks at her fingers and suddenly notices how they hold the pencil and how she is "looking at a combination of yellow and pink, of straight and curved, that had never been seen before and never would be seen again by anyone in the universe, not in this precise configuration anyway"; with such a realization, "all that was familiar would drain out of the world around [her]. Or [she] might look up from a book to find a patch of sunlight pulsing on the floor and feel it leap up to challenge the solidity of the entire scene" (49). Another instance is described like this:

> Something peeled off the visible world, taking with it all meaning, inference, association, labels, and words. I was looking at a tree, and if anyone had asked, that's what I would have said I was doing, but the word 'tree' was gone, along with all the notions of tree-ness that had accumulated in the past dozen or so years since I had acquired language. Was it a place that was suddenly revealed to me? Or was it a substance—the indivisible, elemental material out of which the entire known and agreed-upon world arises as a fantastic elaboration? I don't know, because this substance, this residue, was stolidly, imperturbably mute. The interesting thing, some might say alarming, was that when you take away all human attributions—the words, the names of species, the wisps of remembered tree-related poetry, the fables of photosynthesis and capillary action—that when you take all this away, *there is still something left* (47–48, italics in original).

The first time Ehrenreich has this remarkable experience is about a year before she begins her journal. It is as though a veil of illusion is removed, the veil that according to Ehrenreich's youthful comprehension of Hinduism separates us from the Brahman, "the All" and "perfect One-ness" (43). Words and logic vanish, and Ehrenreich does not understand if it is a *place* that is revealed or a *substance*.

In *Mysticism and Philosophy*, Walter Stace argues that there are two categories of mystical experience, introvertive and extrovertive, each of which has seven characteristics, five of which both categories have in common. They resemble the categories established by William James even though Stace's terms are different, with James's noetic quality corresponding to Stace's objectivity or reality and ineffability to Stace's paradoxicality (experiencing light and darkness at the same time, for example). Stace also points to the importance of a sense of the sacred or divine. As Edward F. Kelly and Michael Grosso put it, extrovertive experiences are "perhaps more common in spontaneous cases and at earlier stages of the mystic way" (504):

> Its primary distinguishing feature is that the ordinary perceptual world remains, but in transfigured form. A multiplicity of objects and events may continue to be perceived through the physical senses, but now they are apprehended as both distinct and yet at the same time mysteriously identical, pervaded by some sort of shared inner subjectivity of consciousness, or light, or life which binds all elements of the perceptual field both to each other and to the perceiving subject. It is as if the multiplicity itself somehow discloses a normally hidden unity. (504–05)

Kelly and Grosso comment that "mystical poets such as Blake, Tennyson, Whitman, and Wordsworth often seem to verge upon this sort of experience" (505). Some aspects of Stace's definition of extrovertive mystical experiences have much in common with the epiphanies described by Ehrenreich. In her experiences, too, the ordinary perceptual world seems to remain, objects are experienced in transfigured form apparently 'pervaded by some sort of shared inner subjectivity of consciousness,' and a hidden unity becomes apparent. Her experiences also recall the descriptions of Evelyn Underhill of how the normal consciousness of thoughts and feelings are suspended and consciousness "is united for an instant with the 'great life of the All'" (qtd. by Kelly and Grosso 507). It also resembles the experiences of Arthur Koestler when "for the first time the veil has fallen and one is in touch with 'real reality,' the hidden order of things, the X-ray texture of the world, normally obscured by layers of irrelevancy" (qtd. by Kelly and Grosso 508). Kelly and Grosso also point to Strassman who "playfully analogizes the brain to a television receiver" through which we can "connect with novel dimensions of reality that are always present, but normally hidden" (550).

In "Unusual Experiences Near Death and Related Phenomena," Emily Williams Kelly, Bruce Greyson, and Edward F. Kelly discuss near-death experiences (NDEs) while suggesting that these are part of a larger group of transcendent experiences that also include mystical experiences. They examine different explanations offered by research so far. Noyes and Kletti (1976), for example, propose that "NDEs are a type of depersonalization, in which feelings of detachment, strangeness, and unreality protect one from the threat of death," whereas depersonalization experiences may be unpleasant in nature, which is not the case with near death narratives. According to Kelly, Greyson, and Kelly, research trying to establish common personality traits linked to near death narratives have not been successful since people from all walks of life and all ages may have these experiences, as may people who are as psychologically healthy as other people (377). One characteristic stands out, however, namely "that near-death experiencers scored higher than a comparison group on a dissociation scale," something that might indicate that they may "be persons who respond to serious stress with dissociative behavior that is adaptive, rather than pathological" (Kelly, Greyson, and Kelly 378).

Ehrenreich herself comes across the concept of 'dissociation,' a state involving a sense of unreality or disruption of consciousness that, if it reoccurs frequently, is regarded as a disorder. Trying to identify what causes these sudden and startling shifts in her perception of reality, she finds that sunlight plays a role[4] and that these experiences tend to occur at liminal points between paying attention to one thing and moving the attention to another thing. Ehrenreich's conversion to Hinduism comes sometime after she has begun to have these experiences and is an attempt to find a way to reach this 'other place.' According to Kelly, Greyson, and Kelly, dissociative tendencies may be related to "*absorption*, or the ability to screen out the external world and focus one's attention either on selected sensory experiences or on internal imagery," and they add that although findings are inconclusive, one study indicates that "people experiencing NDE had slightly higher scores on scales of absorption or fantasy proneness, as compared with a control group" (378). As the following quote shows, for young Ehrenreich, only a horizontal level of human agency is plausible and acceptable within her cosmological framework, not a vertical spiritual dimension of transcendence. Still, she wonders if 'something else' could be causing her dissociations since it is clear that she has no control over them herself. Yet she persists in applying a rational framework and a view that the universe is "made up of tiny dead things" (80):

> 'Something'? Up until now I had thought of the dissociative experience as a 'place,' but since I had no control over my access to it, there was the possibility of some being or agency that swooped down to take me there. If I had no power over the experience, then maybe something else did. But of course there were no candidates to fill such a role. You might say that the major lesson of my upbringing so far was that there was nothing 'out there'—no God, no reliable others, and no help coming, or, for that matter, any threats other than those of human invention. So my uncanny 'jolts,' or sudden fissures in reality, could not represent interventions by some alien being. Rationally speaking, they were nothing more than brief breakdowns of normal perceptual processes, and were ultimately explainable, like everything else, in terms of cellular and molecular interactions. Science confirmed that the universe was dead or at least made up of tiny dead things, mindless particles following their destinies. (79–80)

Looking back at her experience at Lone Pine, Ehrenreich muses:

> [O]n that empty street, I found whatever I had been looking for since the articulation of my quest, or perhaps, given my mental passivity at the moment, whatever had been looking for me. Here we leave the jurisdiction of language,

---

[4] When she moves to Portland, the "otherworldly states" disappear, perhaps because of the grayness (144).

JOURNEYS WITHIN

where nothing is left but the vague gurgles of surrender expressed in worlds like 'ineffable' and 'transcendent.' For most of the intervening years, my general thought has been: If there are no words for it, then don't say anything about it. Otherwise you risk slopping into 'spirituality,' which is, in addition to being a crime against reason, of no more interest to other people than your dreams. (115–16)

At times, Ehrenreich's descriptions of her experiences resemble those of Elizabeth Gilbert in *Eat Pray Love*, for example in her feeling that "[s]omething poured into me and I poured into it" (116): "[she knows] that the heavens had opened and poured into [her], and [she] into them" (117).[5] When she is immersed in the languid, dramatic, sensual landscapes of Florida, the "living breathing Other" again makes itself felt (221).

Ehrenreich's younger self feels that she has "come back from being whacked by a power greater than herself, maybe even from the kind of epiphany that filled biblical prophets with their prophecies" (122). Her older self impatiently wants the younger self to explain in detail what happened, but it cannot be named, the younger self calls it 'that,' this experience of containing all, of seeing "everything in its naked and purposeless significance" (124). Ehrenreich recognizes aspects of the state described in Aldous Huxley's *The Doors of Perception* (although in Huxley's case this state was produced by taking mescaline). Her epiphanic experiences do not convey or challenge any notions of deity but resemble, rather, "an explosion, a calamitous natural process like an earthquake or storm, leaving behind it what is known in science fiction as a 'rent in the fabric of space-time'" (127–28). At some point, Ehrenreich experiences her epiphanies as a form of madness. Her recollections show how we are forced to process and try to understand inexplicable things that happen through whatever logical and cultural framework is available to us. Today's diagnostic terminology did not exist in Ehrenreich's youth, and the only term she finds that to some extent matches her symptoms is schizophrenia. She reads that it "features a general cognitive deterioration, manifested as a loosening grip on reality" and finds that this seems to be the only diagnosis that corresponds to her "occasional excursion into mystical grandiosity" (135). For two decades, Ehrenreich construes her experiences as schizophrenic episodes. Although her

---

[5] "Maybe, from some unimaginable vantage point, I had served my purpose, which was to let this nameless force flow through me so that a circuit could be completed and the universe, for a moment anyway, made whole again" (119).

transcendental episodes continue to occur, she is determined to focus on the worldly, to engage in parental responsibility and political work for "the down-trodden" and "against those who do the down-treading" (197), and she believes that she is more able than other people to see what is 'right' and what is 'wrong.' Her epiphanies, on the other hand, are *beyond* right and wrong, and have had "no moral valence or reference to the human condition" (197). But her quest—wanting to find out what happened during her youthful epiphanies—returns in middle age, to some extent due to personal despair.

Ehrenreich's experiences represent a conflict for a nonbeliever: "If I let myself speculate even tentatively about that *something*, if I acknowledged the possibility of a nonhuman agent or agents, some mysterious Other, intervening in my life, could I still call myself an atheist?" (203). Not only is her atheism a legacy from her parents, it has become a solid and essential part of Ehrenreich's identity and world view: Morality, she thinks, "originates in atheism and the realization that no higher power is coming along to feed the hungry or lift the fallen. Mercy is entirely left to us" (203). In her view, Christianity even has a "nasty, selfish edge" in allowing some souls to come to heaven while condemning others to eternal exclusion. At one point, in a discussion with a minister, Ehrenreich even claims that "the appropriate stance toward an omnipotent God, even the possibility of an omnipotent God, should be hatred and opposition for all the misery he allowed or instigated" (204).

In the end, Ehrenreich concludes that what she is really rejecting is monotheism and ideas of an omnipotent and good God, whereas "amoral gods, polytheistic gods, animal gods—these were all fine with [her]" (213). Looking back to Freud's idea that our notions of God tend to reflect the idealized images of our parents, Ehrenreich muses that her own parents' being so far from ideal may indeed have influenced how she has come to visualize God.

But "nonbelievers have mystical experiences, too," and Ehrenreich's experiences have shown how "God or gods or at least a living Presence [flames] out from every object" (215). In late mid-life, Ehrenreich is able to "acknowledge the possible existence of conscious beings—'gods,' spirits, extraterrestrials—that normally elude our senses, making themselves known to us only on their own whims and schedules, in the service of their own agendas" (and she thinks that she has actually seen such a being) (215). Further, she has also come to the conclusion that she is far from alone in having had such experiences. According to surveys, she notes, "almost half of Americans report having had a 'mystical experience'" (216). Drawing on

Rudolf Otto's writings on mystics (that in turn draw upon Meister Eckhardt), Ehrenreich wants to lay aside any notions of a completely and perfectly compassionate God, since mysticism, as Ehrenreich puts it, "often reveals a wild, amoral Other, while religion insists on conventional codes of ethics enforced by an ethical supernatural being" (226): "The God of religion, the enforcer of ethics, is one thing, the 'Wholly Other' revealed in mystical experiences quite another" (227). "If the Other as perceived by mystics is not benevolent," she continues, "neither is it necessarily malevolent; in fact both descriptions are flagrantly anthropocentric" (227). "Science could of course continue to dismiss anomalous 'mystical' experiences as symptoms of mental illness," she goes on to say, "but the merest chance that they represent some sort of contact or encounter justifies investigation" (229). One might agree with Ehrenreich that "experience—empirical experience—requires [us] to keep an open mind" (23). As for the "Other or Others," she has "the impressions, growing out of the experiences chronicled here, that it may be seeking us out" (237).

In many ways, Ehrenreich's is a success story: measuring her life against her mother's, she finds that she has managed to have "all the things [her mother] craved," "the entire package, plus some," "the adventure, the causes, the friends and the hot romances" (13). Ehrenreich's autobiography leaves most of the friendships and the hot romances aside in order to focus on aspects of spiritual adventure. While she excludes or touches only briefly upon professional development and romantic involvements, however, she does describe some important aspects of her childhood, one example being the aforementioned story about her grandmother throwing a crucifix at the priest.

In "Conditions and Limits of Autobiography," Georges Gusdorf writes that "autobiography properly speaking assumes the task of reconstructing the unity of a life across time" (37). In Gusdorf's view, "it is one of the means to self knowledge thanks to the fact that it recomposes and interprets a life in its totality" (38). "According to Roy Pascal, the first theorist of autobiography in English," further, as David Leigh asserts, "autobiography in its pure form is the reconstruction of the unified movement of one life from a coherent viewpoint" (Leigh xi) Defined along the lines of Gusdorf and Pascal, Ehrenreich's book cannot be called an autobiography, and Ehrenreich herself does not want to call it so, perhaps because she imagines that an autobiography must be more complete or because her book is not, as she says, "the story of me or of that even more imaginary construct, 'my life'" (196). If she had written an actual autobiography, she thinks, she would have started it not with her childhood experiences but from the early 1970s when she was firmly grounded as parent and breadwinner. As I would like to suggest, Barbara Ehrenreich's *Living With a Wild God* is primarily a spiritual autobiography, even though, as the subtitle affirms, it is written by a non-believer.

The presence of an unseen dimension is central also in Kim Chernin's autobiography, *In My Father's Garden: A Daughter's Search for a Spiritual Life* (1996). Chernin's parents were Jewish immigrants from Russia. Her mother, Rose Chernin, was a fervent communist party organizer who was arrested in 1951 for working to overthrow the government. In *My Father's Garden*, Chernin's mother comes across as a hectoring figure who, "with her vision of the politics of total commitment on a grand scale" (Chernin 45), creates a household primarily focused on politics and activism while spirituality and religion, regarded as aspects of the superstructure of society, cannot be tolerated. While the heritage from both parents is important for Kim Chernin, in *In My Father's Garden*, as the title indicates, it is the deceased father who is the central figure on Chernin's spiritual journey, and her story is in fact told to him. Although Paul Kusnitz was a Marxist ped-dling the party paper on Saturdays, he represented an entirely different approach to social change compared to the mother. From her father Chernin learns about "the mysterious consequences generated from small acts of engagement with the world" (45). Kusnitz came from "old religion" and grew up with "the religion of the shtetl, the reading and reciting of ancient texts in a dead language" devoted to a God who, in the father's view, "was said to mean well by his people, yet did nothing to help them in their exile and poverty" (38). Instead, Chernin's father has come to adhere to "Feuerbach's view that it was man who had created god in his own image, thereby attributing to god qualities, capacities, gifts of heart and mind that were man's own attributes" (39). As Kusnitz tells his daughter: "When I was young, it was a liberation for us no longer to believe in heaven. We thought the ways of heaven unjust, unreliable. We believed instead in man's capacity to change the world" (120).

In Chernin's autobiography a spiritual focus is predominant, although specific religious symbols remain absent. For her, God is beyond the creeds of separate religions and can therefore just as easily be found in Eastern-inspired spiritualities. At a certain point, Chernin hears about an Indian woman, Mother Meera, who is residing in Germany. Regarded by her followers as a divine personage, this woman, it is believed, has been sent to help save the world, and she gives *darshans* (blessings) in her home. Chernin writes: "I was happy to know that Meera belonged to a cultural form of worship of which I had been ignorant, in which women saints are worshiped as deities who become incarnate to bring love, memory, a divine message, perform a healing task, repair and perhaps save the world," and she regards Mother Meera as a "Hindu version of the Shekinah" (147–48). Chernin's emphasis is on receptivity: wanting to know more, Chernin finds that "the appropriate response is curiosity," a curiosity without judgement (122), and she feels a strong desire to travel to Germany in order to find out if Mother Meera is indeed divine. At the same time, throughout her narrative, Chernin attempts to look at her own fascination through the rational and explanatory eyes of her father. Trained in psychoanalysis, Chernin knows that she could "be experiencing what is called a projective identification" (something that occurs when a client deposits "faith and doubt" in her analyst so that the latter can "work it over for her and return it to her in an altered form" [123]), and she realizes, further, that the "exalted moods" she has known are "routinely regarded by some people as manic states" (144).

Coming across a book about Mother Meera (Andrew Harvey's *The Hidden Journey*), Chernin recognizes a sense of awakening and transformation that is familiar to her since it resembles the impulse to worship that sometimes comes over her in nature or when the landscape is "charged with presence" (128). She ponders the countless relationships that have existed between gurus and disciples throughout history and how these relationships often make people feel uncomfortable since the "surrender of individual will to the superior knowing of another person … tends to run against our democratic educations" (144–45). Wanting to fall on her knees, Chernin has an experience that is almost Wordworthian in its romantic overtones: "Suddenly I wanted to bury my face in my hands. I felt that I was becoming very small in the presence of something wondrous. I also felt childlike, full of joy and excitement" (128). This sense of wonder in nature, Chernin recalls, was dismissed by her therapist as "the return of a childhood fantasy" (131). The non-spiritual attitude of many people has made Chernin dismiss the "transformative inner experience" and "sensitivity to the consciousness of nature" (131). Learning about Mother Meera—who "says she is here to aid in the transformation and evolution of the world, through the power of divine light, called in Hindu the light of Paramatman, the supreme being," awakens the interest (133). Chernin's thoughts are counterbalanced against those of her prosopoetically present father, who would be deeply skeptical of New Age visions, awakenings, and dreams. However, Chernin's vision could be seen as an example of a contemporary pantheist polyreligiosity combining aspects from different religions and spiritualities: "The gods I knew about, even the great mother, seemed far off, abstract, hypothetical. Sometimes I thought about them as archetypal images that belonged to the psyche. When I felt a wish to worship nature, I imagined that I had projected onto a solitary tree a luminous cloud configuration, a sense of divinity that streamed from the human heart" (125). Listening to a lecture by Andrew Harvey, further, she feels "particularly Jewish, intense, brooding, full of struggle and doubt, not at all a New Age personality" (149). As to whether or not Meera is divine, Chernin arrives at no sure answer. It is certain that Mother Meera is extraordinary, "a focused beam of energy" (172). After her journey to Germany, Chernin remains unsure but decides that Mother Meera at the very least possesses extraordinary compassion. In the end, perhaps, everyone is "potentially divine" (174).

On one occasion, Chernin remembers, her father happens to open her *Tao Te Ching* and come across a passage saying that "To retire when the task is accomplished is the way of heaven" (119). This quote is significant, since it can be related both to the story of dying in Chernin's autobiography and to writing itself. It is as if Chernin has applied this motto to her own book, putting the narrative and symbolic full stops where they need to be instead of extending the narrative unnecessarily. The quote from *Tao Te Ching* can also be related to a reference made on another occasion, to the Havdalah. While the Shekinah, among many other things, is identified with the Garden of Eden, Havdalah, Chernin explains, means division or separation, and refers to the rituals at the end of the Sabbath of wine and herbs. Interestingly, this represents a farewell to the divine visitation of the Shekinah, the "feminine, visible, audible manifestation of God's presence on earth" (136): "the Havdalah marks her departure. Therefore, a box of fragrant spices is passed from hand to hand, to revive the human spirit from the separation" (137). The last words in *In My Father's Garden*—"on the eve of departure"—also point to separations and endings (180).

In My Father's Garden itself could be read as an end-of-Sabbath ritual with Chernin herself as a 'Shekinah' arriving at a dying woman's house during the symbolic final days of her life's 'week,' bringing a sense of God's presence to the death bed. In the second part of the book, Chernin becomes involved in helping this woman. Chernin's grandmother was a healer, and Chernin herself discovers that she has healing abilities. When she is with the dying woman, Chernin finds that her arms "are moving with an intention of their own" enfolding the woman "in a palpable radiance" of spiritual love

(79). In her healing, Chernin "[feels] that [she] is being hollowed out so that a radiant energy can flow through [her] to [the dying woman]. This energy does not seem to be [Chernin's], it arises elsewhere, seems merely to pass through [her] as if [the dying woman] and [Chernin] were threaded to a mysterious world that works in silence, cannot be named, throws itself open to those who are dying" (96). At these times, Chernin "[senses] the presence of that unseen world, as if dying made this world more available than usual" (98). It seems as if "unknown powers seem willing to help [her]" (99). Chernin is leaning "on an unknown world from which [she] has begun to receive the assurance that dying, whether or not an ending, is not to be feared" (104). In a reversal of agency, she reflects that while she has wanted to "find a vocation," "[t]his work has found [her]" (99), the task of assisting the dying. It is when Chernin is attending to the dying woman that her own spirituality reawakens. Unsure of what this means, she muses: "this could mean, in my desperation about not knowing how to help her, I invented a soothing fiction. A spiritual world. It could also mean that her dying and my response to it threw open doors of perception that had always been open, then never quite, then widely thrown open, then banged shut" (151).

Perhaps there is a suppressed spiritual aspect present already in the activist meetings organized by Chernin's mother, since they "always held a religious character" whereby the participants would "thaw away into an ecstatic union with the others," something that was seen by the mother as "entering into the collective" and by the father as "a foretaste of the socialist world" (46). Chernin comments: "There may be a place where socialist humanism and spiritual politics meet, parallel lines finally twisted together by infinity" (44), and she states later that "[t]ransformation has to mean engagement, connection, common purpose" (161). She concludes that "[i]t must be possible to love the human and seek the divine, to be deeply attached to the earth and all its engagements and still be trotting along on a spiritual course" (162).

Ever since childhood Chernin has been endowed with a particular sensitivity, and the presence of an unseen dimension is central for her. She has the "impression [she] is offered knowledge, as if the things we need to know about the world come to us through movements so subtle they have moved on by the time we are aware that something, almost too fine for us, has been and gone" (156). Looking back, she muses: "Each awakening, followed by a deep sleep, each new illumination followed by a forgetting. These isolated, singular events now seem connected to one another, a sequence of transformational steps leading to this very moment" (107).

Inspired, perhaps, by her practice as a counsellor, Chernin's attitude is one of deep listening. For her, receptivity is everything: "if there are messages of compassion currently being sent to us from unknown quarters, it might be very useful to receive and distribute them" (68). Compassion has a revolutionary power, and it may have to *precede* political transformation and be there "before we can devote ourselves to the seemingly impossible task of saving our world" (179).

The use of personification in *In My Father's Garden* is striking. Narration itself becomes personified when Chernin asserts: "Once underway, the story will take care of itself, gather momentum, forget about the listener, charge off on its mission" (117). Parts of the body or nature are given human qualities, they behave like humans and they might have humanlike emotions. At one point, the garden "looks patient, long-suffering," and it is described as possibly endowed with knowledge hidden to humans, but sadly, it "wasn't talking" (89). The use of personification points both to the healing performed by Chernin and, more significantly, to a spiritual dimension. Chernin's hands take on a kind of agency as they become "knowing, autonomous" (96). Things are happening beyond normal volition and agency. The personifications in *In My Father's Garden* create a sense of a universe that is alive and contains unseen dimensions, an unseen world that sends out emissaries or messages whereby agents become somehow ungraspable. This blurred agency is not something her father would have accepted. Chernin thinks that if she had suggested to her father that teachers or messengers are "sent to us" in order to help save the world from chaos or destruction, his answer would have been: "Sent by whom?" (118).

Commenting on writing, narrative form, and reader reception, Chernin suggests that "Stories require a listener who can suspend disbelief long enough to let the tale emerge" (117). This statement would seem to apply not only to her own spiritual autobiography (and that of others), but to spirituality itself. What Chernin seems to suggest is that divinity itself requires listeners who can suspend disbelief long enough to let messages emerge.

"Root and Branch" is the title of the third and final section in *In My Father's Garden*. Nature imagery shapes the depiction of spiritual development, and Chernin's 'new' idea of seeking out Mother Meera is a seed that is taking root. Like special plants, Chernin's developing spiritual thoughts "have grown up mysteriously, in darkness, out of unknowing and disbelief" (142). Continuously, throughout her autobiography, she mulls things over, looks at them from different perspectives, considers rational or psychoanalytic explanations but then feels "tired of explanations" since her most interesting thoughts are "born of ecstasy" (142). At one point she thinks: "I'm sick of accounting for mystical states. I'm just going to let them happen, the more I'm down on my knees the better. Perhaps this is what is meant by surrender" 157). The need to explain everything from a rational perspective can be a hindrance, as these quotes show: "The scientific arrogance, the trust in the rational powers of the mind, the secular humanist pride that we can manage on our own have fallen before the threatened collapse of our civilization" (164).

Although the tradition of Judaism is important, Chernin does not reach back to the old "religion of the shtetl, the reading and reciting of ancient texts in a dead language" (38). Neither does she swallow other dogmas or doctrines uncritically. Her spirituality is pantheistic and polyreligious, celebrating an unseen, intelligent presence that she perceives as divine and that could be called God. At the end, Chernin notes: "I have become a believer. Oh, a believer, but in what?" (143). She goes on: "This is who I am: I am a lover of the mother, of god. What matters to me is this love, this relation, the need to serve in the name of this love, to work in the world so that I am addressing its crisis, its turmoil, its despair" (144). It is noteworthy that here, God is in lower case. Towards the end of her spiritual journey Kim Chernin has a message for her father: "a spiritual awakening may be the most revolutionary experience possible in our time" (176).

Spiritual Voyages Beyond Life:
Contemporary Near-Death Narratives

So we fix our eyes not on what is seen, but on what is unseen, since what is seen is temporary, but what is unseen is eternal.

(2 Corinthians 4: 18)

At the very least, near-death experiences should foster spiritual growth by leading us to question some of our basic assumptions about mind and brain, about our relationship to the divine, and about the universe and our role in it.

(Bruce Greyson 13)

If the modern spiritual autobiography in general has drawn little interest in the academy, there is one sub-genre that has drawn even less interest: the near-death narrative. This category of autobiographical writing brings us into an enigmatic area of investigation of more pronounced soteriological aspects. As the occurrence of near-death experiences has been increasingly discussed in recent decades (in particular after the publication of Raymond Moody's *Life after Life: The Investigation of a Phenomenon - Survival of Bodily Death* in the mid-1970s), autobiographical narratives about these 'voyages' have also become more common.

This chapter will delve into accounts of spiritual 'journeying beyond' that occurs during near-death experiences and that are described in recent publications. Some examples that will be touched upon here include Eben Alexander's *Proof of Heaven: A Neurosurgeon's Journey into the Afterlife (2012)*, Dale Black's *Flight to Heaven: A Plane Crash ... A Lone Survivor ... A Journey to Heaven - and Back. A Pilot's True Story* (2010), Ned Dougherty's *Fast Lane to Heaven: A Life-after Death Journey* (2001), Crystal McVea's *Waking Up in Heaven: A True Story of Brokenness, Heaven, and Life Again* (2013), Mary C. Neal's *To Heaven and Back: A Doctor's Extraordinary*

Account of Her Death, Heaven, Angels, and Life Again: A True Story (2012), Richard Sigmund's *My Time in Heaven: A True Story of Dying ... and Coming Back* (2004), and Freddy Vest's *The Day I Died* (2014).

Near-death experiences have been noted throughout history. One example is found in Plato's *The Republic* Book 10).[1] If we go to the Bible, in John 11, Lazarus "had already been in the tomb for four days" when he was raised from the dead by Jesus. Later on, a dinner is given where Jesus is present as well as Lazarus, and many people have come not only to see Jesus but the miracle of Lazarus' having returned to life (John 12). A more recent example are the lines from *Confessions of an English Opium-Eater* by *Thomas De Quincey* (1821): "I was once told by a near relative of mine, that having in her childhood fallen into a river, and being on the very verge of death but for the critical assistance which reached her, she saw in a moment her whole life, in its minutest incidents, arrayed before her simultaneously as in a mirror; and she had a faculty developed as suddenly for comprehending the whole and every part."

Although they have been the object of scientific examination at least since the mid-nineteenth century with a sharp increase in interest in recent decades, no universally accepted definition or explanation exists to date. The experiences may look different from different cultural and religious perspectives, but the core experiences (being out of the body, seeing a light, being in a different sphere) are remarkably similar. In "Unusual Experiences Near Death and Related Phenomena," Emily Williams Kelly, Bruce Greyson, and Edward F. Kelly offer a metacritical discussion of a number of studies from psychological, physiological (neurochemical or neuroanatomical), and transcendent perspectives made over more than a century. Kelly, Greyson, and Kelly have themselves examined 861 reports. Recent studies "suggest that NDE-like experiences may occur in about 10–20% of patients close to death" (Kelly, Greyson, and Kelly 371).[2] According to Bruce Greyson and Surbhi Khanna in "Daily Spiritual Experiences Before and After Near-Death Experiences," "approximately 9 million people in the United States alone

---

[1] Plato's *The Republic*, Book 10, relates "the experiences of the soldier Er during the time when he had been thought dead and placed on a funeral pyre" (Kelly, Greyson, and Kelly 370). Other examples are two cases described by Brierre de Boismont in 1859, three instances described by Myers (1892), and thirty cases described by Heim of accidents and falls. In the twentieth century Russell Noyes (1972) and Raymond Moody were pioneers (Kelly, Greyson, and Kelly 370, 371).
[2] According to a Gallup poll from 1992, about 5 percent of Americans have had near death experiences.

have reported this kind of experience" (303). So far, the most common explanation in neuroscience has been that near-death experiences are caused by brain processes that may be triggered also when someone is not actually close to death but believes he is, as in an accident when protective psychological defence mechanisms set in. It has been proposed that changes in the chemistry of the brain might "lead to abnormal neuroelectric activity in certain critical brain areas, usually in the limbic system or temporal lobes" and that this will produce hallucinations, according to Kelly, Greyson, and Kelly (378),[3] who, however, refute the theory that a release of endorphins causes NDEs, since endorphin generally produces longer-lasting effects than do NDEs (while "the onset and cessation of NDE and its associated features are usually quite abrupt" [380]). In their view, then, increases in endorphins cannot explain out-of-body experiences (Kelly, Greyson, and Kelly 380). Similarly, ketamine may be released in situations of stress, but although ketamine may produce some of the aspects associated with NDEs ("travel through a dark tunnel into light, believing one has died, or communing with God") "ketamine experiences are often frightening and involve bizarre imagery" (380–81). Refuting the idea that NDEs are produced by low levels of oxygen in the blood, further, Kelly, Greyson, and Kelly ask: "If anoxia and related mechanisms play an important role in the generation of NDEs, why do not most cardiac arrest patients report an NDE? Clearly, anoxia is neither a necessary nor a sufficient condition" (380).

It has been suggested that near-death experiences are strongly influenced by the religious beliefs of a person and that they might be instances of "retroactive confabulation" (Greyson 10). Based upon studies by Karlis Osis, Erlendur Haraldsson, Kenneth Ring, and others, Bruce Greyson proposes in "The Mystical Impact of Near-Death Experiences" that it is not so much the content of these experiences that is affected by one's beliefs and expectations but rather the interpretations made afterwards. Greyson underlines the cross-cultural similarities in near death descriptions from Europe, the

---

[3] While some researchers in psychology have suggested that near-death experiences could be seen as a re-experience of one's birth experiences, others assert that newborns cannot register memories and that near-death experiences of going through a tunnel are just as common regardless of whether or not you were born vaginally or by caesarian. Still others suggest that the tunnel experience might be a reflection not of one's actual birth, but an *archetype* of birth or rebirth.

Middle East, India, and America.[4] Furthermore, children have the same patterns of near-death experience as adults.

Let us turn to some recent autobiographical accounts of near-death experiences and begin with a look at Eben Alexander's *Proof of Heaven: A Neurosurgeon's Journey into the Afterlife* (2012). Although this narrative might not resemble a spiritual autobiography at first glance or even be classified as a traditional autobiography,[5] *Proof of Heaven* and other near-death narratives do build on the classical spiritual journey metaphor. Not unexpectedly, the experience 'out beyond' described in *Proof of Heaven* is metaphorized as a multi-level journey. Materially and geographically, Alexander's account moves from home to the hospital and back home again. On a spiritual axis, it moves from a rational and secular, scientific mind-set to an encounter with God and an understanding of what religion is all about. Epistemologically, it is a journey from limited understanding to an instantaneous and all-encompassing knowledge. It is a voyage into another dimension, the comforting message of which is what Alexander's and many other books in this genre are all about. At the emotional and spiritual center of Alexander's autobiography, the journey beyond is concentrated into three brief, spatially conceived chapters: "Underworld" (Chapter 5), "The Spinning Melody and the Gateway" (Chapter 7), and "The Core" (Chapter 9). These chapters combine and compress the recollections of Alexander, written down after waking up from his coma caused by a severe brain

---

[4] Greyson also points to studies exploring the similarities between NDE experiences and the spiritual philosophies found in the Hindu Upanishads and in "early Babylonian, Egyptian, and Zoroastrian texts, as well as to shamanism, Taoism, Tibetan Buddhism, Gnostic Christianity, medieval Christian religious treatises, Mormonism, and Christian Universalism" (13).

[5] Like many contemporary pilgrimage narratives, Eben Alexander's *Proof of Heaven* includes several different sections. The journey 'beyond' takes up only 14 pages out of 196. There is a reading list, appendices, information about an organization Alexander has co-founded with the aim of spreading information about what he calls his "experience out beyond" [151], "Topics & Questions for Discussion," "Enhance Your Book Club," and "A Conversation with Eben Alexander, M. D." (a conversation Eben Alexander holds with himself or perhaps with an editor who asks the questions). Similarly, Mary Neal's *To Heaven and Back* has a section entitled "Q & A with Dr. Neal." Ned Dougherty's *Fast Lane to Heaven* has a tripartite structure with many 'extras' tacked on such as acknowledgments, prologue, introduction, epilogue, afterword, index, and a section turning to the reader with a question: "Do You Have a Sense of Mission?" This feature of mixing different types of text in fact recalls the Puritan spiritual autobiography which, according to Bruce Hindmarsh, was "something of a hybrid or transitional genre: part self-examination and confession, part biblical exposition, part sermonic exhortation, and part factual narrative" (39).

infection. While his family sees what looks like a corpse, Alexander is 'elsewhere.'

Just as the narrative alternates between different levels and perspectives, the language, tone, and style alternate between, on the one hand, a simple personal prose searching for words to convey what really cannot be conveyed and, on the other, journalistic reportage in a scientific, argumentative style that aims to convince.

Close to death, Alexander is drawn out on a spiritual journey that consists of stages and movements between very different post-death regions that he attempts to describe as accurately as he can, even though his experiences are completely beyond language and logic. Since there is no longer a narrating self or any kind of identity, to describe such experiences, further, represents an almost insurmountable challenge. There is only an indefinable awareness that sees, feels, hears, and smells things that are equally hard to identify. Neither human being nor animal, 'Alexander' shrinks to a "lone point of awareness" (31).[6] As there is no past, no memories of anything, and no orientation in time and space, there is, initially, no frame of reference for comprehending or categorizing what this 'point of awareness' is or experiences. And yet, a sense of progression emerges with a change of scenery so that in the end, 'Alexander's' spiritual journey becomes a tour of a large, after-death territory, whereby 'Alexander' is shown aspects of the spiritual world and imparted knowledge about this dimension while also being told that since his time has not yet come he will have to go 'back.' At this point in the journey 'Alexander' cannot understand what or where 'back' is.

In his attempt to convey an image of these post-death territories, Alexander resorts to oxymoronic, contradictory, paradoxical depictions. The void he initially finds himself in is completely dark at the same time as it is also strangely lit: "Pitch black as it was, it was also brimming over with light: a light that seemed to come from a brilliant orb that I now sensed near me" (47). Described as a primordial, muddy underworld, where 'Alexander' finds himself lodged as if within dirty Jell-O, the first stage is poetically described as a visible darkness, recalling and perhaps referencing Satan's fall and the description of hell in Milton's *Paradise Lost*. To begin with, 'Alexander' is merely an awareness, a "consciousness without memory or identity" (29)

---

[6] In this chapter, the author's names will be placed within single quotes in discussions of the near-death passages in order to distinguish them from the conscious counterparts composing their autobiographical accounts *after* the experience.

who has no idea of what or where he is. Apparently bodiless, he is immersed in this strange, "bleary, blurry, claustrophobic" and indefinable region, where he simply registers first sensations and then feelings: "I didn't have a body," he writes, "—not one that I was aware of anyway. I was simply … *there*, in this place of pulsing, pounding darkness"; "my consciousness wasn't foggy or distorted when I was there. It was just … *limited*. I wasn't human while I was in this place. I wasn't even animal. I was something before, or below, all that. I was simply a lone point of awareness in a timeless red-brown sea" (29, 30–31). The experience is primordial: "Language, emotion, logic: these were all gone, as if I had regressed back to some state of being from the very beginnings of life" (29).

Alexander calls this dark indefinable space the Realm of the Earthworm's Eye, a place lacking in any sense of direction or orientation in time and space. It is as though 'Alexander' has "always been there, and would always continue to be" (30). Slowly, there is a sense of progress and development. At a certain point, he notices something in the immediate environment, things that resemble roots that in turn resemble blood vessels in a womb. Gradually, 'Alexander' becomes aware of a mechanical, metallic pounding that sends vibrations through everything "as if a giant, subterranean black-smith is pounding an anvil somewhere off in the distance" (29).

While initially there is a total lack of differentiation, little by little, 'Alexander' is starting to feel uncomfortably trapped in this "deep, timeless, and boundaryless immersion" (31). At this point, "[g]rotesque animal faces bubbled out of the muck, groaned or screeched, and then were gone again. I heard an occasional dull roar. Sometimes these roars changed to dim, rhythmic chants, chants that were both terrifying and weirdly familiar—as if at some point I'd known and uttered them all myself" (31). He also senses movement around him, "as if reptilian, wormlike creatures were crowding … against [him] with their smooth or spiky skins" (31). At this point, too, he notices smells of faces, blood, or vomit, a smell of death, he thinks.

As 'Alexander' starts to panic, wondering where he could go, "something new [emerges] from the darkness" (32). In the second chapter of his journey, entitled "The Spinning Melody and the Gateway," the 'visible darkness' begins to shift to a radiation of light, and the sound of beautiful and complex music replaces the pounding 'Alexander' has heard in the muddy underworld. There is an opening in the light, and he finds himself moving through it and upward, rapidly, as in a flash. Suddenly he is in a different world, at pains to describe the brilliance and beauty he sees from above, soaring above and looking down at a vividly green countryside and joyful people dancing. If this sounds unreal, Eben Alexander goes to great lengths in his book to emphasize that this place is in fact utterly real. After a while there is someone with him, a beautiful girl who radiates love of a kind that cannot be imagined on earth. This girl communicates with 'Alexander' without using language, it is rather as if her 'words' "[go] through [him] like a wind" (40). She has a message for 'Alexander' that translates into three sentences: "you are loved and cherished, dearly, forever," "You have nothing to fear," "There is nothing you can do wrong" (41).

In the third section about the 'beyond,' "The Core" (Chapter 9), 'Alexander' begins to notice how "flocks of transparent orbs, shimmering beings arced across the sky, leaving long, streamer-like lines behind them" (45). 'Alexander' realizes that these "winged beings," for whom he has no words (they are neither birds nor angels) are "different from anything [he has] known on this planet," they are "more advanced. *Higher*" (45). Here, glorious music is not only heard, it is also *felt*: "Seeing and hearing were not separate in this place where I now was. I could *hear* the visual beauty of the silvery bodies of those scintillating beings above, and I could see the surging, joyful perfection of what they sang" (45). There is a sense of complete union, belonging, and harmony: "Everything was distinct, yet everything was also a part of everything else" (46). Alexander even suggests that "you couldn't look at anything in that world at all, for the word *at* implies a separation that did not exist there" (46).

Let us now turn to the near-death account written by another doctor. With the prominent journey metaphor of the title and an image of cloud-swirled high bridge leading off into a misty softness on the cover, *To Heaven and Back: A Doctor's Extraordinary Account of Her Death, Heaven, Angels, and Life Again: A True Story* (2012), is the autobiographical narrative of Mary C. Neale describing her experience of drowning during a kayaking excursion in Chile in 1999. Neal describes how she leaves life, moves towards heaven, returns to earth, and, for some time after the accident, is able to be in touch with life 'beyond.' The near-death narrative is woven into a factual account of Neal's life as a whole along with flashbacks to other crucial events that, in Neal's view, have had miraculous overtones. Several times before the kayaking accident, Neal finds herself in life-threatening situations. As a teenager, she survives a car accident. With the car rolling down the hill, Neal has time to pray to God and to find complete inner peace. Remarkably, she is able to observe both the dangerous, unstoppable movement of the car and her surroundings with complete clarity and equanimity. Another miraculous instance occurs when Neal and her instructor are scuba-diving in Florida and they are trapped in an underwater cave and lose their bearings when the oxygen starts to run out. Praying to God, Neal soon becomes aware of the movement of fish that seems to indicate a way out. Following the route indicated by the fish, Neal and her instructor miraculously manage to escape death by drowning. In the kayaking accident described in a chapter entitled "Death on the River," by contrast, there seems to be no such escape route. Neal gets trapped deep underwater in her kayak. But, as was the case during the car accident, she remains completely calm while praying to God and asking for his divine intervention, although she is not asking specifically to be rescued. She wholeheartedly accepts God's plan, whatever it might be. Doing so, she arrives at a sense of complete peace and acceptance and has a physical sensation of being held and stroked, almost like a baby. Trapped underwater, sensing God's presence, Neal remains conscious of her situation and has the time to review her own life in all its aspects. Feeling ready to move on, she implores God to hurry up. The rescue operation proves almost impossible, but thanks to the miraculous emergence of a rock to step on, her friends manage to liberate her, without knowing it at first, since they cannot see her. The strong current helps Neal to move out of the kayak even though this liberation comes at a frightful price, as she is forced to bend her knees the wrong way in order to get out of her kayak. She feels no pain, however, and by the time she is finally hauled out of the water her body is purple, and she has stopped breathing. Close to eleven or fourteen minutes have passed from the moment when her absence has been noticed by her companions.

While Neal's soul is "returning to God," and she is "drinking in the beauty" of this she is at the same time able to look back and see her own lifeless body on the river bank, looking "like the shell of a comfortable old friend" (72). Underwater, feeling her soul disengaging itself from her body, Neal feels a 'pop' as her soul rises out of the water. At this point 'Neal' finds herself entering another world where she is welcomed and accompanied by spiritual beings whose purpose is to guide Neal to her heavenly afterlife. In meeting with this "large welcoming committee," the "cloud of witnesses as described in *Hebrews* 12:1" that "seemed to be wildly cheering for [her] as [she] approached the 'finish line,'" Neal experiences a joy beyond anything she has known in life (Neal 69). Even though she cannot identify these spiritual beings she feels that she knows each one of them. She is certain that "they are from God," that she has "known them for an eternity" and that they are "sent to guide [her] across the divide of time and dimension that separates our world from God's" (69):

They appeared as formed shapes, but not with the absolute and distinct edges of the formed physical bodies we have on earth. Their edges were blurred, as each spiritual being was dazzling and radiant. Their presence engulfed all of my senses, as though I could see, hear, feel, smell, and taste them all at once. Their brilliance was both blinding and invigorating. We did not speak, *per se*, using our mouths, but easily communicated in a very pure form. (69–70)

Moving closer to Heaven, 'Neal's' soul is drawn to a great hall of unimaginable brilliance and luminosity that marks a special borderline: "I knew with a profound certainty that it represented the last branch point of life, the gate through which each human being must pass. It was clear that this hall is the place where each of us is given the opportunity to review our lives and choices, and where we are each given a final opportunity to choose God or to turn away—for eternity" (73).

In the chapter on Neal's rescue, the narrative perspective alternates between Neal's own description of the events as she remembers them and the descriptions of her companions as told to her afterwards. Beginning CPR, they urge Neal over and over again to take a breath. Since they continue to ask her to breathe, she "feels compelled to return to [her] body to take another breath before returning to [her] journey" (73). When she understands that her time has not come yet since there is more work for her to do on earth, Neal is first annoyed and then sad, and with "one last, longing glance" at her spiritual guides, she returns to her body (74).

After her near-death experience, Mary C. Neal is transformed. Although she has not really questioned her own belief in God before the boating accident, after the accident, her faith becomes a conviction. Her book does not so much describe a spiritual awakening as a spiritual *reawakening*, whereby the task she sets herself is to convey the promises of faith and to share her experiences with anyone who needs renewed hope. The message, then, is central, and her writing is straightforward and artless and she wishes to reinforce a view of herself as an 'ordinary' person and even a "social introvert" (Neal 9).

A third near-death narrative, Ned Dougherty's *Fast Lane to Heaven: A Life-after Death Journey* (2001) begins in 1984 in the Hamptons at a time when Dougherty, a well-to-do owner of fabulous nightclubs, is living what might look like the American dream of success, wealth, and power. But Dougherty's story very quickly veers off into a sudden 'descent' (chapter 2). After suffering murderous rage against a business associate who has let him down heinously, Dougherty experiences the terror and trauma of a complete physical collapse and cardiac arrest. He then transitions seamlessly

173

(although with increasing panic) into a bodiless consciousness falling into an indefinable dark space of nothingness, "like falling down an elevator shaft" "into an abandoned well without [his] body" (Dougherty 12). Recalling the first stage of Eben Alexander's journey through a dark, muddy realm without borders or points of orientation, Dougherty's experience is somehow more frightening since 'Dougherty' instinctively senses that things can go very wrong here. He may have fallen so far away from God that falling any deeper will lead to a complete end of total non-existence. As in Eben Alexander's and Mary C. Neal's narratives, the near-death story in *Fast Lane to Heaven* is told in bits and pieces alternating with rescue scenes and other flashbacks. Trying at first to communicate with members of the ambulance staff, 'Dougherty' soon realizes that the man working on him looks right through him and seems not even to hear him. Looking down on the man on the gurney, who seems dead, 'Dougherty' then realizes that he is looking down on himself. Soon thereafter, he moves up through the roof of the ambulance, something that, strangely, seems normal to him—until kaleidoscopic views of all the toys he has owned in his life appear in flashes or scenes that vanish one by one while 'Dougherty' hangs suspended about forty to fifty feet above the road. Contemplating the stars, he has the sudden inexplicable thought that he is 'going home' (18). He soon enters a field of energy that "[curls] like an ocean wave and [forms] a perfect tunnel that [stretches] into the heavens," where a "shimmering, luminescent-blue field of energy [begins] to float toward [him]," composing itself into an old friend who has died in Vietnam (19).

Since the experiences Ned Dougherty recounts happened in the mid-1980s, before information about near-death experiences had become widespread, it is understandable that he initially decides not to speak to anyone about his experiences. Searching for ways to comprehend and validate what he has been through he seeks medical help in North Carolina, where chance meetings and consultations open doors to another world. Dougherty happens upon someone who has had a near-death experience and who recommends that Dougherty contact a Dr K. Ramakrishna Rao at the Rhine Institute, who is engaged in research on near-death experiences. Dougherty participates in conferences and listens to experts in the field such as Elisabeth Kübler-Ross (and her documentation of more than 20 000 near-death experiences), to the psychiatrist Bruce Greyson, and the psychologist Kenneth Ring.

Not only is Dougherty's account one of the most detailed, it is also one of the most outlandishly fantastic. One example is the inclusion of fully formed exhortatory speeches by the Archangel Gabriel on the state of the American nation (172–74). Dougherty's account differs from other similar narratives in its astonishingly detailed recall, as in the following passage: "I focused my attention on the composition of the walls of the tunnel as we moved forward. They resembled a massive ocean wave in a tubular form. My curiosity caused me to reach out in the direction of the wall to my right. As I touched its essence, a profusion of crystal-like liquid sparks danced and exploded in brilliant colors. The sparks of bright light were accompanied by the synchronous sounds of crystal-like chimes" (22).

Another near-death narrative, Crystal McVea's *Waking Up in Heaven: A True Story of Brokenness, Heaven, and Life Again* (2013), tells the story of how Crystal McVea dies in hospital due to a severe inflammation of the pancreas. Remembering nothing of the emergency situation in the hospital (a passage that is only indirectly autobiographical as it is described to her afterwards), McVea recalls going to sleep and "waking up in heaven, with God" (10). Going to heaven is instantaneous as time does not work in the same, sequential way as on Earth, McVea explains: when she dies, she closes her eyes on earth and opens them in heaven. In heaven, time as we know it does not exist. Approaching the gate of heaven McVea learns from God that if she passes through these gates, she will not be able to go back. Even though visions of her four children appear, McVea chooses to stay with God: "I knew there could be nothing between God and me. God comes first, and everything else is second" (151). But before they go through the gates, she senses that there is someone God wants her to meet. She becomes aware of a little girl holding an Easter basket and realizes that the girl is herself as a three-year-old, the age when McVea was first the victim of sexual abuse that has led to self-hatred, shame, and a life-long sense of being utterly abandoned. Seeing herself as a small girl makes McVea realize that God has always loved her. As a child, McVea did not feel that God was there for her at all. Since she cannot "fathom such a thing as a loving and completely devoted father," "the concept of God as a loving father [has] no meaning" (34). Retrospectively, she understands that God has in fact been chasing her, "glorifying himself through the garbage of [her] life" (57).

Then, hearing the voice of her mother calling her name, McVea wishes to go back just to let her mother know where she is. God gives a clear answer, telling her that the choice is hers. Turning around, McVea looks down and sees beneath her "what [looks] like crystals, shining like a billion perfect diamonds" (166–67). God gives her one final exhortation: "*Tell them what you can remember*" (167, italics in original). McVea's journey to heaven is conveyed in droplets interspersed within an autobiographical framework recounting her life from childhood to the present. From early childhood, McVea has been the victim of abuse, of her parents' divorce, and of a vicious stepfather who on one occasion shoots a bullet dangerously close to her head. McVea tells her life story because she feels that it is imperative that she reveal the darkness that has been hidden which includes sexual abuse, dysfunctional relationships with irresponsible men, and an abortion that more than anything makes her feel like a sinner. As she is telling her story to groups and individuals she feels that God wants her to share these aspects of her own life along with her near-death experience. The reason for this becomes clear when women who have suffered similar experiences come forward in tears to thank McVea for sharing her traumatic experiences, something that helps these women liberate themselves from years of suffering and know that they have been loved by God all along.

Richard Sigmund's *My Time in Heaven: A True Story of Dying ... and Coming Back* (2004) is one of the most extraordinary accounts of heaven as well as one of the longest (more than half of his book) and the most detailed. With a scene that could be taken from a horror movie, *My Time in Heaven* starts out in a far more terrifying way than any of the other near-death narratives: when Sigmund, dead for eight hours, is wheeled to the morgue, he suddenly sits up and speaks—to the sheer terror of the medical attendants. Sigmund's experience dates back to 1974 when he was in a car accident. He finds himself moving through a cloud (or perhaps it moves though him), a passage that takes a few minutes and brings him into what he calls a receiving area. Right from the beginning, he feels joy and peace. Once arrived in heaven, he witnesses how other people who have just died are coming through a veil to be welcomed by deceased relatives.

Sigmund's heaven stands out in its amazing dimensions and magic occurrences. There are trees whose leaves resemble the teardrops of a crystal chandelier that produce divine sounds reminiscent of chimes. There are walnut trees that grow new walnuts instantly when you pick one of their supremely delicious fruits. Since the body has no physical needs in heaven, eating fruit is done merely for the somewhat strange pleasure of having the fruit somehow melt and run down your throat. Among many outlandish events, Sigmund sees a person make a gesture and "arcs of what looked like fire [springs] off his hand, and they [sparkle] like fireworks that [hang] in the air for a few moments" (72). There are gigantic fountains that look "like ice but [are] a kind of crystal" (74), and statues that seem to be alive. Astonishingly, one fountain is "about ten miles in circumference at the base" and has a "living statue of Jesus" at the top holding a vessel overflowing with "the living blood of our Savior" (78). Painting is done simply by commanding the colours to turn a certain nuance. A woman he sees is weaving a tapestry by speaking to the yarn. The tapestry "is hanging in midair without any visible means of support" (45). Strangely, in Sigmund's heaven there are people who have not died yet; Sigmund sees them and wonders about this. Curious, he asks questions, but he is gently put in his place by angels who tell him that there are things he is not yet allowed to know. Sigmund is told that he has an appointment with destiny, with God. His grand tour of heaven takes him to the edge of the universe, where he sees "all of the universe as a great spiral with a pure white center" (52).

After coming back to life, Sigmund experiences a heightened spirituality: "I have a depth of God in my life now that I never knew was possible.... Every day, I hear the audible voice of God in some manner. Every day, I see the angels of God. And I have seen Jesus on numerous occasions" (130). Sigmund's *My Time in Heaven* ends with a long section on testimonies, miracles, and selected quotes from the Bible. The message of Sigmund's book is that Jesus is coming back soon, and at the end Sigmund turns to the reader, asking the reader if he or she is ready for this.

Dale Black's *Flight to Heaven: A Plane Crash … A Lone Survivor … A Journey to Heaven – and Back. A Pilot's True Story* (2010) is as much a spiritual autobiography as it is a suspenseful adventure tale. At the age of 19, Dale Black is the victim of a 'non-survivable' airplane crash. The first half of his narrative recounts events and the consequences of this crash. For a long time after the crash Black has no memories of his 'flight to heaven,' and when the memories come back, he decides not to tell anyone except his trusted grandfather, who advises against telling it publicly unless Dale is sure that it is God's will that he do so. This near-death experience is unusual both in that Black's memories come back a long time after the accident and in his decision to publish his story several decades after it happened. Like Ned Dougherty in his near-death narrative, Dale Black finds nothing strange in hovering above his own body looking down on a trauma team working on him in the hospital. He is curious and wonders what is going on, while he is not shocked: "That may be my body," he thinks, "but I'm up here. I can't be dead because I feel so alive" (30). Very soon, he is drawn upward by an "irresistible force" (32), hovering first near the ceiling in the operating room, then "feeling lighter and lighter, being drawn down the hallway and swept out the door of the hospital, and then suddenly [he is] gone," whereupon he finds himself in a "stunningly beautiful light that [permeates] everything, going out in every direction but not expanding" in ways that defy logic (97). Black discovers that he has peripheral vision and is able see both of the two angels that accompany him at the same time as he can look backward. His vision is completely changed, and he finds that it is "like being in a 3-D movie": "Suddenly everything has more dimensions, more richness. But that is an understatement. Multiply that by ten thousand and it would be like what I was experiencing. There are no words that capture the scenes that were before me. Utterly breathtaking" (102). It is beyond language: "What I experienced there, words cannot do justice. Even the best words pale before the indescribable" (11).

The celestial city to which Dale Black arrives resembles the one described in Richard Sigmund's book. There are millions of people in this great city suffused with an indescribable light that seems to be identical to the love of God, a light that is like an ungraspable being or a penetrating substance that seems to have weight, warmth, and thickness as well as hypnotic qualities. Black's description deviates from other narratives in that there are several walls in this heaven. Approaching a gate in the wall, Black notices a "mesmerizing substance" coating the entry and "large gold letters emblazoned above the opening" that "[seem] to quiver with life" (106). The golden letters appear to communicate something important, but Black doesn't recognize their form and thus cannot decipher their meaning. Entering this gateway, for Black, is like a fantastic homecoming: "I was immersed in music, in light, and in love. Vibrant life permeated everything. All these weren't just *around* me, they were *inside* me. And it was wonderful, more wonderful than anything I had ever experienced. It felt as if I belonged there. I didn't want to leave. It was as if this was the place I had been searching all my life to find, and now I'd found it. My search was over!" (107). His sense of belonging is total. The connection cannot be more complete: "I felt so special, so loved. I had never felt such a deep sense of belonging" (107). Even though Black does not recognize the beings he meets (they know him, however), he intuitively knows that they are part of his spiritual family across generations, "living, vibrant, eternal [beings], exuding the very life of God" (108). As in many other near-death narratives, people in heaven seem to be their best selves and their best ages (often somewhere around thirty). While Black cannot detect any racial differences, he realizes that people here have "come from many tribes and nations" (108). But the gate seems to be a boundary, and this is where his tour of heaven ends.

Waking up in the hospital, Black notices at once that he is radically changed. There has been "a Copernican shift in [his] thinking" (40). He now feels deep love for everyone he meets. Before the crash, he has been the center of his own solar system, but "[n]ow [he is) a lesser planet that [orbits] around something bigger than [himself]. And that something bigger [is] the one true God" (40). After the accident, Black's relationship to God changes, and God isn't "theoretical anymore. He [is] personal" (70). Despite an utterly severe, and very pessimistic medical prognosis, Black is increasingly certain that God will heal him.

Half of Dale Black's book recounts a very long 'before,' the story of his youth and the events around the crash. This narrative structure corresponds to the central fact that Black's memory only returns several months after the accident. It is only then that fragments from the accident and the time immediately after it return, and in connection with this, glimpses of his 'flight to heaven.' Black makes a distinction between 'mind' and 'heart'—for a long time, his mind does not remember, but his heart does. His memories of his 'flight to heaven' have remained in him like a memory chip, he feels, and without realizing it his whole outlook on life has been reprogrammed. Even though for months afterwards he has no memories of the crash, Dale Black's life is turned upside down and he is thoroughly changed, without becoming a perfect saint. To the contrary, at times he is still disappointed in himself. Even though he has tried to help people in need around the world at his own expense he asks the question: "Why couldn't I have lived an even better life? Since I had clearly seen heaven and was so changed by the experience, why did I fail again and again to be the man I truly wanted to be?" (12).

In Freddy Vest's *The Day I Died* (2014), another near-death narrative, the major part of the narrative is a recounting of events and memories from his childhood (growing up as one of eighteen siblings in a close-knit sharecropper's family in Texas), his youthful mistakes (a failed marriage followed by a footloose and fancy-free period roaming bars and rodeos), and finally the safe heaven and satisfaction of his second marriage and family life. Inspired by his second wife's strong Christian faith, Vest returns to his Christian foundation in life. In July, 2008, the day referred to in the title of his book—*The Day I Died*, Freddy Vest's life takes an unexpected turn. During a rodeo on an extremely hot day, Vest falls off his horse and is dead before he hits the ground. During the forty-five minutes that pass before the ambulance arrives, CPR is administered—despite the odds—and everyone present is praying for Vest's survival.[7] In Chapter 5, "A short ride to heaven," Vest describes his near-death experience. As is the case with Crystal McVea, he is there—instantly. There is no travel or transition, the passage is seamless and instantaneous. Unlike other divinity travellers Vest does not get a tour of Heaven, but he is allowed to see the prayers for his life shooting up like bolts of light coalescing into an explosion of light. Then, he is 'sent back' to earth, as seamlessly and instantaneously as he has arrived in heaven. Afterwards, Vest asks himself: "Had all this happened only in my mind? Or were Jesus and I hanging out somewhere in space? The questions baffled me" (104). He finds the answers in the Bible, more specifically in the account given by Paul in 2 Corinthians: "I know a man in Christ who fourteen years ago was caught up to the third heaven. Whether it was in the body or out of the body I do not know—God knows. And I know that this man—whether in the body or apart from the body I do not know, but God knows— was caught up to paradise and heard inexpressible things, things that no one is permitted to tell" (2 Corinthians: 12 1–4). Vest (like many exegetics) takes this to mean that Paul speaks about himself—that Paul is the man who went up to the third heaven. What is interesting here is the notion of different heavens. Vest concludes: "I was in heaven, but it was not the eternal heaven. That is the place we tend to speak of and envision as heaven. I never saw that place because I did not go there" (106).

In the near-death narratives explored in this chapter, there are a number of themes and patterns that are typical. First and foremost, as we see in most of these accounts, the experience is indescribable. As Freddy Vest puts it in *The Day I Died*: "If I tried for all eternity I could not find words to describe the wonder of it" (62). "No human terms can describe the heavenly things I was allowed to experience," Vest continues: "If only they could" (66). God's world, as Mary Neal describes it in *To Heaven and Back,*" is exponentially more colorful and intense," and there is "an explosion of love and joy in their absolute, unadulterated essence" (70–71). While Neal's encounter with the spiritual creatures fills her with a joy that cannot be described in words, she does attempt to convey something about the difference by comparing the images projected by an old type of television with those of the technologically most advanced whose images in comparison are "almost painfully crisp and

---

[7] This situation echoes what happened to Vest's father, who almost died from a heart attack while out plowing. Vest is convinced that his father survived and lived for another thirty years thanks to his mother's prayers.

clear" (71). When it comes to descriptions of heaven, "[t]he appropriate words, descriptions, and concepts don't even exist in our current language" (71). In *Fast Lane to Heaven*, Ned Dougherty puts it like this:

> Surrounding me in every direction was an incredible vastness of space. Stars and planets in varying degrees of brilliance seemed to stretch into infinity. The universe in which these stars and planets existed was in a realm of indescribable depth. I realized that I was not in the universe as I knew it on Earth, but in another celestial realm. I became aware that the universe in which Earth is located is only part of a more limitless heavenly realm. (73)

Although there are no physical needs in heaven, people do possess dwellings. The picture of heaven in Dale Black's *Flight to Heaven*, for example, includes "brightly-colored picture-perfect homes in small, quaint towns" (104): "If music could become homes, it would look like these, beautifully built and perfectly balanced" (105). Colors are "so vibrant they pulsated with life"; there is a "rainbow of hues" that offer a "sensory feast" (Black 105). In Richard Sigmund's heaven, houses have porches and pillars and are put together through heavenly craft without nails, and some buildings are floating in the air.

Some narratives depict surprisingly material and even materialist heavens. Park benches in Sigmund's *My Time in Heaven* are made of gold, to take one example. Sigmund quotes the lines from Matthew 6:19–20: "Don't store up treasures on earth! Moths and rust can destroy them, and thieves can break in and steal them. Instead, store up your treasures in heaven, where moths and rust cannot destroy them, and thieves cannot break in and steal them."[8] Whereas the lines from Matthew might seem to favour a spiritual rather than a materialist approach to life, Sigmund's heaven is a materialist paradise. There is plenty of gold all over: Sigmund is welcomed onto a golden pathway, the streets are golden, and the gates of heaven are made of gold ("The gold represented the great mercy of God" [27]). And yet, strangely, the material things seem to be alive; if Sigmund listens closely, he can hear them humming. As a reward for their dedication during life, missionaries are given mansions in Sigmund's heaven that are beyond

---

[8] Similarly, in Luke (12 32–34): "Do not be afraid, little flock, for your Father has been pleased to give you the kingdom. Sell your possessions and give to the poor. Provide purses for yourselves that will not wear out, a treasure in heaven that will never fail, where no thief comes near and no moth destroys. For where your treasure is, there your heart will be also."

compare. Sigmund gets to meet his grandparents whose heavenly home is bigger than the White House, a mansion that has an outlandish price tag although of course symbolically: "If it were possible to build on earth, it would cost probably a trillion dollars" (42).

Earthly laws of gravitation do not apply in Sigmund's heaven. People can walk in the air and they can travel distances in a moment's time, they can float off from the top floors of buildings down to the ground, or float playfully beneath the surface of lakes. There is a lake that gives off a glow, and a tree whose leaves give off a glow. Electricity does not exist in heaven, yet there are lights everywhere—but no shadows, since the light is completely even. Many things are unfathomably gigantic. Sigmund notices roses that are four feet tall, for example, and trees that are two thousand feet tall. Heaven is like a planet—"God's personal planet"—"millions of times the size of Earth" (Sigmund 87). There are millions of people in a lake he sees, and the same thing goes for the ocean, the Sea of God's Glory. Avenues can be 150 feet wide. University buildings are "a mile or two long and a mile or two deep," "great buildings with the capacity to hold hundreds and hundreds of thousands of people" (Sigmund 56). 'Sigmund' is also shown an enormous suspended crystal castle that "[seems] to extend for miles in all directions" (103), and he later learns from Jesus that this is where hopes and dreams are kept.

In all of these heavens, anything that causes stress, suffering, and anxiety has been eliminated, first and foremost the fear of death. If there is "nothing dying or decaying," as Dale Black puts it in *Flight to Heaven* (101), then our primary fear is nonexistent, that is, the fear that according to Ernest Becker in *The Denial of Death* pushes us to fill our lives with activities in order to get away from feelings of existential anxiety.

Similarly, all these narratives present visions of time, permanence, and eternity. In Richard Sigmund's heaven, firstly, there is only the present, "no yesterday and no tomorrow" (86). There are different levels of heaven ('Sigmund' gets to see four of them), and it is possible to float up and down between them. An angel tells 'Sigmund': "Time here is not measured in such trivial things as years, but in ages where the glory of God rolls on forever" (96). Similarly, in *Waking Up in Heaven*, Crystal McVea has "the stunning realization that [she] was the ['she'] that had existed for all of eternity, long before [her] time on Earth" (12). With the angels she meets after death, further, she has the feeling that they are her own angels and that they have been a "part of [her] existence and [her] journey forever" (37). In many of these narratives there is a sense of returning to origins, to the beginning of beginnings. In a passage clearly recalling *Genesis*, in *Flight to Heaven* Dale Black notices a holiness hover over the souls gathered in the celestial city like "the Spirit of God brooding over the surface of the deep at the beginning of time" (100). Similarly, as Freddy Vest puts it in *The Day I Died*: "In the physical world we try to live in the moment. In heaven the moment is eternity" (66); and he adds: "Heaven has no beginning or end. There was no looking back or forward and no need to fathom time" (66–67). The intensity of the experience is such that the present is all that exists. In Dale Black's heaven "you don't miss the moment before or long for the moment after" (100)—so very unlike human life on earth that tends to contain a great deal of regret along with dreams or anxieties about the future. In heaven, there is no stress: "Nothing waited for you, because you weren't late for anything" (Black 100). Unlike the experience of humans on earth, "[e]verything [happens] right when it [i]s supposed to happen, and you [are] right there to experience it. In sync. With everything" (Black 100–01). In all of this, moreover, heavenly music is central in its seeming calibration of all celestial movements. In *Fast Lane to Heaven*, finally, Ned Dougherty finds a reassuring sense of permanence: "I [know] that my existence on Earth is transitory. Even the Earth itself is transitory"; "At one time in the past, the Earth did not exist. At some point in the future, it will cease to exist; yet the existence of my soul is eternal" (233).

While the near-death narratives explored here often build on thematic and metaphoric contrasts, the heavens depicted are strikingly and fundamentally free from contrast. The mortal conflicts, the aggressive competition, and the irresolvable discord so prevalent on earth is nonexistent in heaven where beauty, bliss, and perfect unity with God predominate. In *Waking Up in Heaven*, Crystal McVea is overwhelmed with love for God and asks herself why she has not been doing more for God during her earthly life. But this is not regret, she reasons, as she sees regret as a negative emotion. "God wouldn't allow [her] to feel bad about it. There is no feeling bad in heaven" (McVea 150). There is neither death nor negativity in Richard Sigmund's heaven. "There is no fear or dread in heaven," and "no negative emotions; they simply do not exist there" (120). While the narratives are governed by contrasts, then, the events described often lack contrast. In the after-life realm Dougherty comes to, for example, there are no negative thoughts, and even though communication is telepathic and instantaneous, the negative thoughts he has (memories of his own murderous rage that may have contributed to his near-death collapse) cannot be heard by the other spiritual beings. Although preternaturally sensible and receptive in every other way, they are deaf to negativity.

In a discussion of near-death experiences, Bruce Greyson suggests that there are four main aspects: cognitive, affective, paranormal, and transcendent (9). In the works explored here, some of these categories are in evidence. The cognitive feature, firstly, concerns knowledge. One striking aspect of many near-death experiences is their portrayal of a capacity to receive knowledge on inconceivably vast, intricate, and different levels. As already mentioned, in *"Unusual Experiences Near Death and Related Phenomena,"* Kelly, Greyson, and Kelly assert that an "enhanced cognitive function" is "more common among individuals who [are] actually close to death than in those who [are] not so seriously ill" (373). In Dale Black's *Flight to Heaven,* knowledge is automatic and immediate, something that is typical in many other accounts. In *Proof of Heaven,* Eben Alexander writes:

> While beyond my body, I received knowledge about the nature and structure of the universe that was vastly beyond my comprehension. But I received it anyhow, in large part because, with my worldly preoccupations out of the way, I had room to do so. Now that I'm back on earth and remember my bodily identity, the seed of that trans-earthly knowledge has once again been covered over. And yet it's still there. I can feel it, at every moment. It will take years, in this earthly environment, to come to fruition. That is, it will take me years to understand, using my mortal, material brain, what I understood so instantly and easily in the brain-free realms of the world beyond. (81–82)

"Up there," Alexander observes, "a question would arise in my mind, and the answer would arise at the same time, like a flower coming up right next to it. It was almost as if, just as no physical particle in the universe is really separate from another, so in the same way there was no such thing as a question without an accompanying answer." He notes, further, that "[t]hese answers were not simple 'yes' or 'no' fare, either. They were vast conceptual edifices, staggering structures of living thought, as intricate as cities" (83). The meeting with God (or with Om, as Eben Alexander sometimes calls him since 'om' is the sound he "[remembers] hearing associated with that omniscient, omnipotent, and unconditionally loving God" (47) conveys knowledge about the epistemologically extremely advanced constitution and meaning of the entire universe as well as the multiple, interconnected universes that cannot be known or explored from the "lower dimensional space" of the earth although the opposite is possible: "The world of time and space in which we move in this terrestrial realm is tightly and intricately meshed within these higher worlds. In other words, these worlds aren't totally apart from us, because all worlds are part of the same overarching divine Reality. From those higher worlds one could access any time or place in our world" (48–49). In this divine classroom "[insights happen] directly, rather than needing to be coaxed and absorbed. Knowledge [is] stored without memorization, instantly and for good" (49).

In *Fast Lane to Heaven*, Ned Dougherty finds that much of the new knowledge he has acquired in heaven is knowledge that he has already had but has forgotten during his life on earth: "During this part of the experience I thought: 'Oh, yes, of course. Why had I forgotten this?'" (161). God is providing Dougherty with the spiritual knowledge he will need in his return to life, and this new, penetrating knowledge is absorbed by Dougherty on a spiritual level rather than received in words. Surprisingly, although much of the near-death experiences are said to be irreproducible and beyond description, the heavenly music heard by Dougherty (and others) has been reproduced, at least approximately, and Dougherty is able to listen to a sample during a sound laboratory session at a conference. He finds that some of the selections are "similar to or sounding almost exactly like what [he] heard during [his] experience" (187). As in other near-death narratives, Richard Sigmund, too, in *My Time in Heaven*, understands things when he is in heaven that he can neither understand nor remember afterwards. Like several other authors, Sigmund underlines how indescribable his experience in heaven is and how he gains immeasurable knowledge, most of which, however, he is actually not supposed to remember afterwards and "[m]uch of [which] you don't remember because you don't have earthly words to express it" (63). In Sigmund's heaven there are archives with shelves that are "miles long and miles high" and books that are "about fifteen feet tall" (50). When we sin, it is recorded in a book, but on a more hopeful note he also learns that "when we repent, anything that we have done that was wrong or sinful in nature and was recorded in the books is erased for eternity. No one can find the record, not even God" (Sigmund 51). In the archives, tall angels write in these huge books with golden quills. But whereas communication is instantaneous, learning can take time. At the universities in heaven, "many secrets of God were being made known"—many, but obviously not all, since "[t]here is no end to learning" (Sigmund 56). Similarly, although Crystal McVea finds that the "wonderful, beautiful, nourishing sense of knowing" (38) soaked up in heaven becomes inaccessible afterwards, she knows that she and her angels have "exchanged mountains of insight in a constant, free-flowing, wordless, beautiful conversation" (188). The angels that await McVea beyond death are also her teachers and mentors.

Another cognitive feature concerns communication. Many of these near-death narratives depict the beauty and the staggering complexity of a post-death explosion of light and sound, of intricate and instantaneous patterns 'happening' all at once and experienced without any separation between hearing and seeing or between source and receiver. This heavenly ultra-immediacy of total immanence and belonging also marks communication. In *Proof of Heaven,* as soon as Eben Alexander asks himself a question (about who he is, for example, or why he is in this place), a wordless answer "[comes] instantly in an explosion of light, color, love, and beauty that [blows] through [him] like a crashing wave" (46). Thoughts appear not in a "vague, immaterial, or abstract" but in a "solid and immediate" way, and "as [he receives] them [he is] able to instantly and effortlessly understand concepts that would have taken [him] years to fully grasp in [his] earthly life" (46). Similarly, in Mary C. Neal's *To Heaven and Back,* spiritual beings "simultaneously [communicate their] thoughts and emotions, and [understand] each other perfectly even though [they do] not use language" (70). Neal attempts to describe her experience: "We did not speak, *per se,* using our mouths, but easily communicated in a very pure form" (69–70). In Freddy Vest's *The Day I Died,* communication with Jesus is wordless, completely beyond language, and in Ned Dougherty's *Fast Lane to Heaven,* communication is telepathic and entirely nonverbal. Already from the beginning, Dougherty is told that he is going to have to 'go back,' and that it will be a part of his mission to bring the knowledge he has gained back with him. Movement itself is by thought: "I willed it, and the movement was accomplished" (21). In *Fast Lane to Heaven,* Ned Dougherty and his guide at one point approach a suspended amphitheater filled with spiritual beings, thousands of them, who know all about Dougherty's life—"[t]here are no secrets in the spiritual realms" (86)—and who are "communicating, by musical sounds, feelings of goodwill to [Dougherty]," greetings that are "in harmony with the symphonic sounds of energy emanating from the amphitheater" (31).

Since they constitute another way of knowing, prophecies could be seen as a third cognitive feature. During his near-death experience, Dougherty is shown scenes both from his own future and the future of the world. In his own life, he learns, there will be momentous changes. His previous materialistic existence will end and he will instead become involved in helping the poor and needy, learn about ancient civilizations, create a foundation

("Mission of Angels)," write, and travel. As for the future of the world, the Lady of Light he encounters points pedagogically and concretely, with flashpoints to a globe of earth, terrorism, war, and nature catastrophes. Some aspects of the prophecies have already come true, according to Dougherty (for example, "[f]anatical, self-proclaimed religious groups supposedly acting in the name of God" [77]). However, although the future cataclysmic events are terrifying scenarios, they are "not part of God's plan," and they *can* be postponed or abrogated altogether from God's agenda *if* humanity returns to God through prayer and through listening meditations (77). Richard Sigmund, too, comes across prophecies. In *My Time in Heaven*, he finds areas that show things to come. In his childhood heaven Sigmund has already met a smiling Jesus who tells him not to drink, smoke, or sin, since Sigmund is cut out for important work later on. In his adult meeting with Jesus he is told: "I have called you as a prophet to the nations" (114). There will be great revivals, he learns, and Jesus also mentions "some very personal and private things about [Sigmund's] life" (115).

A fourth cognitive feature is the life review that many near-death travellers undergo along with soul-searching questions about their lives. This is part of a learning (or unlearning) process. For Ned Dougherty, the life review is "not just lifelike; it [is] reality itself," and he is also "third-person witness to events that [he has] not previously witnessed" (35–36). Mary Neal passes through a life review with Jesus whereby she comes to fully realize the importance of her choices, words, and actions as well as their impact not only on those close to her, but on people who might be many times removed, and she understands that every decision we make has consequences that are more far-reaching than we can ever imagine.

A fifth cognitive feature is the idea that bypassing the brain or the mind can lead to new knowledge. Some thinkers theorize that the brain itself is in the way and that it is only when the usual, incessant 'clutter' of thoughts is eliminated that pure consciousness can emerge. As Kelly, Greyson, and Kelly see it, there is a "dogma that brain produces mind, or is the mind" (385). They suggest an alternative view whereby the brain is rather more of an obstacle and propose "that brain activity normally serves as a kind of filter" so that when this filter is 'relaxed' there may be an "enhancement or enlargement of consciousness" (385). In a chapter on mysticism, Kelly and Grosso mention Aldous Huxley, who saw "psychedelic agents as impairing or suspending this filtering action and thus permitting the inflowing or uprush of Mind at Large with its intrinsically greater capacities" (550). Kelly and Grosso propose that "what psychedelics have in common with all other means of producing mystical states may consist … in some sort of more global disruption or 'loosening' of the normal mind-brain connection" (551).

Analogously, Dale Black comments on his memories of heaven: "They bypassed my conscious brain. If I thought too much, they resisted revealing themselves" (97). Interestingly, Black's method of letting his brain relax when he is lying on his back in a football field gazing up to the stars resembles techniques of hypnosis, and some thinkers have in fact suggested that hypnosis is the best way to remember lost memories. It is when Black lets go that memories return, "[replaying] themselves like one long, continuous movie" (98). Similarly, as Freddy Vest puts it: "The filter of my intellect was out of the way" (65). No thinking is necessary, and 'Vest' has no thoughts, not even of his family, his horses, or his life on earth. Heaven, he writes, is "not a place of thinking but of being" (65). Mary Neal suggests that the usual mental clutter clears away when we find ourselves in difficult situations, and in this clutter-free space it is easier to hear God's voice. Finally, Crystal McVea writes: "I was flooded with self-knowledge, and all the junk that cluttered my identity on Earth instantly fell away, revealing, for the first time ever, the real me" (12).

It is when the filter falls away that Eben Alexander experiences a complete sense of belonging: "Far from being an unimportant by-product of physical processes (as I had thought before my experience)," he writes, "consciousness is not only very real—It's actually *more real* than the rest of physical experience), and most likely the basis of it all" (150, italics in original). Alexander continues: "What I discovered out beyond is the indescribable immensity and complexity of the universe, and that *consciousness* is the basis of all that exists. I was so totally connected to it that there was often no real differentiation between 'me' and the world I was moving through" (Alexander 154–55).

In the cases examined by Kelly, Greyson, and Kelly, many people who had near-death experiences "describe the experience as being altogether unlike a dream, in that their mental processes during the NDE were remarkably clear and lucid and their sensory experiences unusually vivid, equaling or even surpassing those of their normal waking state" (386). These are of course subjective experiences, but "the frequency and consistency of such reports are impressive" (386), and it is difficult to explain the "occurrence of vivid and complex mentation, sensation, and memory under conditions in which current neuroscientific models of the mind deem conscious experience of any significant sort impossible" (Kelly, Greyson, and Kelly 415).

Rhetorically emphasizing his own rational and scientific attitude, Eben Alexander says: "I'm not a soft-headed sentimentalist. I know what death looks like…. I know the difference between fantasy and reality, and I know that the experience I'm struggling to give you the vaguest, most completely unsatisfactory picture of, was the single most real experience of my life" (41). To add to the sense of realism and to discuss possible 'scientific' explanations for his experience, Alexander also includes an appendix about neuroscientific hypotheses (185–88). For Ned Dougherty in *Fast Lane to Heaven*, not only is the near-death experience "more real than reality"; he says that "[u]nlike normal dreams, which I usually remembered after waking and then forgot, these events became more real as I reviewed them,"; "when I was shown things that had happened around me that I could not possibly have known, that confirmed for me that this was not a hallucination, dream, or fantasy" (98, 103–04). "Everything I describe is absolutely, 100 percent how I remember it—that has always been my one and only rule for sharing my testimony," as McVea puts it (4). Her statement about her near-death experience is typical: "What I experienced in heaven was so real and so lucid and so utterly intense, it made my experiences on Earth seem hazy and out of focus—as if heaven is the reality and life as we know it is just a dream" (McVea 12–13).

Notions of truth are also central in these near-death narratives. A desire for truth, evident already in the titles of many of these publications (examples being 'proof' of heaven in Alexander's title and a 'True Story' in the subtitles of Dale Black's, Mary Neal's, Crystal McVea's, and Richard Sigmund's stories), is uppermost. As Black underlines: "Truth is what prevails and has supremacy in heaven" (104). Significantly, Eben Alexander begins with a quote from Albert Einstein (placed at the beginning of his Prologue): "A man should look for what is, and not for what he thinks should be." This quote could be seen as representative of many of the near-death autobiographies.

Let us now turn to the transcendent features that mark the near-death narratives explored in this chapter. Central in all these narratives are the descriptions and notions of God and descriptions of how an encounter with God totally transforms the near-death travellers. Some report seeing glimpses of God or sensing a presence and sometimes even experiencing an encounter with divinity. In Eben Alexander's *Proof of Heaven*, firstly, 'Alexander' enters an "immense void, completely dark, infinite in size, yet also infinitely comforting" (47). Trying to describe this spiritual realm, Alexander points to a line by Henry Vaughan: "*There is, some say, in God a deep but dazzling darkness*" (48, italics in original); in Alexander's case, "[p]itch black as it was, it is also brimming over with light: a light that seemed to come from a brilliant orb that [he] now [senses] near [him]" (47). This orb, 'Alexander' realizes, is an interpreter between him and God, and the orb turns out to be somehow connected to the girl he has met earlier, "who in fact *was* she" (47), and who is his guide. He continues: "It was as if I were being born into a larger world, and the universe itself was like a giant cosmic womb" (47):

> The fetus floats in the womb with the silent partner of the placenta, which nourishes it and mediates its relationship to the everywhere present yet at the same time invisible mother. In this case, the "mother" was God, the Creator, the Source who is responsible for making the universe and all in it. This Being was so close that there seemed to be no distance at all between God and myself. Yet at the same time, I could sense the infinite vastness of the Creator, could see how completely miniscule I was by comparison. (47)

Looking back on his near-death-experience, Eben Alexander reflects:

> So I was communicating directly with God? Absolutely. Expressed that way, it sounds grandiose. But when it was happening, it didn't feel that way. Instead, I felt like I was doing what every soul is able to do when they leave their bodies, and what we can all do right now through various methods of prayer or deep meditation. Communicating with God is the most extraordinary experience imaginable, yet at the same time it's the most natural one of all, because God is present in us at all times. Omniscient, omnipotent, personal—and loving us without conditions. We are connected as One through our divine link with God. (161)

"The universe has no beginning and no end," Alexander goes on to say, "and God is entirely present within every particle of it" (156). In trying to understand the nature of God, most people bring God down to their own level, and as to the higher spiritual worlds, "[w]e taint, with our insufficient descriptions, their truly awesome nature" (157). Although the universe has no end and no beginning, there are, however, in Alexander's view, punctuation marks, one such punctuation mark being the Big Bang. Alexander has an actual conversation with God, who teaches him remarkable things, such as, for example, that there is not one universe but several and that love is the fundamental principle in all of them. After the journey Alexander thinks: "At last, I understood what religion was all about. Or at least what it was supposed to be about. I didn't just believe in God; I knew God" (148).

Similarly, in *Fast Lane to Heaven*, Ned Dougherty describes how "revelations were conveyed to [him]" (26): "As God was bestowing a radiant energy upon me, I recognized that the energy contained information about universal laws, revelations that were part of God's plan for the universe" (26). In this way, God "[imbues] him with universal knowledge" (25). In *Fast Lane to Heaven*, God is described in images of a strong, white light, resembling sunlight but vastly more powerful but still not blinding. More like an embracing energy, this light enters Dougherty's being from the top of his head. God is a "magnificent presence": "I immediately believed that I was in the presence of God, my Creator. I felt that God was embracing me, and He had love for me, a love greater than any love I had ever known on earth. I realized that God was bestowing His light of love on me, as His light transformed from a brilliant golden light to a pure white light. As I became more accepting of God's love, the light of God became brighter, of a pure whiteness beyond description" (Dougherty 24). In Dougherty's near-death experience, then, God is light and energy. God is embracing him and transmitting a cleansing and purifying, overflowing love. God also shows Dougherty how he has lost track when he gave up searching for universal knowledge. Heaven is a completely different sort of classroom: "I realized that I could communicate directly with God and learn directly from Him," but while he is desirous to learn more about God he is told that "to know Him would take an eternity" (28). He learns that our life as souls goes back to "the beginning of the creation of the universe" and that we are enrolled in "spiritual schools of learning in preparation for further growth and understanding" (28). On one level, earthly life is a school, and we have all been endowed with brains and free will, even though on another level God has already decided the outcome: "It is our goal, individually and collectively, through all history and time, and through all dimensions and space, to reunite and become one with God" (Dougherty 29).

In *Waking Up in Heaven*, Crystal McVea experiences God as a 'being.' Knowing instantly that it is God, and she is overcome with "a profound, endless desire to praise and worship this being" (89). McVea's God does not have a form or a face, and certainly no body, he is "just a blinding profusion of brightness" (89). The light McVea sees is "a trillion times whiter than the whitest white you've ever seen or could imagine. It was brilliant and beaming and beautifully illuminating" (13). It also has a purity, a perfection, a "sensation of cleanliness," as well as love and peace: "It was like being bathed in love" (13). In passages that recall Ned Dougherty's sense in *Fast Lane to Heaven* of a restoration of lost and forgotten knowledge, McVea writes that the light feels "familiar, like something I remembered, or even recognized" (13). McVea perceives no "distinction between God, Jesus, and the Holy Spirit," "[they are] all One" (89). In a description recalling Teresa of Àvila's vision of sensing Jesus on her right side and his presence around her, for McVea, God is brightness, he is on her right side, he is all around her, too, and she is also feeling him. "In heaven," she explains, "we don't have just five senses; we have a ton of senses" (90). There is beauty, joy, and ecstasy, and McVea knows that she is changed forever by this experience. Her love for God has an "intensity and immensity" and she concludes: "There is simply no other love remotely like it" (91). Whereas questions of Theodicé—how to reconcile the evil in the world with the idea that God is both omniscient and omnipotent—might bother us on earth, such questions 'evaporate' in heaven where McVea understands that "God's plan is perfect" and "all the questions [she had] for God [are] answered without [her] even having to ask them" (91). In Crystal McVea's story there is a total sense of belonging: "I was *completely* infused by God's brightness and His love, and I wanted to enter into His brightness and intertwine myself completely with it. I felt a miraculous closeness to God but wanted to feel even *closer* (90).

For Dale Black in *Flight to Heaven*, Jesus is "the Word," "the structure that [holds] it all together. Like the rib cage around the heart. He [is] the creative power that [brings] everything that I [see] into place and [stabilizes] it" (104), and God is the heart of heaven, something that recalls Richard Sigmund's story, where there is a place where "you can feel and hear the throbbing heart of God" (85). In Sigmund's heaven, God has a throne—The Throne of God—at "the very center of the universe, the center of all existence," the place where everything began (88), and approaching this place, the millions of people in and around the fifty miles high Throne Building, feel a "reverential fear" (107). Rather terrifyingly, in front of the Throne there is a basin "filled with the blood of Jesus" (111). Disappointingly, despite all the preliminaries, 'Sigmund' never actually sees God. He senses that there is a 'Being' on the throne that radiates great power. Surprisingly, however, 'Sigmund' is allowed to see one of God's feet and notices that "[h]is foot seemed the size of the United States, and His toe looked the size of Tennessee" (109). There are "waves of liquid love" coming forth from God (111). As already mentioned, the center of heaven is like a heart, and 'Sigmund' understands that "everything in heaven flowed into and out of the Throne. It pulsed like a dynamo" (105).

Jesus appears in most of the near-death narratives studied here, although in difference guises. Finding time to ponder her own life and her relationship to God during her drowning accident, Mary Neal has the under-standing that Jesus is able to be present for her while at the same time being present with everyone else who requires his help. In Richard Sigmund's narrative, too, Jesus is available to everyone, and even though people have to wait their turn to talk to him, Jesus appears to be omnipresent. At one point, he walks onto an auditorium like a rock star to the "thunderous praise, worship, and adoration" of onlookers, and his voice is "like rushing waters, metallic" (86). On this occasion, Jesus speaks about eternity—but Sigmund is "not allowed to remember it" (86). Sigmund's Jesus has a "reddish-brown beard" and a body that is "hard as steel" (113, 116). Jesus takes 'Sigmund' to see hell, an area that turns out to be the exact opposite of heaven with black gates, grotesque beings, flames of punishment, and naked people being raped and tortured (117). Terrifyingly, there are "pits of hell that [are] empty now, but waiting for whole nations," and there is a "place reserved for the devil and his angels: he will have flaming, slimy fire over his head for a thousand years" (119). More reassuringly, with Jesus, 'Sigmund' is "engulfed in a torrent, a flood of the greatest love and most absolute acceptance that [he has] ever known" (120).

In Freddy Vest's *The Day I Died* there are no accompanying angels, nor is there any experience of travelling through a tunnel. Instead, from one moment to another, Vest finds himself with Jesus in a realm of complete freedom where Vest is neither thinking about death nor feeling any sadness or regret. To the contrary, in an instant, everything is perfect, and Vest is "utterly content in [his] eternal destination" (62). He has no doubt at all that he is with Jesus: "It was not my mind that told me so; my mind had been left behind" (62). Being with Jesus is *all* that matters for Vest: "There with Jesus, drenched in the perfect serenity that every human being longs to know, I had it all. The Garden of Eden could not have been better. The undisturbed peace Scripture describes was now mine. No effort was required to achieve it. It just was" (62–63). In Vest's heaven, there are no sensations. Nor does he see any heavenly mansions, angels, or deceased relatives. Instead, Vest's experience of heaven is completely focused on Jesus. Just as in Richard Sigmund's heaven, there is a sense that Jesus is omnipresent. It is as if Jesus is able to clone himself limitlessly and be with everyone who needs him at the same time. And yet, as Vest writes: "His attention was undivided. It did not matter how many had just entered heaven; He and I were alone" (63). Vest's total sense of belonging is expressed in the following words: "It was as though Jesus had wrapped His arms around me and drawn me into Himself, where all that was not of Him dissolved. Every weight and care of the natural life was replaced with His love" (63). Heaven is completely safe and peaceful as well as timeless, in Vest's experience. It is home, and nothing can detract from this sense of all-encompassing unity: "I could not be separated from Him. Everything was Him and Him only. I experienced the oneness I'd read about in Scripture," and Vest is 'consumed' by this: "I was with Him, but also in Him. Really, there was no difference between the two. His presence was all-encompassing. Nothing was outside of Him or beyond Him" (64). This, however, does not mean that 'Vest' is equal to Jesus: "He was my exalted Lord and King. I was His subject and thrilled with the arrangement" (64).

Another recurring transcendent feature is the appearance of angels. Most of the authors encounter spiritual beings, welcoming guides, "transparent orbs" or "winged beings" in Alexander's case (45). Are they birds or angels? Alexander wonders. "But neither of these words do justice to the beings themselves, which were quite simply different from anything [he has] known on this planet. They were more advanced. *Higher*" (Alexander 45). According to Mary Neal in *To Heaven and Back*, angels turn up more than 250 times in the Bible. Usually, we are not aware of angels, but Neal believes that "there are angels all around us every day of our lives" and that they "are the ones orchestrating the 'coincidences' that occur so commonly in our lives" (99). In Neal's view, in real life, angels can appear in many shapes and guises such as fish or birds or as the Chilean men who "[materialize] out of nowhere" to help carry Neal from the river bank to an ambulance after her drowning accident (75). For some time after her near-death experience, Neal is still able to move between worlds. While still in the hospital, on one occasion, she is suddenly transported into a sunny field where an angel is sitting on a rock, a "messenger, Christ, or teacher," and she knows without a doubt that "he [is] of God, in God, and from God" (98). Neal believes that it is with Jesus she is talking in this field, and she describes him thus: "He was wearing some sort of flowing robe and exploded with beauty and brilliance. His hair was long. His features were indistinct," and "He conveyed the impression of complete love, compassion, kindness, and infinite patience" (216). In her conversation with this angel Neal learns that "[w]e are each given the opportunity and privilege to come to earth for different reasons," to develop certain character traits (such as kindness or self-control) but above all to become more Christ-like. As spiritual beings, our journeys on earth are charted by God while we ourselves are "able to make a basic outline for our life"; "[w]ithin the algorithm are written branch points in our lives at which times we may exit, returning to God, or we may be redirected to a different task and goal" (98). In a later meeting with the angel Neal knows will be their last she realizes that much of what she has learnt is going to be "placed beneath a veil"; she feels that she "could later choose to lift the veil and recall all of the words said to [her] if [she] really [wants] to, but [she] also [knows] that [she is] expected to let them remain veiled" (106).

While Crystal McVea's near-death experience does not include any deceased relatives, she does go through a tunnel in the company of her own two angels towards a bright light that she knows is the gate of heaven. The angels seem to have a slender form but McVea cannot really determine their shape since they are emitting so much light. She feels safe, secure, and free with these angels, and there is "instant and complete communication," a "profound connection and an eternal bond" (38). In Dale Black's story there is no tunnel but a pathway along which he discovers that he is accompanied by two male angels. Crystal McVea and Richard Sigmund, too, are accompanied by two angels on his grand tour of heaven. One of the chapters in Richard Sigmund's book is devoted to "Classes of Angels" and their rank and duties. Some angels keep records of all our thoughts and deeds, 'Sigmund' learns, and he sees an angel with a heavy-looking book (that "might have weighed several hundred pounds on earth" [97]). There are armies of huge angels endowed with flaming swords that exit heaven to come down and help us on earth.

Part of the transcendent aspects, prayer is central in most of these near-death narratives. In all the difficult or life-threatening situations that occur on her spiritual journey, Mary Neal turns to God in prayer. In a chapter entitled "The Power of Prayer," many people pray for Neal when it is uncertain that she will survive the night. Gradually, Neal's understanding of prayer is transformed. At one point, her vision is blurred, and she is unable to read or watch television. Turning to the Bible, she is only able to read the three verses from 1 Thessalonians that exhort us to "Rejoice always, pray continually, and give thanks in all circumstances" (1 Thessalonians 5:16–18).

What stands out in all of these narratives is the total conviction of the reality of what the authors have experienced beyond death. This is a feature in many accounts of mystic experiences and out-of-body experiences as well. The writers themselves in no way doubt what has happened. Even though they are unable to fully communicate what they have experienced, for these writers, heaven is real. Words fail, language becomes inadequate. And yet, these authors feel compelled to communicate in some measure what they have experienced since they feel that it is their mission to convey as best as they can the message of God's reality and Heaven's certainty. The accounts do not labour to delineate social and historical circumstances, nor do they wish to challenge or develop theological concepts or religious creeds beyond the simple picture of God's presence and the purpose of faith.

As already emphasized, most of these narratives build on contrast. Structurally, the narrative in Eben Alexander's *Proof of Heaven*, firstly, alternates between two levels. Spatially, it moves in two directions: downwards (as when Eben Alexander is skydiving and parachuting and when he is sinking into a murky, muddy lower post-death region, and upwards (as when he is soaring into the highest spiritual realms). The body is mainly associated with falling imagery while the spirit soars high above our accustomed material and worldly existence.

As if echoing the description of the apostles Peter and John, who are described as "unschooled, ordinary men" (Acts 4:13), another common trait is that these writers see themselves as ordinary people who are exposed to something extraordinary before being called back to life to tell their stories. Narrative contrast is commonly created by portraying the protagonist as an utterly ordinary person. Crystal McVea sees herself as "a run-of-the-mill American mom living in the heartland" (4), "ordinary in every way" (221). Freddy Vest portrays himself as "a simple man" (101): "All I have to offer is an extraordinary story about heaven, from the life of an average guy—me" (115). Richard Sigmund holds himself up as completely ordinary and has no idea why God has chosen him: "I am the most ordinary man you have ever seen" (79). In this way, the stories they tell stand out as even more extraordinary compared to the persons who have these experiences. The approach, tone, narrative, and scope range from the ordinary to the unfathomable, from the commonplace to the grandiose, from the quotidian to the miraculous, and from fear and tragedy to joy. In *Proof of Heaven*, Eben Alexander places his rational, scientific before-death self in stark contrast to the rock certainty after his near-death experience. Ned Dougherty, on the other hand, contrasts his earlier materialistic, success-oriented, fast-lane persona, "by nature cynical and disbelieving" (212), with his prophetic after-near-death personality. Another striking contrast is the one between a scientific language, approach, and world view, and a post-linguistic, epistemologically elusive dimension. There is also a contrast between the material body and a bodiless state, between the apparently linear and chronological time as we know it and the timeless realm of an all-engulfing (in the first part of the story) or all-encompassing (in the higher dimension) present. In Eben Alexander's book there is also a striking contrast between the boundaries of our rationally conceived known everyday world, and the boundaryless and memoryless consciousness of the identityless point of awareness he is in the Realm of the Earthworm's Eye. There is the material, earthly world and, as Alexander puts it, "that world out there—a world so vast that as you journeyed in it you could lose your very sense of your earthly self and become a pure part of the cosmos, the God-soaked and love-filled darkness" (169).

All the stories discussed here—Eben Alexander's *Proof of Heaven*, Dale Black's *Flight to Heaven*, Ned Dougherty's *Fast Lane to Heaven*, Crystal McVea's *Waking Up in Heaven*, Mary C. Neal's *To Heaven and Back*, Richard Sigmund's *My Time in Heaven*, Freddy Vest's *The Day I Died*—build on a classical three-point plot of the time before, a turning-point experience, and a profound transformation. Eben Alexander goes from rationalist and skeptic to believer or, more precisely, knower ("I didn't just believe in God; I knew God" [148]). Like Alexander, Dale Black has regarded himself as a scientific-minded and pragmatic realist who has come to total faith in God, in Black's case to the extent that he decides to put more faith in the healing of God than in an operation his doctor tells him is necessary if he wants to walk again. Black trusts in God and is healed. Ned Dougherty's *Fast Lane to Heaven* is the story of a self-made man who turns away from the sins of materialism, arrogance, and abuse towards a life of faith and service for others.

One aspect that will not be discussed here is the development of paranormal abilities after near-death experiences reported by Kelly et al. Ned Dougherty finds that "a number of significant mystical experiences [are] now occurring to [him] on a regular basis" after his near-death experience, and he is "guided by inspiration and interior locutions" (213). The telepathic communication Dougherty has experienced during his near-death experience continues and he finds that he can see and understand people's auras (127). In a chapter on mystical experiences (states that may resemble near-death experiences), the perceptual, cognitive, and expressive capacities of individuals may be changed, according to Kelly and Grosso, who "have encountered several individuals who informally reported noting sudden and dramatic increases in their perceptual acuity, reading speed, problem-solving ability, memory capacities, and the like," changes that were "permanent or slowly fading over periods of weeks to months" (523). Reports about mystics of all times whether of Hindu or Christian or other spiritual traditions are full of instances of the miraculous.[9]

Although she does not want to return to life, after her near-death experience Crystal McVea realizes that her life has changed and that she is changed herself and liberated from the heavy mental baggage she has been burdened with for so long. McVea has gone from being "plagued by doubts and fears" to "an absolute certainty about who [she is]" (12). Not only does she go from being (or regarding herself as) a sinner, she goes from being a doubter—"the ultimate skeptic, demanding proof, setting conditions, challenging God" (138)—to having complete faith in God. She has become less materialistic and more balanced, and she says: "Nothing bothered me or made me angry anymore, and I overflowed with compassion and love" (181). She goes from "[t]he sinner and the skeptic, the one with all the questions" (39) to someone who is absolutely certain about issues of faith.

In a final chapter entitled "Logical Conclusions," Mary Neal delineates the lessons she has learned from her spiritual journey: a firm belief in the support, love, and the promises of God, a conviction that God has set certain tasks for her to do, and a belief that heaven is real. She concludes by turning to the reader with the proposal of keeping a journal for six months to a year, noting good and bad things which will lead to the detection of "evidence of God's work in your life" and to the discovery of miracles (208). Freddy Vest's trip to Heaven is a "life-altering experience—so intense," he says, "that I dared not speak of it lightly. Not even my family would know the story until a couple days after I came back" (91). Commenting on the consequences of his heart attack, his wife says: he is "calmer and gentler than ever" (87). Although he is doing God's will, however, Vest's life has not gone from sinning to saintliness. He confesses to not being "spiritually ablaze every moment" (112), and sometimes, he would prefer to do his own thing!

The texts discussed in this chapter resemble sermons in their missionary impulse and impetus to share the remarkable sights seen and insights reached. Indeed, in many of these near-death narratives, there is a clear missionary intent. Crystal McVea writes: "God wants me to share my story with others in the hopes that they, too, can accept His salvation" (231). Wondering why he was 'sent back' to earth, Freddy Vest finds the answer in Jeremiah 1:7: "You must go to everyone I send you to and say whatever I

---

[9] One report mentioned by Kelly et al. is that of Herbert Thurston from 1952 examining "innumerable volumes of Catholic hagiography in search of serious evidence of supernormal phenomena in the lives of the saints" (528).

command you." In other words, Vest, comparing himself to the prophet Jeremiah, speaks to people about his journey to heaven because he feels that God is asking him to so, but he does not strain to tell it to everyone. But there is a clear purpose: "He sent me back so that I might bear witness to you, because He has a plan for your life too!" (116). *The Day I Died* has a strong missionary intent, and Freddy Vest assures other Christians about what awaits them after death: they will go to Heaven. Anyone who is unsure is encouraged by Vest to believe, to take Jesus into their hearts, and accept Jesus' sacrifice. Dale Black's *Flight to Heaven*, similarly, is a missionary tale, since both Black and his wife (in a short postscript) invite the reader to embrace faith in God.

One question that arises when reading these near-death narratives is how to explain their great popularity. Personal and spiritual development has become one of the megatrends of our time. The popularity of the near-death narratives could be understood within this framework. One might also surmise that they are related to our fear of death. In Western society, death has become hidden away and almost denied, something that could increase cultural fears of death and dying. That is how Freddy Vest explains the wonder of the message of heaven: "If you think about it (and Scripture bears it out), all fear boils down to the same root: the fear of death" (107). Vest goes on to say: "When it is answered with God's ultimate peace—when you know that death has been settled through the death and resurrection of Jesus Christ—nothing can make you afraid" (108). This assurance is reserved for Christians alone: "Those who call Him Savior can rest in peace for real and forever. That is why the Christian need not fear anything, not even death" (108), something that, according to Vest, is "one giant gulp of hope!" (108).

Many of these near-death narratives elicit incredulity. Some of the episodes described are hard to believe, and one must reserve the right to regard them with a great deal of skepticism. It is also difficult to determine the nature of many of the authors' visionary or mystic experiences, often construed as divinely ordained episodes enmeshed in a coherent, logical story whose teleological progression forward points to individual and global salvation, as in some cases with prophetic visionaries playing a decisive role as alarm-clocks or inspiring lights. But we could leave aside the issues of veracity and credibility connected with these publications. Whether these stories are veridical or not, they seem to point to timeless existential needs while indicating what is missing in contemporary culture. With the plus sides of heaven in relief, the minuses of contemporary culture emerge more clearly. Whereas notions of truth, reality, identity, and permanence connected with the grand narratives of western history have been problematized by post-modernist thinkers, the need for such notions seems not to have not gone away. While life in contemporary society is riddled with fears, pressures, and stress, in heaven there is total peace. As Freddy Vest puts it: "No question lacked an answer. No fear could flourish. There were no needs at all and no demands to be met. Pressure was nonexistent" (63). Heaven, as Freddy Vest succinctly sums it up, is "the bliss we all crave" (111). The near-death experiences discussed here may be as subjectively true as they are culturally conditioned, and it is on this level that these 'outlandish' journeys may add to the understanding of spirituality in our time.

Whatever the veracity and factuality of the near-death experiences narrated in these spiritual autobiographies, then, one might agree with Bruce Greyson's words in "The Mystical Impact of Near-Death Experiences": "At the very least, near-death experiences should foster spiritual growth by leading us to question some of our basic assumptions about mind and brain, about our relationship to the divine, and about the universe and our role in it" (13).

Spiritual Autobiography Today

While people living hundreds of years ago eked out their existence within an all-encompassing religious framework that permeated scientific and cultural pursuits as well, human beings in the West today generally do not explain the mystery of life with references to God. Events or accidents that happen are rarely explained as the rewards, punishments, or warnings from God. At the same time, researchers in theology and religious studies note that while the interest in the God of monotheistic Abrahamic religions has been decreasing in Europe there is an increasing interest in other forms of spirituality, something that indicates that there is still a great existential need for religion and spirituality. While traditional institutions and religious authorities seem to be losing power, private cosmologies and 'alternative' spiritualities are gaining ground. In his article "Renaissance of Religion: Clarifications to a Disputed Topic," Hans Joachim Höhn proposes that even if society is increasingly secularized, religious practice will continue in post-secular society, and the demythologization expected upon the progress in science and technology has not taken place. Employing a negative food metaphorics, theologian Werner Jeanrond finds that contemporary spirituality in the West resembles a vast supermarket selling a variety of religious junk food, a fare that may not satisfy a hunger for God's alterity. Religion becomes a commodity among others to be consumed.

During the twentieth century, the development of the discipline of psychology led to a distinction between religion on institutional levels and religion as a private experience, something that influenced the development towards a division between church and state. In the most recent decades, spirituality has become a commodity among others to be consumed thanks to the ideas of humanistic psychology but also to the discipline of psychology itself as well as to an individualist and materialist consumer society, according to Jeremy Carrette and Richard King in *Selling Spirituality: The Silent Takeover of Religion*. As with any commodity, there is a risk of addiction, and this type of individualized and privatized spirituality has become a drug in a culture of excess, a cultural Prozac that can only offer passing feelings of bliss, a "psychological sedative for a culture that is in the process of rejecting the values of community and social justice," a spirituality that is "co-opted by the desiring machine of consumerism" (83). Worse, while people today believe that they have freed themselves from the dogma of traditional and oppressive religions, unwittingly, in their consumption of new spiritualities, they have become the victims of and even slaves to the insidiously authoritarian 'thought-control' of globalized capitalism:

> While 'New Age' followers dance the gospel of self-expression they service the financial agents and chain themselves to a spirituality of consumerism. While they selectively ravage the feel-good fabric of ancient cultural and religious traditions, their disciplines and practices can easily isolate them from the resources of social justice and community to be found within those traditions. (Carrette and King 78)

What Carrette and King call "psychological-capitalist spirituality" offers an illusion: the "illusion of a unified self is the market subject, the consuming agent, necessary for the function of late capitalistic societies. Its illusion is that the self somehow exists in isolation, when it is in fact a product of a complex network of economic, political, cultural and social interactions" (80). For Carrette and King, an individualized and privatized spirituality is inevitably linked to "a closed self" (81). In ways that recall both classical thinkers such as Auguste Compte and modern secularist philosophers such as Alain de Botton, Carrette and King propose a utilitarian and instru-mentalist view of religion and spirituality as a means to social integration and social justice. Whereas theirs is a functional theology that finds religion useful when it changes the world or provides a good *group* feeling, the most fundamental raison d'être of religion remains inaccessible if one dwells only in a horizontal dimension of social change. As long as the primary purpose and priority of a spirituality is not to work for 'alternative' models of social justice, it is merely a sedative in the view of Carrette and King, a spirituality deserving the derogatory label of a 'capitalist spirituality' that actually *causes* "individual suffering, loneliness and isolation" and that "operates according to the dictates of global capitalism" and the "colonization of our collective cultural heritage" (85, 171). Even though the authors affirm that they are "not denying the reality of the individual agent," their approving reference to David Smail's view that we need "a moral reformation of our public, not our private ways of life" (qtd. by Carrette and King 81), gives an indication of the extent to which Carrette and King emphasize societal perspectives. In fact, their social justice goal places religion and spirituality in a subordinate role. While drawing upon the Indian parable of the blind men and an elephant in rightfully arguing that selective western uses of Asian spiritualities merely capture small aspects of an ungraspable greater whole, in their insistence on the socially transformative aspects of religion, Carrette and King themselves see only a part of the needs for and purposes of religion: "The use of an idea such as 'spirituality' is *always* bound up with political questions, even when the term is defined in apparently apolitical terms (in which case it supports the status quo" (172). In the view of Carrette and King, capitalism, the Market, and neoliberalism are agents that have agendas, explicit goals, and even a missionary activity "to convert the people of the world into consumers" and worshippers of "the new religion of the contemporary (postmodern) world," that is, capitalism; and there is a "missionary project" going on in mass media, education, and advertising whose theology is neoliberalist (174).[1]

Carrette and King's typology of modern spiritualities is intriguing, but their Marxist-inflected inversion of the 'accomodationist' aspects of spiritual and personal development literature in charging that it seeks "to pacify feelings of anxiety and disquiet at the individual level rather than seeking to challenge the social, political and economic inequalities that cause such distress" (22) is simplistic, and their views of the purposes of spirituality and religion remain rationalist, secularist, and instrumentalist.

If we posit the new expressions of spirituality as part of a 'return of religion,' we may ask if the writers of spiritual autobiographies are sellers on a market of world views and life philosophies or if they are new intermediators on the boundary between immanence and transcendence. Similarly, we may ask if the contemporary spiritual autobiography should be compared to a self-help literature that, as Jo Woodiwiss puts it in "What's Wrong with Me? A Cautionary Tale of Using Contemporary 'Damage Narratives' in Autobiographical Life Writing," "encourages the construction of narratives that identify an inner world of damage at the expense of the external world, and in doing so ultimately render events or experiences irrelevant to the construction of one's autobiography" (186). Such a need to

---

[1] Promoting anti-capitalist or *alter-mondialiste* views of politics and spirituality and ideas of community as sites of resistance, Carrette and King support Third World liberation theologies and movements such as the Zapatistas, Socially Engaged Buddhism, and movements building on Gandhi and Hindu Vedanta traditions (180).

reorganize one's life story and to find 'new stories' is indeed predominant in the literature of self-help and self-improvement. Although a discussion of this literature is outside the scope of the present study, it is interesting to note its similarities and parallels to the contemporary spiritual auto-biography.

Today, "educated in a therapeutic discourse of the emotions" we "turn our own 'cases' into stories, and become the authors of our own plot," as Nicholas Rose puts it in *Governing the Soul* (257). Jo Woodiwiss argues that a particular narrative framework informed by the therapeutic culture in which we live dominates in contemporary self-help accounts, narratives of progression whose conscious or unconscious starting point is damage of some kind (childhood trauma, abuse, or the uprooting of adoption) leading to an end point of healing, a journey that is propelled by the individual assuming responsibility for her own healing. In these self-improvement tales the individual is encouraged to look inwards in order to identify both the causes of and solutions to her own suffering. If, as Woodiwiss suggests, our therapeutic culture "encourages us to focus on the inner world of our psychologies and construct ourselves as damaged and in need of healing" this 'healing' is often seen as resting on an 'authentic' self, a "'true self,' a pre-damaged self that can be returned to" (185). These texts offer support and inspiration to change one's life while encouraging women to turn inwards and search for the root of their problems, dissatisfactions and unhappiness inside themselves. The contemporary self-improvement literature has a "dominant storyline of damage and recovery" and an "identification of damage and the journey to healing and recovery that becomes the central narrative," a story infused with "a relentless optimism" (Woodiwiss 186):

> Whilst there is a degree of optimism in these texts there also lurks a warning and an element of blame for those who fail to exercise their inner power and claim their right to happiness. Increasingly the biographies or stories we are encouraged to tell, direct us to recognise, or even search for, an authentic self—a pre-traumatised, pre-damaged (or pre-adopted) self that can be returned to and, through healing, can 'grow-up' to be the person she would or should have been—a person who is happy and satisfied with their lives, but who knows deep down that if she isn't, it's her own fault. (Woodiwiss 190)

Such contradictory views on the roots of suffering and the road to healing may be found also in the spiritual autobiography. Another contradiction stems from the fact that religion often calls for a surrender of the self while autobiographical writing could be seen as a self-centred and even self-glorifying act. Concerning the dilemma of balancing between an emphasis on one's spiritual progress on the one hand and humility on the other, Philippe Gasparini writes (in a discussion of the work of Grégoire de Naziane): "S'il se pretend favorisé par la Providence, il pèche par orgeuil, s'il ne lui rend pas grâce, il se montre ingrat: ce dilemme, récurrent dans la littérature mystique, reste ici sans solution" (103). In *The Self and the Sacred: Conversion and Autobiography*, on the other hand, Roger M. Payne finds that conversion may endow the converted person with an authority that enables him or her to write about their experiences.

Robert Bell argues in "Metamorphoses of Spiritual Autobiography" that "[u]ltimately all these lives are modeled upon the great patterns of Christian sainthood, Christ and Paul" (108). In *Grace Abounding to the Chief of Sinners*, for example, Bunyan "depicts a plain man's growth in grace; his story contains sections corresponding to the standard stages of regeneration: conviction of sin, vocation, justification, sanctification, and glorification" (108). Bell shows how the stories of saints become important comparative milestones for many authors of spiritual autobiographies, something that for some writers leads to a comparison of the writer's life to the life of a particular saint, and this may endow the writer with a certain authority. Other times, spiritual autobiographies could be seen as confessions, whereby the reader is cast in the role of priest-confessor. In Bell's view, there is a "radical transformation of autobiography in the century between Bunyan and Rousseau" (123). With Rousseau's *Confessions*, there is something new: "the uniqueness of the story," on the one hand, but, on the other hand, "[s]elf-indulgence and self-exposure have replaced self-denial and rebirth as the organizing principles of autobiographical narrative" (123). Such an "emphasis on individual experience and self-realization repudiates two cardinal tenets of the Augustinian model: the uniformity of personal experience, and the dichotomy between the fallen and reborn selves" (121).

In spiritual autobiographical narratives there is often an interplay of institutional discourse (the great existential and theological stories) and everyday accounts (the little stories of small selves in front of God). As was the case with the protagonists in the early spiritual autobiographies, many of the modern journeys begin with difficult life experiences that push the author-protagonists onto paths of spiritual quest. The impetus to the spiritual search may be an experience of devastating personal loss such as the loss of a partner or a parent that "[plunges] the writer into the most crucial of religious struggles: that of finding an adequate notion of God ('naming the whirlwind') and that of affirming eternal life in the face of death," as David Leigh puts it in *Circuitous Journeys: Modern Spiritual Autobiography* (9). In the case of Augustine, it is "the loss of a close friend," and "Augustine begins at this time to search for *permanence*. Absorbed in this search, he begins to reflect on the radical contingency and temporality in human life" (Leigh 14). For the writers studied by David Leigh, the spiritual autobiography is "the creation in symbolic form of the self-affirmation of the person as transformed from lost to found, from seeker to discoverer, from alienated to reunited with a higher and deeper One" (26).

Genuine faith must build on both contemplation and action. As Teresa of Àvila asks: "What value can be there in faith without works?" (27). Werner Jeanrond comments, further: "without contemplation we risk functionalizing God and in an activist manner attempting to force God's reign. Without action, we are escaping this world ... into a pseudo world" (44). But one or the other of these approaches may be predominant on the spiritual path undertaken. In the contemporary spiritual autobiography, two interdependent pathways to spiritual transformation open up, one apostolic, action- and goal-oriented, and the other more contemplative.

Sara Miles' approach in *Take This Bread: A Radical Conversion* (2007) could be placed within an apostolic American tradition of interactive blending of politics and religion (one can think of Billy Graham, Ronald Reagan, Eisenhower, Jerry Falwell, Martin Luther King Jr., and many others). In a goal-oriented theology it is important to claim to know what God's will is, since God's will should determine what is to be done, whereas a contemplative tradition may leave more room to dwell on the unknowability and mystery of divinity itself.

In its physicality, materiality, and concrete realism, Sara Miles' narrative echoes the realism of Augustine and Bunyan, a realism that "depicts unexceptional action which takes on profound spiritual implications" (Bell 112). In *Take This Bread,* spirituality is apostolic in its orientation toward a specific mission, the food pantry set up by Miles. Here, *doing* rather than *being* is uppermost, and action takes precedence over prayer and contemplation just as faith takes precedence over doctrine. The main focus is on community, collective action, and on the physical and concrete praxis of sharing food rather than on theological or intellectual sophistication. Whereas some of the autobiographies in this study focus mainly on God, *Take This Bread* is focused on Jesus in a very concrete sense while the image of God remains fuzzier. We learn that Miles wants to "reach the next level of conversation with God," but not how she understands the nature of God.

Perhaps God is synonymous with meaning. Miles sees herself as "just another rather hopeful and screwed-up adult hungry for *meaning*" (132, my italics). It is not really clear exactly how God is visualized. Approvingly, Miles quotes a preacher who says: "I don't have the slightest idea what God is like, really. All I know is what I see God doing, in my own life and in the lives of the people around me" (257–58). The closest we get to a definition of Miles' theology is that, since sharing food is "a real experience of the divine," God is "about feeding and being fed" (197, 196). The divine is beyond us— "God [is not] manageable" (221)—it is we as humans who need religious ritual while God does not 'need' this at all: Miles does not "think God [needs] humans to practice religion at all: God [does not] need to be appeased by sacrifices or offerings or perfectly memorized quotations from the Bible spoken in the right order" (221). Furthermore, to "confuse the rituals with an ultimately unknowable God" is dangerous, in her view, since this can lead to crusades and worse (221). Throughout *Take This Bread*, then, the emphasis is on action.

If the works in this study could be located on a spiritual axis of vertical and horizontal dimensions in terms of the spiritual experiences they narrate, Sara Miles' autobiography would be placed on a firm horizontal ground of immanence, physicality, materiality, and action. Significantly, it is when Miles starts "distributing communion" that she has a "truly disturbing, dreadful realization about Christianity: You can't be a Christian by yourself" (96). This is disturbing because "sooner or later, if [she keeps] participating in communion, [she'd] have to swallow the fact of [her] connection with all other people, without exception" (96). Still, to *do* rather than to *be* is uppermost, and Miles, significantly, likes "the idea of *deaconing* as a verb rather than *deacon* as a title or an identity" (94). Emphasizing blood and flesh, Sara Miles affirms and celebrates the transcendence found in immanence rather than the immanence found in transcendence.

In *Take This Bread*, food is central both as a material reality and as a metaphor linked to the body and to communion. At first glance, it might seem curious that the food described in *Take This Bread* ranges from the unappetizing to the disgusting. On closer consideration, however, this makes perfect sense. The unappetizing references signal a stance of inclusivity, an embrace of diversity and openness to people and situations within a contemporary American social, spiritual, and political context. The negative food references in *Take This Bread* should be read in relation to a celebration of the subversive and an attraction to the neglected underside of the socially approved surfaces of religious practice. If conventional celebrations of food focus on *haute cuisine*, Miles delves with relish into the greasy, the spoiled, and the raw as if to emphasize her commitment to the 'raw' and 'spoiled' people in American society: the marginalized and the downtrodden. Faith, for Miles, is not "about abstract theological debates" or about issues such as: 'Does God exist? Are sin and salvation predestined?'" (97). Rather, there is a corporate sense of community, a "suggestion that God could be located in experience, sensed through bodies, tasted through food; that [her] body [is] connected literally and mysteriously to other bodies and loved without reason" (64).

While narratives such as *Take This Bread* seem to insist on objectivity and credibility, the narrator-protagonists are of course not merely reflecting the past and reproducing their roles in events but also (re)producing their stories and identities in the present. Introducing herself as a journalist who has worked in war zones and engaged with equal enthusiasm in political debates and bisexual love affairs, Miles elevates her narrative to the mythical and heroic in her description of how "[h]oly communion knocked [her] upside down and forced [her] to deal with the impossible reality of God," how conversion challenges her "relentlessly" and how "God [forces her] to deal with all kinds of people" (xiv). Since her conversion does not lead to "a set of easy answers and certainties," Miles has to 'wrestle' with Christianity (xv). Her new life after her conversion in 1999 leads to "something huger and wilder than [she has] expected: the suffering, fractious, and un-boundaried body of Christ" (xv). Being knocked upside down, relentlessly challenged, having to wrestle in the huge and the wild, Sara Miles finds that, for her, faith has everything to do with action and very little to do with words, doctrine, or catechism.

Precipitated by life's anomalies, setbacks, and sorrows that upset pre-viously held expectations of a linear progression toward individual success and happiness, spiritual development often involves a paradigm shift precipitated by crisis. In *Understanding Religious Conversion*, Lewis Rambo argues that in most cases, "[s]ome form of crisis usually precedes con-version," and this "crisis may be religious, political, psychological, or cultural in origin" (44). Nancy Shumate, similarly, takes the view in *Crisis and Conversion in Apuleius' Metamorphoses* that crises and conversion can be regarded as part of a spiritual paradigm shift. In *Towards a New Under-standing of Conversion*, further, Ulf Görman introduces the term 'the evangelical paradigm' and suggests that crises are central in descriptions of conversions. After a paradigm shift, there is an epistemological reorientation and a transformation of the ways of understanding the world. Mystics, as

Werner Jeanrond underlines, have known that receiving the grace of God always leads to radical change in all our relations, first of all, of course, in our relation to God, but also in all our relations to other human beings as well as in our relations to ourselves; none of these relations will be the same if one lives *coram deo*, as Jeanrond cites Martin Luther (42). In Jeanrond's view, mystics are often radicals and sometimes rebels.

In his discussion of autobiographical sources in *The Evangelical Conversion Narrative*, Bruce D. Hindmarsh looks back to Augustine, whose *Confessions* he regards as "a remarkably precocious spiritual autobiography without precedent in the ancient world" (4).[2] Whereas an autobiography, as Hindmarsh writes, "simply promises to retrace the history of a life," "at a deeper level it is always an apologetic of the individual. Autobiography is one of the ways to answer the question of what my life means" (5). Whereas a memoir tends to be "episodic and anecdotal," the conversion narrative is "highly emplotted" with a "strongly etched beginning, middle, and end, and a sense of wholeness" (6). Hindmarsh states further that "the narrative shape of these evangelical stories was clearly provided by the larger story of salvation history in the Bible.... It is sometimes assumed that the modern and bourgeois form of autobiography is characterized by its rejection of such ready-made universal patterns—concerned with the wholly immanent meaning of each unique life as the product of unique choices," but "the bourgeois narrative still surely represents another pattern" (8).

As Hindmarsh points out, "Aristotle's temporal syntax of beginning-middle-end is also a moral structure" (7). In Karen Armstrong's *The Spiral Staircase: My Climb Out of Darkness* (2004), a tripartite narrative movement beginning in darkness (with Armstrong's spiritual confusion arising from her time in the convent, the loss her God, and her attacks of epilepsy), moves through a series of successes and setbacks, and arrives finally at the light in ways that recall the lines in Eliot's Ash Wednesday VI about "The dream crossed twilight between birth and dying," a "time of tension between dying and birth." *The Spiral Staircase* might seem to narrate a process of *decon-*

---

[2] Augustine's autobiography is unlike any of the models provided by ancient biographers, such as Plutarch, whose 'lives' were by and large the *res gestae* or 'great deeds' of famous men. It differs from the autobiography of St Patrick, for example, which is an account of St Patrick's "outward vocation as a charismatic missionary," written "in part to correct false accusations and misrepresentations of his mission" (Hindmarsh 22). "The *Confessions* was in a literal sense *sui generis*. Augustine was also precocious enough to reflect upon what he was doing. In Books 10 and 11 he turned from his narrative to consider the nature of time, change, memory, and identity" (Hindmarsh 4).

version over a period of time. And yet, the end result is the opposite: although Armstrong's life at the end of the narrative is not focused on prayer, it is oriented towards silence and religious scholarship that lead to a deep spiritual serenity. Indeed, Armstrong's later work focusing on compassion could be seen as a form of prayer for a better world. Several remarkable ups and downs lead to Armstrong's decision to immerse herself in religious studies in a broader sense. Departing from the foundational metaphors of Eliot's poem "Ash Wednesday," so important to Armstrong, we can distinguish several turning points in Armstrong's life in the guise of disasters: failing her final degree in Oxford, losing a teaching job, losing a job at television. These are events that form the bulk of the middle part of the narrative. At the beginning of *The Spiral Staircase*, Karen Armstrong still regards herself as a Catholic. At the end, she belongs to no church, and appears instead to have moved towards an interfaith perspective. After an immersion in studies of the Crusades, in particular, she comes to the conclusion that religious certainties are dangerous since they do not allow for a consideration of the perspectives of others. At the end of the narrative, Armstrong's core beliefs have been transformed, and there is a "climbing upward" "toward the light" (306). A long distance has been covered from the initial 'darkness' of the title to the final word in the book—which is 'light.'

Armstrong discovers the truths inherent in the ancient myths in which the hero "must venture into the darkness of the unknown, where there is no map and no clear route," something he must do on his own in order to find his own truths. The Holy Grail was, according to Armstrong, "a watershed in the spiritual development of the West" (268), and "[t]he destination of the Grail Knights," finally, "is not the earthly city of Jerusalem, but the heavenly city of Saras, which has no place in this world. The forest represents the interior realm of the psyche, and the grail itself becomes a symbol of a mystical encounter with God" (269). Similarly, turning inward, Armstrong 'turns again,' recalling the protagonist in Eliot's "Ash Wednesday." This 'turning' is a conversion of sorts, a turning away from orthodox doctrine, conformity, and blind obedience toward an orthopractic spirituality centred on the compassion of the Golden Rule. Theology resembles poetry, and is best approached in silence, she concludes: "Like the words of a poem, a religious idea, myth, or doctrine points beyond itself to truths that are elusive, that resist words and conceptualization" (284).

In Lauren Winner's autobiographies—*Girl Meets God: On the Path to a Spiritual Life* (2002) and *Still: Notes on a Mid-Faith Crisis* (2012)—a complex, extended metaphor of matrimony as related to the spiritual journey is central. Indeed, the matrimonial metaphor is a key directional image that infuses much of Lauren Winner's writing. It is crucially intertwined with the stages of the spiritual journey itself with its accelerations, turning points, impasses, stases, and arrivals. First of all, matrimonial metaphors are appropriate in spiritual writings because of their biblical connotations. In *Real Sex: The Naked Truth about Chastity* (2005), Winner observes:

> Marriage serves as the biblical analogy par excellence to the relationship between God and His people. Over and over in sacred scripture, that relationship is described as a marriage. When the people of Israel are faithful to God, Israel is described as a bride; when she turns away from God, she is called a harlot. Similarly, the writers of the New Testament found that one way to capture the relationship between Christ and the church was to draw an analogy to husband and wife. Through these analogies, marriage is substantively linked to community. (*Real Sex* 50)

Moreover, matrimonial metaphors are appropriate because connubial bliss could be compared to the bliss of mystic experiences. In *Why God Won't Go Away*, Andrew Newberg suggests that "the neurological machinery of transcendence may have arisen from the neural circuitry that evolved for mating and sexual experiences. The language of mysticism hints at this connection: Mystics of all times and cultures have used the same expressive terms to describe their ineffable experiences: *bliss, rapture, ecstasy,* and *exaltation*" (125). It seems that "mystical union and sexual bliss ... [have] similar neural pathways," and mystics "speak of losing themselves in a sublime sense of union, of melting into elation" (125), and he goes on to say that "[a]n evolutionary perspective suggests that the neurobiology of mystical experience arose, at least in part, from the mechanism of the sexual response. In a sense, then, mystical experience may be an accidental by-product, but this does not necessarily diminish the meaning of spiritual experience" (126). Newberg underlines that "by explaining mystical experience as a neurological function, we do not intend to suggest that it can't be something more" (126). Similarly, in William James's chapter on mystic experiences in *Varieties of Religious Experience*, we learn that the states of mystic experience are ecstasies often conveyed through images referring to "nuptial union," whereby, according to James, "[i]ntellect and senses both swoon away in these highest states of ecstasy" (319).

Pilgrimage has been another path to illumination, insight, and union with God. Looking into the history of pilgrimage and different types of pilgrimage ranging from healing to devotional, William Schmidt, an ordained minister and a spiritual counsellor, suggests in "Transformative Pilgrimage" that "one element that seems present in all types of pilgrimages centers around the personal change it evokes in the participants," whereby "the term 'transformational' ... is a useful overarching category to cover most all pilgrimage commitments" (xi). In pilgrimage narratives, transformation is usually connected with a special and sacred place. As Karen Armstrong writes in *A History of God: The 4,000-Year Quest of Judaism, Christianity and Islam*, "The idea of a holy city, where men and women felt that they were closely in touch with sacred power, the source of all being and efficiency, would be important in all the monotheistic religions of our own God" (16). Indeed, the importance of a sacred, transformative place is central in the pilgrimage narratives explored in this study: Lee Hoinacki's *El Camino: Walking to Santiago de Compostela* (1996), Conrad Rudolph's *Pilgrimage to the End of the World: The Road to Santiago de Compostela* (2004), Arthur Paul Boers' *The Way Is Made by Walking: A Pilgrimage Along the Camino de Santiago* (2007), Tony Kevin's *Walking the Camino: A Modern Pilgrimage to Santiago* (2007), and Linda C. Magno's *Bliss: My Pilgrimage to Santiago de Compostela* (2011).

Even though any pilgrimage has a goal, the result of the pilgrimage—what happens when the goal has been reached and one has gone home—is often left out in pilgrimage narratives. If, as E. Alan Morinis states, "[t]he return to the everyday is a component of almost every pilgrimage," this return is *not* a component of almost every pilgrimage *narrative*. Morinis writes further that "[w]hile the sacred place is the source of power and salvation, it is at home once again that the effects of power are incorporated into life and what salvation is gained is confirmed. The return journey and the reincorporation of the pilgrim into social life are the test of the pilgrimage. Has there been change? Will it last?" (27). If Morinis is right that the "return journey and the reincorporation of the pilgrim into social life are the test of the pilgrimage," then many contemporary pilgrimage narratives remain inconclusive. But perhaps Nancy Frey is right that questions about change and transformation need to be formulated differently: "Within a linear worldview journey's end is usually equated with the goal, effectively negating the return. What happens when the goal is the way and not the shrine and the end comes while making the journey or after the goal is reached or once the pilgrim returns home?" (179). Victor Turner and Edith Turner suggest in *Image and Pilgrimage in Christian Culture: Anthropological Perspectives* that the metaphor of an ellipse is the most fitting if one takes the whole pilgrimage into account, including the road back home, which is usually very different from the pilgrimage route itself:

> even when pilgrims return by the way they came, the total journey may still be represented, not unfittingly, by an ellipse, if psychological factors are taken into account.... When he returns, so travelers' accounts repeatedly inform us, his aim is to reach home as swiftly as he can, and his attitude is now that of a tourist rather than a devotee.... The road is thus two roads; the apt metaphor is an ellipse, not a straight line (22–23).

In Anne Rice's *Called Out of Darkness: A Spiritual Confession* (2008), a different journey is enacted. This is a story that could be analyzed with the help of typological patterns used in biblical exegesis. In Rice's autobiography, the narrative delineates first a 'fall' into atheism and later a return to her Church whereby her story could be seen as paralleling the biblical story of the loss of paradise and redemption through Christ. In Rice's case, attending a non-Catholic college leads to a different view of good and evil and to a loss of the Catholic faith of her childhood. Metaphorically speaking, Rice tastes the forbidden fruit and is cast out of the Garden of Eden of her Catholic childhood. After this, she suffers an aversion to Catholicism for four decades. It is when she moves back to New Orleans in 1988 and becomes once again immersed in a vibrant Catholic community and notices that the Church has become "somehow more inclusive and accepting than it had been" (173) that Rice gradually returns to faith. Paradise—that is, faith—is regained in the end, and although it is in a modified form, there is a sense of a homecoming in the end.

Recalling the traditional spiritual journey from the darkest night of the soul to the light of God, Elizabeth Gilbert's *Eat, Pray, Love: One Woman's Search for Everything Across Italy, India, and Indonesia* (2006) begins in a "dark period of loss" (24). Crisis sets the narrative in motion, and Gilbert embarks on a one-year a pilgrimage to three countries, Italy, India, and Indonesia, in a search for God from a polyreligious perspective including Buddhist, Taoist, and Christian traditions and spiritual disciplines. Narrative structure and organization carry deep significance. *Eat Pray Love* has an intricate tripartite structure that not only holds the story together but that infuses the whole narrative with deeper layers of meaning, as it points to a conceptual framework relating the spiritual search to Christian and other religious traditions within which the inner and outer journey can move forward geographically and spiritually while affording backward glances on the level of memory. Indeed, according to David Leigh's *Circuitous Journeys*, many authors of modern spiritual autobiographies "employ an explicitly tripartite grid for their autobiographies ... while others use simple chapter divisions that readily separate into three major structural sections with significant parallels in the persons, events, and symbolic objects of each section" (5–6).

In India, Gilbert unexpectedly has what could be seen as a mystic experience and an encounter with God. Mystical experiences are ineffable, according to William James in *Varieties of Religious Experience*, since "[m]ystical truth exists for the individual who has the transport, but for no one else" (314). James gives countless examples of experiences that resemble Gilbert's. Saint Teresa of Àvila, for example, writes that after a mystical experience one cannot doubt "that she has been in God, and God in her" (qtd. by James 317)—a description that closely resembles that of Elizabeth Gilbert.[3] Are mystical experiences real, then, or are they self-deluding illusions, hallucinations, or symptoms of mental derangement? Following researchers in neurology, Andrew Newberg points to important differences between hallucinatory experiences and spiritual experiences of unity. While the former may be frightening or involve "feelings of religious grandiosity," the latter are usually joyful or even ecstatic and "involve a loss of pride and ego" (110). But although there is research that posits epileptic seizures as the cause of mystic experiences, arguing that St. Paul, Joan of Arc, Saint Teresa of Àvila and even "the conversion experience of Mormon patriarch Joseph Smith" were caused by "ecstatic partial seizures" or "an intracranial tuberculoma" (Newberg 111), others contend that "[f]or most patients the involvement of the hippocampus in temporal lobe epilepsy precludes any memory afterward for what happened during a seizure" (Kelly, Greyson, and Kelly 384). Hallucinations and seizures, further, often involve only one sensory aspect and are usually recognized as unreal afterwards, whereas mystic experiences often involve more than one sensory experience and are seen as entirely real afterwards (Newberg 112). Gilbert's experience in *Eat Pray Love* is not hallucinogenic: "It was the most basic of events. It was heaven, yes. It was the deepest love I'd ever experienced, beyond anything I

[3] Other examples include that of Malwida von Meysenbug who felt "impelled to kneel down, this time before the illimitable ocean, symbol of the infinite," to pray "as [she] had never prayed before, and [she] knew now what prayer really is: to return from the solitude of individuation into the consciousness of unity of all that is" (James 306). James also mentions the *Autobiography of J. Trevor*, in which Trevor writes about the "Real Presence" and about being "aware that [he] was immersed in the infinite ocean of God" (qtd by James 308).

could have previously imagined, but it wasn't euphoric. It wasn't exciting. There wasn't enough ego or passion left in me to create euphoria and excitement" (209).

Mystic experiences have a number of aspects in common with near-death experiences. A number of these features have become well-known. These include a sense of bliss, peace, and happiness, a sensation of going out of one's body and sometimes hovering above it, going through a tunnel and entering a different space, meeting persons, souls, or spiritual beings that may be known or unknown, and experiencing a review of one's life. Near-death experiences may contain a combination of these aspects and they may happen in different sequences. Outlining fifteen elements, Raymond Moody observes in *Life after Life: The Investigation of a Phenomenon: Survival of Bodily Death* that a maximum of twelve of these were included in any individual near-death experience among those he studied in the mid-1970s. Studies suggest that the degree of closeness to death may determine experiences so that "alterations in the sense of time, unusually rapid thinking, and a revival of memories are more common in near-death events that are sudden and unexpected than in those that may have been anticipated," that "an encounter with a brilliant light, enhanced cognitive function, and positive emotions, were more common among individuals who were actually close to death than in those who were not so seriously ill," and that "[p]eople actually close to death were also more likely to report encounters with deceased persons than those who were not" (Kelly, Greyson, and Kelly 373).[4]

One of the near-death narratives examined here, Eben Alexander's narrative in *Proof of Heaven* (2012), moves between and contrasts relations to his present family, the childhood family into which he was adopted, his (long unknown) birth family, and his 'family' as experienced in the spiritual realm. Moving from the unreflected awareness of ultra-immanence in a place without meaning or memory to an underworld realm of timelessness

---

[4] Near-death experiences of moving towards a bright light have also been described in fiction. In a forthcoming interdisciplinary study, *Lazarus' Silence: Near-Death Experiences in Fiction, Science, and Popular Culture*, Laura Wittman will re-examine the Lazarus tale in literary works. "It is the first cultural history of near-death experiences in the twentieth-century West, and it puts literary rewritings of the Biblical Lazarus story – by major authors such as Leonid Andreyev, Miguel de Unamuno, D. H. Lawrence, Luigi Pirandello, Graham Greene, Georges Bataille, André Malraux, and Péter Nádas – in the double context of popular versions of coming back to life in testimonies, fiction, and film, and of evolving medical and neuroscientific investigation. Its central questions are: how near-death stories shape our understanding of consciousness; and how they affect our care for the dying" (https://dlcl.stanford.edu/people/laura-wittman).

and on to an immersion in a maternally conceptualized divine space, 'Alexander' has a sense of being born into a universe likened to a "giant cosmic womb" evoked through biological metaphors of pregnancy and gestation (47). Literally and geographically, *Proof of Heaven* depicts a journey from home to the hospital and back again, spiritually, a journey from a rational and secular, scientific mind-set to an encounter with the divine, and epistemologically, a journey from limited knowledge and understanding to an experience of instantaneous and all-encompassing knowledge. Other near-death narratives follow a similar pattern and share the same sense of conviction about the reality of the experience.

As already suggested, three of the stages of spiritual development delineated by Lewis Rambo—crisis, quest, and consequences—have turned out to be the most relevant for an analysis of the autobiographies chosen here. As we have seen, the writers in this study focus to different degrees on these three stages in their autobiographical narratives. Commonly, the first stage, crisis, is given fairly short shrift, while the searching stage associated with spiritual quest is more fully elaborated. This is particularly true of the pilgrimage narratives that tend to outline rather briefly their different starting points, say surprisingly little about arrivals at the geographical and spiritual destinations, and even less about the consequences of the pilgrimage, that is, its lasting effects. As already suggested, pre-crisis stages (such as Rambo's 'context' and Teresa's 'first mansion') are generally deemphasized in these modern spiritual autobiographies, except for Anne Rice's *Coming Out of Darkness* where the description of her Catholic childhood takes up a large part of the narrative. In a discussion of Rice's autobiography, Larry Culliford's terms in *The Psychology of Spirituality: An Introduction*—belonging, searching, and homecoming—would also fit rather well. In Sara Miles' *Take This Bread*, to the contrary, context and background are only touched upon whereas the consequences of Miles' conversion constitute the main part of the narrative. Generally, however, in the spiritual autobiographies examined here, the stage of quest is the most important.

A search for oneness, a focus on the endpoints of pilgrimages, on food and on matrimony are central in some of the texts analyzed in this study. Many other crucial symbols and metaphors, intertwined with central theological concepts, are associated with a search for unity, transcendence, and permanence. If spiritual autobiographies give us knowledge not usually accessible, they may offer a royal road into domains that are otherwise difficult to access. They may not give any definite answers. In *The Map of*

Heaven: How Science, Religion, and Ordinary People Are Proving the After-life, Eben Alexander writes:

> At our very center, deep beneath the surface character we have built up in the course of this lifetime, there is a part of us so central, so timeless, and so fundamental that mystics have been politely disagreeing for centuries as to whether it is the place where we intersect with God, or whether it is God itself. My understanding is that Eastern religions generally equate this deepest and most central part of us directly with the Divine, while Western religions tend to keep a distinction between the individual soul or self and God. (120–21)

Georges Gusdorf's essay, "Conditions and Limits of Autobiography," has an existential depth in its comments on how we all tend to see ourselves as the center of the universe and our own lives as highly significant, thinking that we matter and that there will be a void when we disappear. This is where autobiography can play a role: "In narrating my life, I give witness of myself even from beyond my death and so can preserve this precious capital that ought not to disappear" (29). Unlike the autobiographies of famous men whose narratives tend to be a "revenge on history" of the "victim who puffs himself up as a victor" "providing a sort of posthumous propaganda for posterity" (Gusdorf 36), other autobiographers for whom "the private face of existence assumes more importance," turn inward: "The act of memory is carried out for itself, and recalling of the past satisfies a more or less anguished disquiet of the mind anxious to recover and redeem lost time in fixing it forever" (37). The "mature man or the man already old" can thus assure himself "that he has not existed in vain; he chooses not revolution but reconciliation" (Gusdorf 30). Gusdorf goes on to say:

> Autobiography appeases the more or less anguished uneasiness of an aging man who wonders if his life has not been lived in vain, frittered away haphazardly, ending now in simple failure. In order to be assured, he undertakes his own apologia, as Newman expressly says. Perhaps Cardinal de Retz is ridiculous with his claim to political insight and to infallibility, since he lost every game he played; but it may be that every life, even in spite of the most brilliant successes, knows itself inwardly botched. So autobiography is the final chance to win back what has been lost. (39)

As we have seen, spiritual autobiographies differ from other autobiographies in their focus on *one* aspect of life, leaving big chunks of experience aside. Moving, frequently, from crises on social-horizontal levels to peace, insight, or transformation on vertical levels of transcendence, the contemporary spiritual autobiography often narrates a story focused on *one* particular relationship, that between an individual and an unseen divine dimension. Consequently, patterns depicting movement from loss and failure to epiphanic realizations of fundamental existential and spiritual truths predominate. Since many of the authors of the works studied here feel that they have arrived at something and see their lives as transformed their texts could be called narratives of transformation. Some of the stories are recounting the ultimate in personal and spiritual development, or the passionate *pursuit* of it: enlightenment, illumination, and transformative encounters with an ultimate reality or God.

While Augustine's addressee is God, the aim of his *Confessions* was also to inspire other men: "To whom am I narrating all this?" he asks; "Not to thee, O my God, but to my own kind in thy presence" (Book Two, Chapter III). Similarly, in *The Interior Castle*, Teresa of Àvila finds that cost what it may, if she can "lead but one soul to praise Thee a little better," her efforts will have been worth it (95). In *Walking with Stones: A Spiritual Odyssey on the Pilgrimage to Santiago*, finally, William Schmidt is not looking for doorways for the sake of his own spiritual progress only. He wants his story, his pain, and his joy to become markers for those who follow in his footsteps. Along the Camino, there are prayer stones that Schmidt picks up. These stones travel with him part of the way as "reminders to prayer and inviting God's sacred presence into [his] feelings of joy and sorrow on each day," and are left behind at certain points on cairns along the road as literal depositions that are testimonials.

Along similar lines, the spiritual autobiographies of the writers explored here could be seen as depositions on the cairns of writing. In this way, the metaphorical prayer stones left behind may serve as doorways for readers to walk through on their own spiritual journeys.

Works Cited

Primary Sources

Alexander, Eben. *Proof of Heaven: A Neurosurgeon's Journey into the Afterlife*. New York: Simon & Schuster, 2012. Print.

Armstrong, Karen. *The Spiral Staircase: My Climb Out of Darkness*. New York: Anchor, 2004. Print.

___. *Through the Narrow Gate: A Memoir of Spiritual Discovery*. London: St. Martin's Griffin, 2005. Print.

___. *Beginning the World*. London: St. Martin's Press, 1983. Print.

Black, Dale, and Ken Gire. *Flight to Heaven: A Plane Crash ... A Lone Survivor ... A Journey to Heaven – and Back: A Pilot's True Story*. Minneapolis, Minnesota: Bethany House, 2010. Print.

Boers, Arthur Paul. *The Way Is Made by Walking: A Pilgrimage Along the Camino de Santiago*. Foreword by Eugene H. Peterson. Downer's Grove, IL: Intervarsity P, 2007. Print.

Chernin, Kim. *In My Father's Garden: A Daughter's Search for a Spiritual Life*. Algonquin, 1996. Print.

Dougherty, Ned. *Fast Lane to Heaven: A Life-after Death Journey*. Charlottesville, VA: Hampton Roads, 2001. Print.

Ehrenreich, Barbara. *Living with a Wild God: A Non-Believer's Search for the Truth About Everything*. London: Granta, 2014. Print.

Gilbert, Elizabeth. *Eat, Pray, Love: One Woman's Search for Everything across Italy, India, and Indonesia*. New York: Penguin, 2006. Print.

Hoinacki, Lee. *El Camino: Walking to Santiago de Compostela*. University Park, PA: The Pennsylvania UP, 1996. Print.

Kevin, Tony. *Walking the Camino: A Modern Pilgrimage to Santiago*. 2007. Melbourne: Scribe, 2013. Print.

Magno, Linda C. *Bliss: My Pilgrimage to Santiago de Compostela*. CreateSpace Independent Publishing Platform, 2011. Print.

McVea, Crystal, and Alex Tresniowski. *Waking Up in Heaven: A True Story of Brokenness, Heaven, and Life Again.* Foreword by Laura Schroff. New York: Howard, 2013. Print.

Miles, Sara. *Take This Bread: A Radical Conversion.* New York: Ballantine, 2007. Print.

Neal, Mary C. *To heaven and Back: A Doctor's Extraordinary Account of Her Death, Heaven, Angels, and Life Again: A True Story.* Colorado Springs, CO: Waterbrook, 2012. Print.

Rice, Anne. *Called Out of Darkness: A Spiritual Confession.* 2008. London: Arrow, 2009. Print.

Rudolph, Conrad. *Pilgrimage to the End of the World: The Road to Santiago de Compostela.* Chicago: U of Chicago P, 2004. Print.

Schmidt, William S. *Walking with Stones: A Spiritual Odyssey on the Pilgrimage to Santiago.* Bloomington: Trafford, 2012. Print.

Sigmund, Richard. *My Time in Heaven: A True Story of Dying … and Coming Back.* 2004. Maxwell, Iowa: Whitaker House, 2010. Print.

Vest, Freddy. *The Day I Died.* Lake Mary, FA: Charisma House, 2014. Print.

Winner, Lauren F. *Girl Meets God: On the Path to a Spiritual Life.* New York: Shaw, 2002. Print.

___. *Real Sex: The Naked Truth about Chastity.* Grand Rapids, MI: Brazos, 2005. Print.

___. *Still: Notes on a Mid-Faith Crisis.* New York: Harper, 2012. Print.

___. *The Voice of Matthew.* Nashville: Thomas Nelson, 2007. Print.

Secondary sources

Alexander, Eben. *The Map of Heaven: How Science, Religion, and Ordinary People Are Proving the Afterlife.* New York: Simon & Schuster, 2014. Print.

Allport, Gordon Willard. *The Individual and His Religion: A Psychological Interpretation.* New York: Macmillan, 1960. Print.

Anderson, Linda. *Autobiography: New Critical Idiom.* London: Routledge, 2001. Print.

Armstrong, Karen. *A History of God: The 4,000-Year Quest of Judaism, Christianity and Islam.* London: Heinemann, 1993. Print.

Atchley, Robert C. "Everyday Mysticism: Spiritual Development in Later Adulthood." *Journal of Adult Development* 4.2 (1997): 123–34. Print.

Àvila, Teresa of. *The Interior Castle or The Mansions.* Translated by a Benedictine of Stanbrook. Abridged and edited by Hugh Martin. London: SCM Press, 1958.

Barbour, John D. *The Conscience of the Autobiographer: Ethical and Religious Dimensions of Autobiography.* Basingstoke: Macmillan, 1992. Print.

___. *Versions of Deconversion: Autobiography and the Loss of Faith.* Charlottesville: UP of Virginia, 1994. Print.

Becker, Ernest. *The Denial of Death.* 1973. New York: Free Press Paperbacks, 1997. Print.

Bell, Robert. "Metamorphoses of Spiritual Autobiography." *ELH* 44.1 (1977): 108–26. Print.

Brownson, Orestes. Excerpt. In Edwin S. Gaustad, ed. *Memoirs of the Spirit: American Religious Autobiography from Jonathan Edwards to Maya Angelou.* Cambridge, UK: William B. Eerdemans, 1999. 79–91. Print.

Bruss, Elizabeth. *Autobiographical Acts: The Changing Situation of a Literary Genre.* 1976. Ann Arbor, MI: University Microfilms International, 1989. Print.

Campbell, David E., Robert D. Putnam, and Shaylyn Romney Garrett. *American Grace: How Religion Divides and Unites Us.* New York, NY: Simon & Schuster, 2010. Print.

Callahan, Maureen. "Eat, Pray, Loathe." Review of Gilbert, Elizabeth. *Eat, Pray, Love: One Woman's Search for Everything across Italy, India, and Indonesia.* *New York Post.* December 23, 2007. http://nypost.com/2007/12/23/eat-pray-loathe/. Accessed April 20 2016.

Carrette, Jeremy, and Richard King. 2005. *Selling Spirituality: The Silent Takeover of Religion.* London: Routledge, 2008. Print.

Cartwright, Kelly B. "Cognitive Developmental Theory and Spiritual Development." *Journal of Adult Development* 8.4 (2001): 213–20. Print.

Chesterton, G. K. *The Catholic Church and Conversion.* London: Burns, Oates & Washbourne, 1926. Print.

Clifford, Anne M. *Introducing Feminist Theology.* Maryknoll, NY: Orbis, 2000. Print.

Cohen, Erik. "Pilgrimage and Tourism: Convergence and Divergence." In *Sacred Journeys: The Anthropology of Pilgrimage.* Morini, A., ed. Westport, CT: Greenwood. 47–61. Print.

Culliford, Larry. *The Psychology of Spirituality: An Introduction.* London: Jessica Kingsley, 2010. Print.

Dalziell, Rosamund. "Speaking Volumes: About Auto/biography Studies in Canada." *ESC* 32.2–3 (2008): 211–27. Print.

Campbell, David E., and Robert D. Putnam, *American Grace: How Religion Divides and Unites Us.* New York: Simon & Schuster, 2012. Print.

Dallam, Marie W. "Introduction. Religion, Food, and Eating." In *Religion, Food, and Eating in North America* (Arts and Traditions of the Table: Perspectives on Culinary History). Ed. Benjamin E. Zeller, Marie W. Dallam, Reid L. Neilson and Nora L Rubel. New York: Columbia UP, 2014. xviii–xxxii. Print.

Davidsson Bremborg, Anna. "Creating Sacred Space by Walking in Silence: Pilgrimage in a Late Modern Lutheran Context." *Social Compass* 60 (2013): 544–60. Print. *Pilgrimsvandring på svenska*. Lund: Arcus, 2010. Print.

De Man, Paul. "Autobiography as De-Facement." *The Rhetoric of Romanticism*. New York: Columbia UP, 1984. 67–81. Print.

De Quincey, Thomas. *Confessions of an English Opium-Eater. London Magazine* September 1821. https://www.gutenberg.org/files/2040/2040-h/2040-h.htm Accessed 16 July 2015.

Eakin, Paul John. *Fictions in Autobiographpy: Studies in the Art of Self-Invention.* 1985. Princeton, NJ: Princeton UP, 2014. Print.

Eden, Trudy. "Introduction." *Food and Faith in Christian Culture.* Ed. Ken Albala and Trudy Eden. New York: Columbia UP, 2011. 1–7. Print.

Edwards, Jonathan. "Personal Narrative." In Edwin S. Gaustad, ed., *Memoirs of the Spirit: American Religious Autobiography from Jonathan Edwards to Maya Angelou.* Cambridge, UK: William B. Eerdemans, 1999. 19–33. Print.

Egan, Jennifer. "The Road to Bali." Review of Gilbert, Elizabeth. *Eat, Pray, Love: One Woman's Search for Everything across Italy, India, and Indonesia. New York Times.* February 26, 2006. http://www.nytimes.com/2006/02/26/books/review/26egan.html?pagewanted=all. Accessed 9 July, 2015.

Fowler, James W. *Stages of Faith: The Psychology of Human Development and the Quest for Meaning.* San Francisco: Harper Collins, 1995. Print.

Franklin, Benjamin. *The Autobiography and Other Writings.* Selected and Edited with an Introduction by L. Jesse Lemisch. New York: New American Library, 1961.

Frey, Nancy. *Pilgrim Stories On and Off the Road to Santiago. Journeys along an Ancient Way in Modern Spain.* Berkeley: U of California P, 1998. Print.

Gasparini, Philippe. *La tentation autobiographique: de l'Antiquité à la Renaissance.* Paris: Éditions du Seuil, 2013. Print.

Gaustad, Edwin S. ed. "Introduction." *Memoirs of the Spirit: American Religious Autobiography from Jonathan Edwards to Maya Angelou.* Cambridge, UK: William B. Eerdemans, 1999. xiii–xix. Print.

Gilbert, Elizabeth. *Big Magic: Creative Living Beyond Fear.* London: Bloomsbury, 2015.

Greyson, Bruce. "The Mystical Impact of Near-Death Experiences." *Shift: At the Fronters of Consciousness* 17 (Dec 2007-Febr 2008): 9–13. Print.

Greyson, Bruce, and Surbhi Khanna. "Daily Spiritual Experiences Before and After Near-Death Experiences." *Psychology of Religion and Spirituality* 6.4 (2014): 302–9. Print.

Gusdorf, Georges. "Conditions and Limits of Autobiography." In *Autobiography: Essays Theoretical and Critical,* ed. James Olney. Princeton: Princeton UP, 1980. 28–48. Print.

Görman, Ulf. *Towards a New Understanding of Conversion.* Lund: Teologiska Institutionen, 1999. Print.

Hamilton, D. M., and Jackson, M. H. "Spiritual Development: Paths and Processes." *Journal of Instructional Psychology* 25.4 (1998): 262–70. Print.

Hartman, Geoffrey Galt. "Conversion and the Language of Autobiography." *In Studies in Autobiography.* Ed. James Olney. Oxford: Oxford UP, 1998. 42–50. Print.

Hawkins, Anne Hunsaker. *Archetypes of Conversion: The Autobiographies of Augustine, Bunyan, and Merton.* Lewisburg: Bucknell UP, 1985. Print.

___. *Reconstructing Illness: Studies in Pathography.* West Lafayette, IN: Purdue UP, 1999. Print.

Hindmarsh, D. Bruce. *The Evangelical Conversion Narrative: Spiritual Autobiography in Early Modern England.* Oxford: Oxford UP, 2005. Print.

Hull, John M. "Spiritual Development: Interpretations and Applications." *British Journal of Religious Education.* 24:3 (2002): 171–182. Print.

Hutch, Richard A.*The Meaning of Lives: Biography, Autobiography, and the Spiritual Quest.* London: Cassell Religious Studies, 1997. Print.

Höhn, Hans Joachim. "Renaissance of Religion: Clarifications to a Disputed Topic." From: *Herder Korrespondenz,* 12 (2006): 605–8. Webmaster's own, not authorized translation. http://www.con-spiration.de/texte/english/2006/hoehn-e.html. Accessed July 9, 2015.

Irenaeus: Against Heresies. *From: Ante-Nicene Fathers, Vol. 1. Edited by Alexander Roberts.* 180. The Gnostic Society Library. http://gnosis.org/library/advh1.htm. Accessed 21 April 2016.

James, William. *The Works of William James. The Varieties of Religious Experience.* Ed. Frederick Burkhardt. Cambridge, MA: Harvard UP, 1985. Print.

Jay, Paul. "What's The Use?: Critical Theory and the Study of Autobiography." *Biography.* 10.1 (1987): 39–54. 7 May 2015. http://muse.jhu.edu/journals/bio/summary/v010/10.1.jay.html. Accessed 9 July 2015.

Jeanrond, Werner G. *Guds närvaro: Teologiska reflexioner 1.* 1998. Lund: Arcus, 2006. Print.

Johnston, Margaret Placentra. *Faith Beyond Belief: Stories of Good People Who Left Their Church Behind.* Wheaton, IL: Quest, 2012. Print.

Katz, Steven T. "Language, Epistemology, and Mysticism." In Steven T. Katz, ed., *Mysticism and Philosophical Analysis* (22–74). Oxford UP, 1978. Print.

Keller, Barbara. "Toward a Multidimensional Conception of Faith Development: Deconversion Narratives in Biographical Context." *Autobiography and the Psychological Study of Religious Lives.* 75–93. Print.

Kelly, Edward F., and Michael Grosso. "Mystical Experience." In *Irreducible Mind: Toward a Psychology for the 21st Century.* Lanham, MD: Jason Aronson, 2006. 495–575. Print.

Kelly, Edward F., Emily Williams Kelly, Frederic Myers, and Adam Crabtree. "Unusual Experiences Near Death and Related Phenomena." In *Irreducible Mind: Toward a Psychology for the 21st Century*. Lanham, MD: Jason Aronson, 2006. 367–421. Print.

Klein, Stanley B., Tim P. German, Leda Cosmides, and Rami Gabriel. "A Theory of Autobiographical Memory: Necessary Components and Disorders Resulting from Their Loss." *Social Cognition*, 22.5 (2004): 460–90. http://www2.fiu.edu/~ereserve/010029638-1.pdf

Knox, Melissa. "Protean Identity: Religion and Contemporary American Autobiography." *Forum for Inter-American Research: The Journal of The International Association for Inter-American Studies*, 6.1 (2013): http://www.interamerica.de/. Accessed 9 July 2015.

Knudsen, Britta Timm, and Anne Marit Waade. "Performative Authenticity in Tourism and Spatial Experience: Rethinking the Relation between Travel, Place and Emotion in the Context of Cultural Economy and Emotional Geography." In Knudsen, Britta Timm and Anne Marit Waade, eds. *Re-investing Authenticity: Tourism, Place and Emotions*. Leeds: Channel View, 2010. 1–19.

Kort, Wesley A. *Textual Intimacy: Autobiography and Religious Identities*. Charlottesville and London: U of Virginia P, 2012. Print.

Koskinen-Hagman, Marcus. *Latent Trait Models of Intrinsic, Extrinsic, and Quest Religious Orientations*. Lund: 1999. Print.

Leigh, David J. *Circuitous Journeys: Modern Spiritual Autobiography*. Bronx: Fordham UP, 2000. Print.

Lejeune, Philippe. *On Autobiography*. Ed. P. J. Eakin. U of Minnesota P, 1989. Print.

Littberger, Inger. *Omvändelser: nedslag i svenska romaner under hundra år*. Eslöv: B. Östlings bokförl. Symposion, 2004. Print.

Love, Patrick G. "Differentiating Spirituality from Religion." *Character Clearinghouse*, 2015. https://characterclearinghouse.fsu.edu/index.php/articles/perspectives/74-differentiating-spirituality-from-religion. Accessed 27 July 2015.

Lynch, Kathleen. *Protestant Autobiography in the Seventeenth-Century Anglophone World*. Oxford: Oxford UP, 2012. Print.

McFague, Sallie. *Metaphorical Theology, Models of God in Religious Language*. Philadelphia: Fortress, 1982. Print.

Merton, Thomas. *The Seven Storey Mountain*. London: SPCK, 2009. Print.

Moody, Joycelyn. *Sentimental Confessions: Spiritual Narratives of Nineteenth-Century African American Women*. Athens, Georgia: U of Georgia P, 2001. Print.

Moody, Raymond Jr. *Life after Life: The Investigation of a Phenomenon: Survival of Bodily Death*. New York: Bantam, 1976. Print.

Morinis, Alan, Ed. *Sacred Journeys: The Anthropology of Pilgrimage.* Foreword by Victor Turner. Westport, CT: Greenwood, 1992. Print.

Morinis, E. Alan. "Introduction: The Territory of the Anthropology of Pilgrimages." In *Sacred Journeys: The Anthropology of Pilgrimage.* Morini, A. , ed. Westport, CT: Greenwood. 1–28. Print.

Morrison, Karl F. *Conversion and Text: The Cases of Augustine of Hippo, Herman-Judah, and Constantine Tsatsos.* Charlottesville: U of Virginia P, 1992. Print.

Newberg, Andrew, Eugene D'Aquili, and Vince Rause. *Why God Won't Go Away: Brain Science and the Biology of Belief.* 2001. New York: Ballantine, 2002. Print.

Newman, John Henry. *Apologia Pro Vita Sua.* Edited by Ian Ker. London: Penguin, 1994. Print.

Norman, Alex. "Spiritual Tourism: Religion and Spirituality in Contemporary Travel." Thesis. The University of Sydney, 2004.

Norris, Kathleen. *Amazing Grace: A Vocabulary of Faith.* New York: Riverhead, 1998. Print.

NPR STAFF. "Writer Anne Rice: 'Today I Quit Being A Christian'". August 02, 2010. http://www.npr.org/templates/story/story.php?storyId=128930526. Accessed 20 April, 2016.

Ochs, Carol. *Women and Spirituality.* New York: Rowman and Littlefield, 1996. Print.

Olney, James, ed. "Autobiography and the Cultural Moment: A Thematic, Historical, and Bibliographical Introduction." In *Autobiography: Essays Theoretical and Critical.* Princeton: Princeton UP, 1980. 3–27. Print.

___. *Metaphors of Self: The Meaning of Autobiography.* Princeton: Princeton UP, 1972. Print.

Oser, Fritz K., and Paul Gmünder. *Religious Judgement: A Developmental Perspective.* Birmingham, AL: Religious Education P, 1991. Print.

Pascal, Roy. *Design and Truth in Autobiography.* Cambridge, MA: Harvard UP, 1960. Print.

Payne, Roger M. *The Self and the Sacred: Conversion and Autobiography in Early American Protestantism.* Knoxville: U of Tennessee P, 1998. Print.

"Pilgrimage with Simon Reeve. France to Italy." Documentary television series. BBC. 2013.

Popp-Baier, Ulrike. "Life Stories and Philosophies of Life: A Perspective for Research in Psychology of Religion." In *Autobiography and the Psychological Study of Religious Lives.* Ed. Jacob A. Belzen and Antoon Geels. Amsterdam: Rodopi, 2008. 39–74. Print.

Rambo, Lewis. *Understanding Religious Conversion.* New Haven: Yale UP, 1993. Print.

Ricœur, Paul. *The Symbolism of Evil.* Boston: Beacon P, 1969.

Richards, I.A. *The Philosophy of Rhetoric*, 1936. New York: Oxford UP, 1965. Print.

Roiphe, Katie. "Should you read the best-selling *memoir Eat, Pray, Love?*" Review of Gilbert, Elizabeth. Eat, Pray, Love: One Woman's Search for Everything Across Italy, India, and Indonesia. July 3 2007. http://www.slate.com/articles/arts/books/2007/07/summer_reading.html. Accessed 7 May 7, 2015.

Rousseau, Jean-Jacques. *Les Confessions.* 1782. http://www.litteratureaudio.com/livre-audio-gratuit-mp3/rousseau-jean-jacques-les-confessions-2.html

Rose, Nicholas. *Governing the Soul.* London: Free Association, 1989. Print.

Ryan, Michael. "Self-Evidence." Rev. of Philippe Lejeune's *Le Pacte Auto-biographique* [Paris: Editions du Seuil, 1975]. *Diacritics: A Review of Contemporary Criticism* 10.2 (1980): 2–16. Print.

Schmidt, William S. "Transformative Pilgrimage." In *The Spiritual Horizon of Psychotherapy.* William S. Schmidt and Merle R. Jordan, eds. New York: Routledge, 2013. 65–76. Print.

Schott, Sarah Bill. "Pilgrims, Seekers, and History Buffs: Identity Creation through Religious Tourism in Late Modernity." In *On the Road to Being There: Studies in Pilgrimage and Tourism in Late Modernity.* Swatos, W. H. Jr, ed. Leiden: Brill, 2003. 297–327. Print.

Sholem, Gershom. 1967. *Den judiska mystiken.* Trans. Joachim Retzlaff. Preface by Salomon Schulman. Stockholm: Brutus Österlings, 1994. Print.

Shumate, Nancy. *Crisis and Conversion in Apuleius' Metamorphoses.* Ann Arbor: U of Michigan P, 1996. Print.

Sigurdson, Ola. "Beyond Secularism? Toward A Post-Secular Political Theology." In *Modern Theology* 26:2, April 2010. 177–96. Print.

Sim, Stuart. "Spiritual Autobiography." *The Literary Encyclopedia.* First published 01 January 2001. http://www.litencyc.com/php/stopics.php?rec=true&UID=1377. Accessed 20 April 2016.

Smith, Robert. *Derrida and Autobiography.* Cambridge: Cambridge UP, 1995. Print.

Stace, Walter T. *Mysticism and Philosophy.* Philadelphia: Lippincott, 1960. http://wudhi.com/mysticism/ws/index.htm. Accessed 20 April 2016.

Streib, Heinz. "Deconversion." In *The Oxford Handbook of Religious Conversion.* Eds. Lewis Rambo and Charles E. Farhadian. Oxford: Oxford UP, 2014. 271–96.

Tolle, Eckhardt. *A New Earth: Awakening to Your Life's Purpose.* 2005. London: Penguin, 2006. Print.

___. *The Power of Now: A Guide to Spiritual Enlightenment.* London: Hodder and Stoughton, 2011. Print.

Tomasi, Luigi. "Homo Viator: From Pilgrimage to Religious Tourism via the Journey." In *From Medieval Pilgrimage to Religious Tourism*. Swatos, W. H. Jr, and Luigi Tomasi, eds. Westport, CT: Praeger. 1–24. Print.

Turner, Victor, and Edith Turner. *Image and Pilgrimage in Christian Culture: Anthropological Perspectives*. New York: Columbia UP, 1978. Print.

Underhill, Evelyn. "Preface." *Mysticism: A Study of the Nature and Development of Man's Spiritual Consciousness*. 1911. http://www.sacred-texts.com/myst/myst/myst02.htm. Accessed 20 April 2016.

Weintraub, Karl Joachim. *The Value of The Individual: Self and Circumstance in Autobiography*. Chicago: U of Chicago P, 1978. Print.

Wilber, Ken. *The Collected Works of Ken Wilber. The Spectrum of Consciousness. No Boundary. Selected Essays*. Boston: Shambhala, 1999. Print.

Wink, Paul, and Michele Dillon. "Spiritual Development Across the Adult Life Course: Findings From a Longitudinal Study." *Journal of Adult Development* 9.1 (2002): 79–94. Print.

Wittman, Laura. Stanford University website. https://dlcl.stanford.edu/people/laura-wittman. Accessed 17 March 2016.

Wolff, Kurt H. "Surrender and Religion." *Journal for the Scientific Study of Religion* 2.1 (1962): 36–50. Print.

Woodiwiss, Jo. "What's Wrong with Me? A Cautionary Tale of Using Contemporary 'Damage Narratives' in Autobiographical Life Writing." In *Writing the Self: Essays on Autobiography and Autofiction*. Eds. Kerstin W. Shands, Giulia Grillo Mikrut, Dipti R. Pattanaik, and Karen Ferreira-Meyers. Stockholm: Södertörn UP, 2015. 183–93. Print.

English Studies

1. Kerstin W. Shands (ed.), *Collusion and Resistance: Women Writing in English*, 2002
2. Kerstin W. Shands et al. (eds.), *Notions of America: Swedish Perspectives*, 2004
3. Kerstin W. Shands (ed.), *Neither East Nor West: Postcolonial Essays on Literature, Culture and Religion*, 2008
4. Kerstin W. Shands & Giulia Grillo Mikrut (eds), *Living Language, Living Memory: Essays on the Works of Toni Morrison*, 2014
5. Kerstin W. Shands et al. (eds.), *Writing the Self: Essays on Autobiography and Autofiction*, 2015
6. Kerstin W. Shands, *Journeys Within: The Contemporary Spiritual Autobiography*, 2016